PADDY
McGUINNESS

→ MY LIFEY ←

EBURY
SPOTLIGHT

Virgin Books, an imprint of Ebury Publishing
20 Vauxhall Bridge Road
London SW1V 2SA

Virgin Books is part of the Penguin Random House group of companies
whose addresses can be found at global.penguinrandomhouse.com

First published by Virgin Books in 2021
www.penguin.co.uk

A CIP catalogue record for this book is available from the British Library

Hardback ISBN 9781529109351
Trade Paperback ISBN 9781529109368

Printed and bound in Great Britain by Clays Ltd, Elcograf S.p.A.

The authorised representative in the EEA is Penguin Random House Ireland,
Morrison Chambers, 32 Nassau Street, Dublin D02 YH68

Dedicated to Mum, Dad and Angie.
Always in my thoughts.

 CONTENTS

INTRODUCTION

How do! Welcome to my life story. Come in, look around, make yourself at home. I've done a lot of mad old things throughout the years, and that's before I started working in television. Sitting here typing away, I find myself constantly thinking about what to tell you. This is totally new to me. I've not read a book cover to cover, let alone written one. I mean, do you want to know about when I was a kid and the stuff before teledom, or is it just the show business side of things you want to read about? So I decided to write about it all. Well, what I can remember at least.

First things first, the title of my book, *My Lifey*. It is my life and there's no doubt that catchphrase is very much a part of television vernacular. I've got to say, though, I wasn't short of titles. Here's a few I toyed with:

Girl Power
The McGuinness Book of Records
Take Me Out of the Bookshop
The Bolton Wanderer

1

INTRODUCTION

Let the Life See the Story
Catchphrases and Comedy
Phoenix Writes
Top Shelf to Top Gear
Lucky? Me?

Girl Power was the working title for a long time. When I sat down and started to properly look at my life, from playing outside on the cobbled streets of Bolton to walking down the red carpets in London, there was always one constant in my life: strong women. All my life experiences so far, the highs and lows, decisions, work, relationships, have all been shaped by or involve strong women. Don't get me wrong, there's been a few good men (good name for a film, that) along the way but the most important role models in my life have always been female.

The reason it changed from *Girl Power* to *My Lifey* was way beyond my pay grade. It turns out there's a whole team of marketing brainiacs at these publishing houses, the upshot being that no one will have a clue that it's a book about myself. Apparently the excitement of opening a book about the Spice Girls only to find a picture of me with my trousers down, drunk, leaning on a Bentley would've caused a few problems.

So here we are. I'm Paddy McGuinness and this is *My Lifey!*

CHAPTER 1

MINI ME

I was brought up in an era when bins didn't have wheelies,
television had three channels and a smoothie was
a bloke called Julio Iglesias. Read on.

I was born in 1973 and raised in Bolton, Lancashire, a mighty town in the north-west of England. I lived with my mum in a little two-up two-down terrace in the Daubhill district, on Auburn Street. Auburn Street was my world growing up and it was such a happy place to be. Thinking about it now makes me feel quite emotional – I suppose one of the things about writing a life story is revisiting all those long-forgotten memories, good and bad.

I do consider myself fortunate that my prime playing-out years were in the seventies and eighties. There was less traffic on the roads, no Xboxes, no PlayStations, no iPads. Well, we kind of had the early prototype of the iPad, we had Etch A Sketch. (google it). Nature's iPad: no need to delete your search history after using an Etch A Sketch. Just give it a little shake and you were good to

3

go. Which, ironically, is the thing you do that leads to deleting the search history on an iPad!

I'm aware that a lot of you reading this may have been born after 1990, so some of the references may leave you a little confused as to what the hell I'm talking about. In fact, if I just do you a random list of stuff from the seventies and eighties, you can look them up now and it'll save you a job once we carry on with the story. Even though I may not mention every one, pretty much all of them played a part in my childhood and growing up. (P.S. This book is also available electronically for all you whippersnapper millennials!)

Reference list

TOYS/GAMES – Stretch Armstrong, Kerplunk, He-Man, the Six Million Dollar Man, Rubik's Cube, Cabbage Patch Kids, Tamagotchi, Action Man, Pac-Man, Pong, Kerby, Crossfire, Connect 4.

COMPUTERS/ELECTRONICS – Atari, ZX Spectrum, Amstrad CPC 464, Commodore 64, Sega, Game Boy, hi-fis, Frogger, Donkey Kong.

PEOPLE – Cilla Black, Larry Grayson, Terry Wogan, Bruce Forsyth.

TV – *The Love Boat*, *Starsky and Hutch*, *The A Team*, *Tomorrow's World*, *Baywatch*, *Happy Days*, *Terrahawks*, *Thundercats*, *Space 1999*, *Buck Rogers*, *The Fall Guy*, *Prisoner Cell Block H*, *World of Sport*, *Bullseye*, *Ceefax*, *Treasure Hunt*, *Hi-de-Hi!*, *Brush Strokes*, *Just Good Friends*, *Blankety Blank*.

THINGS – cassette tapes, VHS tapes, video recorders, Walkman, Raleigh Chopper, Matey bubble bath, Acdo washing powder, lucky bags, fags, penny trays, *Smash Hits*, digital watches, Slush Puppies, Yellow Pages, Thomson Local, door curtain strips.

For most of my early childhood I was out playing with my friends morning, noon and night. I distinctly remember climbing a lot of things. In the seventies and eighties, risking life and limb was the norm. Buildings, trees, walls, people: if it could be climbed, I'd be up it. Laughter, grazed knees and endless summer holidays are what stick in my head. The old saying 'we were poor but we were happy' was so true for me.

My mum was Mum *and* Dad. She was Mad. Sounds wrong, that. Dum? Oh God, that sounds even worse! I think the posh word for what I'm saying is a portmanteau, like Brad and Angelina used to be Brangelina. Basically she wore both of the parenting hats and she was my world. Her full name was Patricia Winifred Leonard but everyone knew her as Pat. Some of our Asian neighbours christened her Pat L (Patel), which I never got at the time. She was the numero uno, girl-power-to-the-max strong woman in my life. She was a single parent holding down two jobs, cleaner and barmaid. I never felt like I missed out on much being brought up in a one-parent family. I suppose that's all I knew, really. It's only when you get older that you fully appreciate what your parents sacrificed for you.

She never had any men around and she certainly never stayed out overnight without me. I liked it being just me and my mum. I always found it a bit strange whenever I went to a mate's house and their dad was there. They always seemed miserable and bad-tempered. Yep, these blokes seemed to be permanently angry, which in hindsight is totally understandable – most of them worked nights in factories. If ever I went round to a mate's house in the day, their dads would usually be asleep, and you daren't wake them. You'd creep into the kitchen for a glass of water, your mate shitting himself, whispering, 'Please don't wake my dad up.'

If you went round and they were awake, they'd normally be sat on the couch, oozing bad energy, looking at the telly through bloodshot eyes, telling you to piss off because they'd been working all night and they didn't want noisy effing kids running around.

Looking back, why would they have been happy? Working every hour God sends to put food on the table. All those dreams of scoring that winning goal in an FA Cup Final or having their own business crushed a little bit more every time they clocked on at work. I loved that I didn't have to tiptoe around an angry bear at home, although my mum did have her moments.

I saw my dad at the weekend. That suited me just fine. For one, my dad was always happy, probably because he didn't have to deal with all the stresses of raising a child. He had already been married previously and had a grown-up family, but I didn't know about them until I was an adult. He lived on his own, loved his job (he was a lorry driver at the time), and got to see me at the weekends then hand me back over to my mum for all the non-fun stuff the rest of the week: washing, cooking, cleaning, brushing teeth.

Dad had me quite late in life so when I was a kid he was already in his fifties. He'd served in World War Two, worked down the pit as a coal miner and also been in the scrap industry. All hard-grafting jobs and I always remember him being strong and physically fit. He had those great big working-man hands, veins bulging out the back of them. Despite his age, he never seemed old to me. He was never tired or frail – in fact, compared to most of my mates' younger dads, he was fitter than the lot of them! We'd always be play fighting or mucking about in the back yard with an air rifle, shooting holes in a Yellow Pages – something my mum was never happy about.

He was really chilled out, considering he had two families on the go. I never saw him stressed. He never spoke about any problems or worries he had, and seeing him lose his temper was rarer than an MP apology. He made me laugh all the time and I thought he was the best thing since sliced bread, while I probably gave my mum a bit of a hard time because she was the one instilling the rules. Talk about good cop, bad cop. I remember once telling my mum, through the innocence and immaturity of childhood, that I loved my dad more than her. To this day that still haunts me. How must that have made her feel? Bringing me up on her own, and I hit her with a statement like that! When you're a child you don't realise how hurtful you can be. My mum made so many sacrifices for me.

Everyone knew my dad as Joe but I found out about ten years ago that his actual name was Patrick. This blew my mind somewhat because I hadn't the slightest idea we had the same name for thirty-odd years! Having said that, I wasn't named after my dad. My parents named me Alexander. It was my nan, on my mum's side, who wanted a Patrick in the family. She was so keen for me to be called Patrick she bribed my mum with the offer of buying her a new pram if she changed my name. So that was that, I was named Patrick and given the middle name Joseph, after my dad, who was called Patrick. I also got my dad's surname. The changing of names definitely went in my favour. 'With your host, Paddy McGuinness!' flows much better than 'With your host, Alexander Leonard!'

Waiting for my dad to pick me up on a Saturday morning and take me out for the day was the best thing ever. I'd get so excited when I heard his little yellow Fiesta pull up. He'd always drive over this grid outside our house and as soon as I heard that distinctive clunk, I'd race to the living room window and wave to him, nearly bursting with excitement. My dad would usually treat me to a toy or something when we went out. Also he'd have me in tears of laughter. He had a wonderful ability to tell funny stories and that definitely had an effect on me and my future career. What I do for a living now has massive elements of both my mum and dad's influence. Although totally different styles, they both had very good senses of humour.

I never looked at my parents as a couple and I struggle to imagine them ever being together. The one good thing is I didn't have to go through the heartache of seeing them divorce, mainly because they were never married. If I'd ever seen them kissing or showing affection to each other I'd have probably imploded. If they'd held hands I think I'd have emigrated. I used to struggle seeing someone kissing on a TV show if my mum was sat with me. Like I said, I was brought up by my mum on her own; my dad lived with us for a short period of time. When I say short, well, I was born in 1973 and he moved out in 1974.

These were my parents, yet they seemed a million miles apart. I don't think they had much time or patience for each other. In fact, as the years went by I noticed more and more their dislike for one another. I hated to see them arguing because those slanging matches usually resulted in my dad not coming around for a few weekends, which was heartbreaking for me.

I also have brothers and sisters. Some I know, some I don't. I'll get to all that later, much later – like in my forties later. Let's start with the ones I know.

My older brother, Tony (same mum, different dad), I didn't really get to know until my twenties. He's a few years older than me, 14 to be precise. Mum had been struggling financially, so Tony lived with my grandad. Back then having a child out of wedlock wasn't the norm, especially when the dad was nowhere to be seen, so kids often lived with grandparents or other family members while the mums went to work. I saw little of Tony growing up, so I didn't realise I had a brother for many years. I vaguely remember him arriving on Auburn Street once on a motorbike, but I wasn't really aware he was my brother. I never gave it much thought. I was a kid and had better things to worry about, like playing out with my mates.

Eventually, Tony emigrated to New Zealand and that was that. I didn't see him again for nigh on 25 years. I remember speaking to him on the phone in my late teens but that was about it really. We've definitely made up for all that lost time now, though.

I also had an older sister, Angela, who wasn't my sister biolog-ically but I definitely looked at her like she was. Angela, or as she was known to everyone, Angie, was the best ever. She came from a big family who lived in an area called Darcy Lever. Darcy Lever, or Darcy, was where my mum and all her brothers and sisters were brought up. To give you an idea of what Darcy was like, it made Auburn Street look like Mayfair. It was a rough and ready area, full of big families, and everybody knew everyone. Angie was from a family known as the Whittles. We had nothing, but Angie's family had double nothing, so my mum took her in as one of her own.

That kind of thing happened a lot. Everyone just mucked in and got on with it. I remember laughing so much and constantly smiling when Angie came on the scene. I loved having someone around who was so much fun, and I'd tell anyone who cared to listen that she was my big sister.

Angie taught me some major life skills, like how to butter bread properly.

'Go right up to the corners, Patrick, and make sure you get the crusts.'

Or grated carrots covered in salad cream. I mean, in terms of life skills it's not up there, but at the time I was totally amazed.

I also remember her saving my life once. My love of climbing and adventure led to me hanging out of my bedroom window at the age of six. Up shit creek without a paddle and clinging on for dear life, Angie came bolting into the bedroom to pull me back in through the window. She never told my mum about it – we'd have both got a bollocking – but that was just Angie, always there for me. My big sister who I loved to bits.

* * *

Mobile phones were a pipe dream then. To get me in for tea my mum relied on a more primitive means of contact – shouting! Everyone's mum used to do it. Back then you'd always hear a mum bellowing out their child's name from the doorstep. No matter where you were playing at the time – it could've been the next county – you always heard your mum's shout. I'd disappointedly tell my mates that I had to go home for my tea.

'But, Mum, we've only been playing out for nine hours!'

'Just get in and get your tea!'

I don't recall having set meal times in our house. Teatime was usually any time between three and seven. A mind-blowing event for me, as a kid, was going to a mate's house and seeing a family all sitting round a table to eat their tea. I literally had no idea what was going on, or why people would do such a thing. It just seemed so strange to me. When we had our tea, I'd be sitting with my mum in front of the telly, a plate on my lap, a few slices of bread on the chair arm and a drink on the floor by my feet. That was the norm and it felt good, apart from the bollockings I used to get for accidentally kicking the drinks over. Being at a table was cold and formal. I couldn't relax like that. It wasn't what people like us did.

Aside from the seating arrangements, my mate's dinner came as a bit of a shock to me too: Spam and chips. I was only around seven or eight at the time and I remember thinking, *Wow, these people are so classy.* My mum was a really good cook so most things were made from scratch: pies, cakes, stews, Yorkshire puddings, mashed potatoes, all the old-school stuff. To me, though, Spam out of a tin was upmarket. There was even a knife to go with the fork on the table, something I never had when I ate. The fact that my mum's food was a million times better and took longer to prepare didn't really come into my head. At that age, a tin of Spam took precedence over a roast dinner.

What I remember most about growing up on Auburn Street were all the fantastic strong women, proper characters. They'd be either sat on their front steps or leaning on the windowsill with a cup of tea in one hand and a fag in the other. Smoking was massive back then. I don't think I'd ever seen an adult who didn't smoke. Every house you went to had a smoky blue haze in the air. I reckon kids growing up then must've been passively smoking about 40 packets of cigarettes a week, which is some going for anyone under the age of 12.

Most of the day consisted of playing out on the streets and running back and forth to the shop for various neighbours.

'Patrick, nip to the shop and get Mrs Houseman a packet of fags and a bottle of steri, love.'

Another thing my mum would send me to the shop for was a 'separate' or 'sepi'. This was a single cigarette. It's mad how all these kids would be in the corner shop buying sepis for their mums and dads. Eight years old and asking for a 10p sepi. You'd run back home in the hope of a 2p reward.

The women on the street would often be on their knees scrubbing the doorsteps of houses they'd never own, because that's what you did. There was real pride in a clean front doorstep. These women were hard as nails and, as a kid, if you were out of line, you'd get a clip round the ear from whoever was nearest. Although saying that, my mum very rarely had to raise her hand to me: just one of her mum stares was enough of a deterrent to keep me in line. A look from any one of the women on our street was enough to terrify the life out of any wayward boy, let alone if they shouted at you. It was a case of do not piss these ladies off or you'll come a cropper, big time. I was a street kid and as rough as they come, but the minute my mum or anyone else's mum shouted at me, I was indoors and behaving. We all were because those women didn't take any shit.

The corner shop that sold those sepis was a big part of most working-class areas, and ours had a belting penny tray. Well, it had a penny tray along with a 2p and 5p tray. Shrewd bargain hunters like myself would never go near the 5p tray, though. I liked to stretch out my 5p spends. I was bargain hunting before David Dickinson was brown.

We actually had two corner shops. Hang on, that'll be one corner shop with another shop at the side of it? My brain hurts already.

Auburn Street also had an ironmongers and a regular shop. By 'regular' I mean it sold things like cigarettes, sweets, crisps, bread, milk. Oh, and it sold a bit of meat they kept in the stockroom at the back. Food hygiene, along with health and safety, wasn't top of everyone's list back then.

CHAPTER 1

One of my mum's jobs was as a cleaner at the local bingo hall, the Tivoli. The Tivoli was a massive old place, and if Angie wasn't around to babysit, my mum used to take me with her while she cleaned. The bingo hall was so big that I'd bring my bike with me, a bright yellow Raleigh Boxer. While my mum and the other ladies worked, I'd set off exploring the building.

When you're seven years old everything is an adventure, and an old bingo hall was no exception. There was this massive expanse of pink lino in the main hall, just in front of where they'd call out the bingo numbers. Once the women had finished mopping, it would be glistening and perfect for one thing – skids! I would set about perfecting the most spectacular ones on that freshly cleaned floor, which wasn't easy when you're being chased by a group of angry cleaning ladies. I was ducking brushes and had cleaning cloths thrown at me, but it was worth it for the perfect skids on the perfect floor.

It felt special being in that big building on our own, and when it was their break we'd all sit in the main hall eating cold bacon butties that my mum had wrapped up in waxy bread-packet paper that morning. Looking back, I'd forgotten how much I enjoyed going to the bingo hall with my mum. I loved being around those women, even the ones who attacked me with their mopheads.

* * *

Before I was born my mum worked in the cotton mills on a loom. It was a loud, noisy, clock in/clock out factory and she grafted there to provide. She'd been a fantastic swimmer when she was young and could have competed at national level, but when you were brought up in a poor area there were a lot of what-ifs. Back then, my mum's parents weren't taking her to swimming lessons to hone her skills; they were telling her to get out of the house and get a job. That kind of attitude was passed down to the next generation. It wasn't that my mum couldn't be arsed to take me to swimming clubs or football practice, she was just too busy working.

My dad never once took me to a football match. I'd see boys going to watch Bolton with their dads, or wearing dead-smart football boots, but I never felt jealous. I just thought, *This is how it is.* I used to think, *Well, they've got money, so they can do that. We don't, so I can't.* Simple. Despite never having football boots, football kit or even my own ball, it never put me off loving it. There'd always be someone with a ball, and back then we'd play in whatever was on our feet – trainers, shoes, slippers.

A good few years ago, myself and a good mate of mine, Jonathan Wilkes, wrote a pantomime parody called *Pantos On Strike.* I told him that I'd have to go and see a few pantos before we started as I'd never seen one. He couldn't believe it. Where I grew up, the festive entertainment was throwing snowballs at passing buses or holding on to the backs of cars while being dragged round the streets in the snow – dangerous but brilliant!

I went to watch Jonny in a panto at the Stoke Regent Theatre and I remember being surrounded by excited kids. You couldn't move for flashing wands, deeley boppers and cartons of pop. I was sat with a coffee thinking, *What the fuck am I doing here?* Five minutes later I was singing along with a pair of flashing bunny ears on.

I loved it! It was great seeing all the kids singing and shouting, but it was tinged with sadness. I had a little wobble thinking about how I never got to experience this kind of thing, and I wondered if these children realised how lucky they were. (All that magic quickly vanished when I visited Jonny's dressing room after the show. The sight of Buttons sat having a shit will live me forever. Anyhow, I digress, we're still in the early years.)

I must stress that I had a really happy childhood. I don't want this to be a 'woe is me' kind of vibe. My mum loved me to bits and that's all that mattered. Even as I got older and found out Angie wasn't my biological sister, the love was so strong that it actually didn't matter. Angie eventually got married to a builder called Ian. They built a house together and I spent all my summer holidays there – they were really happy times. I loved Angie, and I still miss her. She passed away far too early and it really broke me. Angie fell down the stairs at home and that was that, a total accident and she was gone all too soon.

I wish she was still here now to enjoy the success with me, meet my kids and just be a part of our lives. All the financial security that success brings … It would've been nice to treat her. No matter what I achieve in life, I don't think I'll ever be truly happy. All the people I wanted to make proud are no longer around.

The other thing I really struggle with is losing contact with Angie's immediate family. They had a daughter, Rebecca, who I watched grow up, and they adopted a little boy named Craig. Some of my happiest childhood memories were staying at their house but after Angie's death I didn't visit again. Maybe it was the trauma of loss, knowing things would never be the same again. I really don't know, but it's one of those things that I struggle with in my personal life. I often think of them all but can't bring myself to go and visit. I think it's a mixture of clinging on to the past and the fear of seeing their life being totally different now. In my head they're all still doing what they were doing back then. Losing that contact was and is weird, but all those happy memories still stay with me. That's the good thing about memories. They're yours to keep forever. No one can take them away from you. My uncle Tony told me that, and he was right.

The way I treat my children now and the way I spent my childhood are a million miles apart. I remember bath night used to be every Sunday in our house – even that in itself seems odd. I'll throw mine in the bath or shower most days, but for me, and loads of other kids, it was once a week and that was that. Hot water meant putting on the immersion heater and that cost money – it wouldn't matter if I'd been rolling around in mud all day, you got one bath on a Sunday, end of. And get this, my mum used to put washing-up liquid in my bath. Actual detergent! Why waste money on shampoo and bubble bath when we had washing-up liquid? It wasn't even Fairy either, it was some stuff she used to clean with at the bingo hall.

I wasn't on my own. I remember Peter Kay telling me his mum used to put Acdo washing powder in his bath. Compared to him, I was living the dream with washing-up liquid. I could only sit in that bath for ten minutes tops, any longer and my eyes would start burning. How I got through my childhood without some kind of skin condition or sight loss is beyond me. It wouldn't have surprised me if my mum had chucked the pots and pans in with me. What do you want a sponge for? We've got a perfectly good Brillo pad here. I couldn't even rinse it off properly because we didn't have a shower. My mum had this hose thing that she'd wedge onto the bath taps that acted like a shower, if a shower was made out of cream rubber with no mixing valves. It was either freezing cold or scalding red hot. In fact, up until the age of about five, I actually had my baths in the kitchen sink, with my feet hanging over the edge.

After I got out the bath, and as soon as my skin stopped tingling, my mum would sit me in front of the gas fire. I didn't see a radiator until I was 10 or 11, and up until the age of 15 I didn't know they warmed up. The TV would be on but it was on a meter – my mum had to put 50p in a little box at the back and that'd give us about six hours of viewing. I'd sit there watching something like *Magnum* or *Crazy Like a Fox* while my mum went through my hair with a metal comb and nit lotion. I didn't have the heart to tell her fleas wouldn't survive one of her detergent baths.

It wasn't until I stayed at my first proper girlfriend's house that I discovered there was an alternative to washing-up liquid when it came to bath products. Her name was Claire and she lived with her mum, dad and brother in a three-bed semi-detached (very posh). *I'm marrying into royalty here,* I thought. They had an actual shower too, a proper one, not a bit of hosepipe hanging off the taps. I'll never forget the first time I used it. I remember standing there naked, thinking, *How do I work this contraption?* Once I figured it out, I was blown away, literally! The pressure on that thing compared to my mum's rubber hose nearly took the skin off my face. It was then I had my second awakening. They had fancy shampoo!

Fucking hell, I thought, sniffing it. *This is posh.*

It was honey blossom and something or other. I didn't want that shower to end; it was just so nice not to smell like a bingo hall kitchen. After that, I was hooked. You'd find me flicking the tops off shampoo bottles in the local supermarket and smelling them, trying to decide which one I was going to have next.

One day Claire handed me some conditioner – that girl opened my eyes to a world of wonderment! Like most teenage lads, I ended up dousing myself in anything I could get my hands on: Insignia shower gel, Lynx underarm, Brut aftershave. I'd walk in a room thinking, *God, I'm box fresh tonight,* when in fact I probably smelt like the stock room at Superdrug. In retrospect that four or five years I spent with Claire were probably the cleanest I've ever been.

Yet, like most young lads, it wasn't long till I started looking for that infamous greener grass on the other side of the fence. When you're young you don't realise how good you've got it with a steady girlfriend – I certainly didn't. That's one of those life lessons you learn the hard way, usually when it's much too late. No matter what people told me, I thought I knew it all. I was always about acting up with my mates and trying to please the people who didn't really matter. If you're reading this, Claire, thank you for introducing me to fancy shower gel and thank you for being a fantastic first girlfriend.

* * *

I used to walk two or three miles to primary school, on my own, along main roads and in and out of different estates. My mum was fiercely protective of me but there was never a sense that I was going to come to any harm. I wouldn't dream of letting my kids walk to school now, well, not unless they had a taser. The seventies and early eighties seemed like such an innocent, carefree time. I'm sure it wasn't all Raleigh Choppers and space hoppers but to me it just felt safe. Where we lived, in Daubhill, there were loads of pubs, small businesses and family-run shops. It was full of life and we all knew one another. There was one little pet-grooming place on my route to school. It had a tiny, old-fashioned telly on the counter with a bell on the top that I'd ring every day, driving the owners mad. It was one of my little routines on my way home from school and I loved it.

There was a lamppost outside my primary school, and every day my mates and I would compete to see who could get to it first. The lamppost king was usually the one who got up earliest. I'd never managed it. Why? Well, I've always been a big sleeper. I love sleep. Even as a kid with boundless energy, I slept like an absolute bastard, still do. So, this one summer night, I came home from school, eight years old, knackered as usual, and fell asleep on my bed straight off. Consequently, I was awake bright and early the next morning. Yes! This would be the day I was first to the lamppost. I jumped out of bed, got dressed and rushed down the stairs to my mum, who greeted me with a puzzled expression.

'Where are you off to?'

'School,' I said.

'School? You've not got school.'

'I have, and I want to be first to the lamppost.'

'Patrick—'

'I'm going, Mum. I'm going to miss my chance if I talk to you any longer.'

She watched while I gathered my things together and rushed out the door. Sure enough, when I got to the lamppost by the school gates, no one was there. I'd done it, I was king of the lamppost! In fact, there weren't even any teachers about, leading me to think that I wasn't just early, I was mega-early. I'd nailed it. For an hour and a half I stood there. Nothing. No one to witness my finest hour, my triumph.

Eventually, a couple of my mates who'd been playing in the area walked past, staring at me, confused.

'What you doing, Paddy?'

'I'm waiting for school to start, what do you think I'm doing?'

'School? What you talking about? School finished hours ago.'

'You're only saying that cos I got to the lamppost first.'

'I'm not! There's no school now. Not till tomorrow morning.'

The truth was, when I'd got home from school, I'd fallen into a virtual coma on my bed for an hour or so, then woken up, still half-dreaming, convinced it was morning. And being mid-summer, it was bright long into the evening. So, yes, I was early for school. A day early.

I couldn't believe my mum had let me go to school at six o'clock at night! She said I was so adamant that she thought it best to just let me get on with it.

I wish I had more photographs of where I grew up, but unlike now, when you take 40 pictures of the meal you're about to eat, we never took hardly any back then. It was a novelty having your photo taken and it took a week to get your film developed at Boots or Max Spielmann. I think that's what made photographs special, that anticipation. When you finally got them you'd all be laughing and talking about them. You even looked at the negatives! Nowadays, every photo of my kids on my phone is special but I've got so many I never really look at them.

The images of my childhood are only in my head. There are no pictures of us all playing out in the street, or of the old ladies sitting outside their houses on their freshly scrubbed doorsteps, or of the daily race to be king of the lamppost – that would've been a definite selfie moment. On reflection, though, I'd have then been trolled by everyone at school for getting it wrong.

One thing I hated when I was a kid was church. I'm Catholic but I used to have nightmares about priests. We had two of them at my school, Father Woods and Father Malloy. They were old, stern and more than a bit frightening, and consequently I was shit-scared of going into church. When people talked about churches as beautiful, peaceful places to be, I couldn't get my head around it. That wasn't my experience at all, and I couldn't fathom why anyone would choose to go there. You daren't speak or smile and you certainly wouldn't mess around. They were cold, unwelcoming places with all these statues bearing down on you, and right there in the middle of it all, Jesus nailed to a cross, all naked and bloody. Then there were the rules and traditions of Catholicism, foisted upon you every time you walked into church, or even at school.

'Don't speak, do this, don't do that, get out, have you blessed your-self, go to confession.'

In confession we were taught to confess our sins. I was six! What did they think I'd done?

'Bless me, Father, for I have sinned. I mixed the blue and brown plasticine together.'

'OK, that'll be twelve Hail Marys and eighteen Our Fathers.'

Totally ridiculous! It was an unhappy, negative place for me. In fact, I was that terrified of church, I had recurring dreams that I'd woken up to find Father Woods and Father Malloy standing around my bed. A whole wall of them, in duplicate, just staring at me. It was always so real and freaked me out as a young kid, and I wonder, even now, how did those images get in my head at that age? Why priests standing around me in such a forbidding manner? It's not like anything that could be deemed abusive ever happened at my school, well, apart from the odd nun beating us up. The priests never even looked at us half the time.

It wasn't until I was in my thirties that I actually enjoyed being in a church. A mate of mine's son was getting christened. The priest was openly gay and had a totally different way of doing things. It was a million miles from the Fathers Woods and Malloy days.

There was noise and atmosphere. People were smiling, chatting and laughing.

'Oh, yes, bring the kids in,' he said to everyone arriving at the church. 'Let them run around and enjoy themselves.'

CHAPTER 1

I thought, *This is how a church should be: inclusive and welcoming.* I loved how that priest was with his congregation. It reminded me of the mosques my Muslim mates went to when we were kids. They used to look forward to going, and their religion was centred around a real community feel, which to me is important. Not even sure why I've just told you that. The memory just popped into my head so there you go.

 **CHAPTER 2**

ALWAYS LEARNING

When life gives you petrol, hide the matches.

I clearly remember when we first moved to a posh house. When I say moved house, we didn't go far – just two doors up – and when I say posh, it had freshly painted walls and a new front door. Our new place was a Housing Association terrace rather than a council house and it had an open staircase in the kitchen. Even the tiny back yard was a step up by virtue of the fact that it had two little six-foot patches of grass in it, which was a first for us. I was thinking, *Look at that, we've got a garden.*

In the days leading up to the move I'd been staying with Angie and Ian. The memory of coming back from Angie's and walking into that new house is still vivid. There was bright sunshine bouncing off the walls, and the kitchen cupboards were white Formica with no handles on the doors – proper space-age and modern. My mum was in the kitchen and she had such a smile on her face. She was in a good mood; she was happy. It was lovely to see.

My bedroom was at the back of the house and it had a big airing cupboard in there that housed the hot-water tank. A few years later this caused me a major problem. While out playing with a mate we stumbled across a box full of adult literature on some scrubland we were messing about on. Everyone had different names for these kind of magazines – jazz mags, porn mags, bongo books and grot mags (not to be confused with popular children's TV character Grotbags) – but we called them knacky mags, still do to this day, no idea why. Do they even still sell them? Anyhow, this box was crammed to the brim with knacky mags. Now, if you've never been a 13-year-old boy, to give you some idea of what this was like, the emotions were akin to winning the EuroMillions. There must've been a hundred different knacky mags in that box, the only trouble being they were soaked in petrol. Someone was obviously about to burn them and got disturbed and just left them there. Their loss, our gain. We weren't going to let a bit of petrol put us off.

We split them 50/50 and off we went, with a spring in our step, to our individual houses. I walked in with 50 petrol-soaked knacky mags stuffed up my jumper and ran straight upstairs to my room. The adrenaline was still pumping. *How the hell am I going to get these dry? I know, I'll put them in the airing cupboard, right on top of the red-hot water tank, that'll dry them out in no time. Genius!*

I climbed on to the airing cupboard and placed them straight on top of the tank. My mum was only small so I knew she'd never see them that high up. Like being king of the lamppost, again victory was mine. While the drying phase took place, I decided to nip back out to play. About an hour later I heard my mum shouting my name. It was nowhere near teatime yet so what could she possibly want? As I got closer to our front door, the petrol fumes started to hit me. The knacky mags were a whisker away from setting the house and most probably the entire street on fire. My mum's eyes were streaming and bloodshot.

'Patrick, what's that smell coming from your bedroom?'

Obviously I couldn't say, 'Relax, Mum, it's just those fifty petrol-soaked *Razzles* I popped up in the airing cupboard to dry out.'

I aired them out in a wheelie bin for a few days and then they were good to go. To this day I get butterflies in my stomach whenever I smell petrol. This can get a little bit awkward when I'm hosting *Top Gear*.

I've got so many fantastic memories from living in that little two-up two-down Housing Association terrace. One of the wonderful things about life back then was people would leave their unwanted furniture out in the back streets. You could find some gems, and by gems I mean second-hand sideboards and the like. I remember once finding a mattress at the back of someone's house. If I saw a mattress lying on the floor now I wouldn't even stand on it, never mind pick it up and drag it home and put it in my bedroom.

'Look, Mum, I've got a new bed.'

For years I slept on two second-hand mattresses that had been found out the back of other people's houses. The first one my mum had had given to her and the other was the one I found in a back street. It's madness but it all seemed pretty normal to me back then. When you're a kid, hygiene isn't at the top of your priorities list. I didn't even think about what could've been crawling around in it.

Having said that, I wasn't a complete savage – I put the second one underneath the first one.

Most life skills I learned in my younger years were through making mistakes or from older mates. A mate of mine, Taz, taught me how to shave. Firstly, Taz wasn't his real name. Daubhill has a large Muslim and Hindu community and Taz lived in the next street. Taz had another brother, Peter (again not his real name), who was also shaving. Let me clear up this whole name thing. Back in the seventies when Muslim and Hindu families first moved into the area, names like Aaqib, Parvez and Mitesh couldn't be comprehended by most people – and by most people I mean white people who couldn't pronounce those names properly. 'In … Iniab … Inibini? Oh, we'll just call you Ian.'

Everyone was given British names, which for most of my mates must've been not only offensive but also very confusing.

'Jason, ask your mum if she'll do us one of those nice curry things.'

'Who's Jason? My name's Jatin.'

My mum used to bollock my mates if they called me Paddy! 'His name isn't Paddy, it's Patrick!' she'd shout at them. How do you think Bilal's mum felt when I knocked on her door and said, 'Hiya, is your Peter in?'

I didn't have a clue till I got older. When I found out some of my mates' real names I felt like a right twat. Casual racism aside, to be fair Taz is still Taz now, even among the Muslim community and his family. Anyway, he was a few years older than me and he had proper whiskers. One day he called round to mine and I opened the front door looking like a tomato with teeth.

Taz: 'Fucking hell, Paddy! What have you done to your face?'

Mum: 'His name's Patrick!' (No mention of the F-word.)

Taz: 'Sorry.'

I explained that I'd been trying to shave but it'd made my face go all red. Probably because I was using a rusty old Bic that my dad had left behind years earlier. (Hang on, my dad hadn't lived with us since 1974? Oh Jesus, it must've been my mum's for her legs.) Taz talked me through how to shave properly. How to hold the razor, which way to stroke, how to get round those awkward bits.

'Go this way,' he said, demonstrating, 'and don't put aftershave on your face straight away cos it'll sting like fuck.' Especially as the aftershave I was using wasn't even real. You could buy fake Jazz and Kouros aftershave from Bolton Market at the time. I remember the first time I sprayed some on. I was wearing a white T-shirt, which the fake Jazz instantly turned yellow. You can imagine what it did to my skin. Luckily the years of bathing in washing-up liquid had toughened me up.

Growing up in such a multicultural part of Bolton, I learned a lot, apart from actual names. I learned about Muslim and Hindu traditions. Their way of life, clothes, food. I once went to a mate's house where we all sat on the floor to eat our tea.

I whispered to him, 'Where's the forks?'

'We don't use them. We eat with our fingers.'

'Fair enough, that's how I eat a bag of chips.'

I was fortunate to have those experiences at such a young age. Those families I mixed with growing up were exactly the same as every other family in the area. Mums would be arguing with dads, kids were getting bollocked for kicking their ball against a neighbour's wall, all the usual family ups and downs. I was blessed with seeing other ways of life, but really all I'd seen was that we were all exactly the same – poor!

We lived on Auburn Street till I was about 17. By then the smell of petrol had disappeared and I was sleeping on an actual shop-bought mattress. A £15 one, to be precise, from a shop called Quintens in Bolton. Around this time my mum's health was deteriorating so the Housing Association moved us to a bungalow in an area called Deane. The bungalow was like a castle compared to our old terraced house. It had a drive with little black metal gates and a wraparound garden. It was also an end bungalow so technically it was a semi-detached!

It's funny, when you have nothing, the minute you get something you immediately want to show off and tell everyone. I couldn't wait to bring my mates, or a girl, round to the bungalow and say, 'Here, look at that, we've got a drive and someone comes round from the council to mow the lawn once a month.' My mum still didn't have any money, but having that something extra, something we'd never had before, made me feel like we were doing well. When you've not got much it's the best time to show off a bit because no one slags you off for it. All your mates were in the same boat most of the time, so they'd all buzz off it with you. These days, I'd never brag to my mates about the nice things success has afforded me. You almost go the opposite way when you start earning a few quid. I consider myself very fortunate but I wouldn't dream of banging on about it to all and sundry. I guess that's my working-class Catholic guilt rearing its head. I've seen people on social media flashing wads of cash or showing off their expensive watches and I don't get it. I prefer the mantra 'Walk softly and carry a big stick.'

Back in the day, though, it was all about, 'See these trainers? Thirty quid, they were,' 'Check out my new stereo, it's got a CD player!' or 'Look at that, we've got a proper shower.' Although that proper shower did get me into a bit of bother with my mum.

Due to our bungalow being sheltered accommodation, it had those red emergency pull cords hanging from the ceilings everywhere, and in the shower there was a fold-out seat attached to the wall. One day my then girlfriend and I had the place to ourselves and decided to jump in the shower for a bit of afternoon fun, as you do. The bungalow shower was hot and steamy. I was sat on the disability chair (romantic) and my girlfriend was sat on me, you get the picture. In the throes of teenage passion, the chair, with us sat on it, snapped off the wall. I went from Richard Gere to Frank Spencer in an instant. I threw my arm out to grab the nearest thing to stop us falling, which happened to be the red emergency cord – in hindsight not the best thing to grab but you can forgive me for not thinking clearly at the time. The emergency alarm went off, which consisted of a very loud air-raid siren type noise and – which I didn't realise at the time – a big plastic box on the outside of the bungalow with a flashing red light and the word 'HELP' on it. My girlfriend was on the bathroom floor, surrounded by debris, the shower was still going, and I was running around the bungalow pissed through, naked, trying to figure out how to turn it off. The

Batphone (a sheltered housing phone with a big red panic button on it) started ringing. I picked up in a blind panic.

'Hello!'

'Hello, love, it's the housing warden. Is everything OK? We've got an alarm notification here?'

What was I supposed to say? 'Not really, I was just shagging on the disability chair in the shower and I seem to have ripped half the wall off.'

What I actually said was, 'Erm, sorry about that, I think I've accidentally caught the red cord.'

With that the alarm suddenly stopped. *Thank God for that*, I thought. It wasn't until I walked back into the hallway, still wet, still naked, that I was greeted by my girlfriend, still wet, still naked … and my mum! She'd just turned off the alarm. The silence was deafening. It's not often I'm speechless – there's normally a way of talking yourself out of a bad situation – but this was definitely not the time for blagging. It didn't take Luther to figure out what had happened. It was a fair cop, guv. It was so tense I was half expecting the theme tune from *EastEnders* to kick in. Getting caught in the act by your parents is always traumatic, but I'd really outdone myself with this one. The next few weeks were toe-curlingly awks. I couldn't look my mum in the eye and when the tiler came round to fix the wall, I thought, *For fuck's sake, do not ask how this has happened.* Eventually, after a decade or two, I think I finally got over the embarrassment.

* * *

I was incredibly shy as a teenager. I still am now. Folk find that hard to believe but I really am. Back then the thought of walking into a room full of people would traumatise me to the point where I'd avoid it unless absolutely necessary. I missed full lessons at school and college for fear of walking in once the class had started. Even now, walking out onstage or standing in front of a TV studio audience fills me with anxiety. It goes right back as far as I can remember.

My mum would always do the weekly shop at Bolton Market. Sometimes on her way home she'd call into one of the pubs she worked in as a barmaid, the Pike View Hotel. It definitely wasn't a hotel, it was an old-school little boozer on Daubhill. It had two different rooms, the vault and the tap room. The vault, or volley, was for hardcore drinking and smoking, but the tap room was for the sportier types, with drinking, smoking and darts.

My mum would call me from the payphone in the pub to come and pick the shopping up. Fresh chicken and veg doesn't keep that well at the foot of the bar in the volley. Even though I was always laughing and joking around with my mates, walking into that pub was extremely difficult. When I opened the door, I'd walk straight over to my mum, looking down at the floor, not making eye contact and certainly not speaking to anyone. The blue haze of cigarette smoke would be hanging thick in the air and it'd be full of people getting tanked up during the day.

I'd climb up on the windowsill of the Pike to see if my mum was at the bar first. God forbid I'd have to walk around the pub looking for her. She always stood in the same spot. If I couldn't see her there I'd usually walk back home, only to then get another phone call.

'Patrick! Where are you? These pissing chicken legs are defrosting.'

My mum was always happy in a pub. She worked in most of them on Daubhill and there'd always be someone in there she knew. I actually hated it when she'd been drinking. I didn't like seeing her drunk because that wasn't my mum. Looking back now, I realise that was her only release. Being a single parent living in a two-up two-down terraced house, with a son to look after, I think I'd look forward to a beer.

I'd dread any of the regulars speaking to me, and this acute shyness stayed with me. Later on in life, therapy revealed that my shyness probably stems from feeling ashamed about something when I was very young and I ended up unearthing a really embarrassing experience from when I was about six years old. I wouldn't say I had an accident in my underpants, more a 30-car motorway pile-up. I thought I was breaking wind but my body had other ideas – it was the shart to end all sharts. At the time I was mortified and confused. Where the hell did that come from? I didn't even want to tell my mum. I was really embarrassed.

For Christmas the previous year, my dad had given me a blue plastic box for carrying little Matchbox cars in. There were no cars in it, mind, but it's the thought that counts. Anyway, on the day I followed through in my undies, that blue plastic carrier was, I decided, my way out of humiliation.

I opened it up, took the two little shelves out, whipped off my undies and stuffed them inside. If I'd been a bit older, I'd have just chucked them away, but when you're six, you don't have access to that sort of logic, so hiding them in a Matchbox carrying case seemed like the best way forward. Genius! No one would be any the wiser, despite the smell of shit in the living room, but I hadn't thought that far ahead.

It must have been a Sunday, because later that day one of my mates came round to play, by which time I'd forgotten all about 'the incident'. After a while playing, my mate started pulling a face.

'What's that smell?' he said.

I didn't cotton on at first but by the time I did, he was opening the case to investigate. Too late.

'Urgh! Skiddy undies!' he shouted.

I was absolutely mortified, to the point where I didn't know what to say or do with myself. At school the next day there were cries of 'You got dirty undies!' and 'You've got skids in your pants!' from the other kids. I mean, to a six-year-old, discovering your mate's shitty pants stuffed in a toy was big news, so he had of course told everyone. At that delicate age, something like that can be so traumatic that it stays with you. The shame of it had scarred me to the point that I found it difficult to speak to people or even look them in the eye. Harris and I once ripped Fred's undies off during an episode of *Top Gear*. There was something in there that'd put a yule log to shame. We were howling with laughter and to a bloke that's nothing major – but when you're six and the entire school is talking about it it's very different.

Another big hang-up I had as a kid was the fact that my ears stuck out. I hated them, and consequently always kept my hair long and curly so they were well and truly covered up. One day at school, a girl told me she thought I'd look nice with my hair pushed back behind my ears, so I bit the bullet and gave it a go. This turned out to be a huge mistake, as the sight of my sticky-out ears was the subject of much hilarity, with everyone laughing and taking the piss, including the girl.

This fear of being exposed is sometimes still very real, even now. My wife Christine often says to me that I don't let people in, that I'm secretive. I don't mean to be but I know she's right. I have this skewed notion that if I let people in they'll have some sort of angle on me. Take my fear of flying, which I've had for most of my adult life. For the longest time, I never spoke publicly about it. To me, if people knew I had this deep-seated, some might say irrational, fear, then they'd somehow have something over me.

Walking into cafes and shops in the village where I live now, I still instinctively keep my head down, intent on avoiding eye contact with other people. It's not that I don't want to be friendly, it's just an odd feeling I get in my stomach when I walk into a room full of people I don't know. I suppose the job I do doesn't really help that. The more famous I got, the more I'd avoid people. It's strange, isn't it? I've chosen a profession that relies on people recognising and interacting with me, the one thing I've always struggled with. If I go into a restaurant or bar, I always ask for a table at the back or something tucked away.

I can handle it these days, now I'm aware of why it's happening, but back in my teenage years it caused me all sorts of problems. That internalising of thoughts and feelings, that fear of being exposed, manifested itself as a real physical illness that nearly killed me during my college years. Well, that and severe money worries.

SOLE PROVIDER

It was the best of times, it was the worst of times.

I was envious of people I knew who never had to give their parents money for their keep. They weren't necessarily well off, but they usually had a mum and dad at home who both had jobs, so they never really needed to chip in towards rent and food. For me it was pretty much straight from leaving school you got a job and this would allow me to give my mum around 35 quid a week for my keep. So when I decided I wanted to get some further education at college after leaving school, the idea of telling my mum wasn't a very fun prospect. I was the one bringing a wage in and for that to stop was a major deal. I was labouring at the time. It was all cash in hand but I didn't care, so long as I had enough to give my mum for keep. Kids like me didn't have the luxury of taking gap years or continuing with education.

I loved science at school. It was one of only three subjects I was any good at, the other two being English and RE. I totally get the importance of a good teacher. I did well in those three subjects because the teachers made the lessons interesting and engaging. My science teacher, Mrs Walker, and my RE teacher, Mrs Mullen, were fantastic. They got the best out of me, encouraging my enthusiasm and engaging with me whereas all the other teachers only asked the smart kids for answers. Towards the end of school, and due to Mrs Walker, I decided I wanted to work in science, maybe get a job as a lab technician. I left school with an A and the next step on the ladder was to study for a BTEC diploma in science at Bolton College. My mum wasn't keen.

'But you're gonna have to work, Patrick, we need the money,' she said when I broke the news. No young person should have to worry about this kind of dilemma but unfortunately that's the way it was for me and no doubt countless others out there as well.

I understood where she was coming from. I knew my mum loved me to bits, she'd always worked and provided for me when I was younger, but now she'd given up work due to ill health. Still, putting that kind of responsibility on my shoulders caused me a lot of stress and anxiety, to the point where I eventually became very ill.

I knew I'd have to get a job while I was at college to sway my mum into giving me an easier time, but then I found out I could get a grant from college of about £300, twice a year, so I told my mum she could have that. These were the kind of deals I needed to make if I wanted to push on in life. Hand over all the money for books and things in exchange for doing a course that requires you to have books and things. Anyhow, my mum eventually agreed, and for the first year that's what happened. The problem was, it wasn't nearly enough for us both to live on, plus I had no money left to buy the things the grant was meant for. Books, stationery, bus fares and lunches all went out the window. If that wasn't enough to stress about, it wasn't long before my mum was asking me when the next lot of grant money was coming in. In the end, I got myself a part-time job, stacking shelves at Morrisons, where I worked nights and days. I also had a Saturday job at Warburtons, such was the need I felt to provide for my mum. All that along with trying to study for a college course that I had no books for felt like a lot to cope with. What am I on about, felt? It *was* a lot to cope with, I was 17!

I'd teamed up with a good little gang of mates at Bolton College. This included some of my old school mates and a few new pals as well. Peter Stott (Stotty) and John Beaulieu (Bully) I went to school with and still know and see to this day. (Stotty was the lad who helped get me on at Morrisons and Warburtons. The Saturday job at Warburtons turned out to be one of the worst jobs I ever had – nice one, Stotty.) Then there was Parvez (Niggi), who smoked more weed than Bob Marley and Cypress Hill combined, and Derek Grant (Del), who was a couple of years older than me but we went to the same primary school. There was also Olly and Emu, Niggi's brothers, Paul Morris and a lad called Jacko, who got that nickname for doing a belting MJ impression in the days before the Jesus juice and child sleepovers. As a gang, we were like the United Colors of Benetton: three white lads, two black lads, three Asian lads, and anyone else who tagged along.

Del was big built, with a beard, and he always seemed older than the rest of us, even though there was only a couple of years' difference. He was 19 but looked 25, and had his own flat, which we all thought was amazing. Del was that lad who'd walk out the showers at school with a full quota of pubes. Even though it was very basic, we all loved hanging out at Del's flat listening to music, smoking and playing *Street Fighter*. If you sat on his couch, your arse was on the floor because you went straight through it, and he never had any food in. Instead he'd knock us up a plate of dumplings, which always went down well. He lived on dumplings and pints of water with about ten sugars in it. Everywhere you look these days it's all protein bars and power shakes. Del was a unit on flour, water and sugar.

We spent more time hanging out at Del's flat than we did in college. He was a bright lad but like the rest of us came from nothing. He used to talk about being a doctor – I remember walking into his flat one day to find him in front of his bathroom mirror cutting the inside of his own eyelid open with an old razor blade to get rid of a cyst.

'Del, what the fuck are you doing, son?'

'Just a bit of operating, Ginn, I couldn't get in with the doctor.'

(All my mates have different nicknames for me. Most of my school mates and telly bods call me Paddy, all my college mates called me Ginny or Ginn, people I worked with at Bolton Council called me Pat and with my family I'm always Patrick. Anyhow, I digress, back to Del's flat.)

The entrance buzzer to Del's never worked, so every morning me and Stotty would climb on to the bins and jump up on to the first-floor balcony of the high rise and then walk the rest of the way up the stairs. We'd bang on the door for ages to wake him up, and he'd usually open the door with a plastic bag on his head, something to do with conditioning treatment on his Afro. Out of all my black mates, Del was the only one to answer the door with a Morrisons bag on his head.

On the day we got our grants, Del went straight down to Curry's and bought a Toshiba hi-fi stack system – done! All his money gone in one go. To me this was madness because like the rest of us he didn't have any money. I, of course, gave all mine to my mum, but even if I'd had it to myself I wouldn't have done it all in on just one thing. I was good at rationing, even then, and I'd have made it last.

The problem with Del buying a brand-new Toshiba that day was there was no electricity on. Eventually, though, we managed to put some money on the electric card, and I spent the rest of the day with the boys smoking and listening to R&B and hip-hop. Some would say that's a waste of a day but for us it was the best time ever.

During my second year at college, things got tricky, and that's when I got seriously ill. I was under a lot of pressure from my mum to keep the money coming in, but I was becoming more wayward, hanging around with my boys and neglecting my college work. I knew I'd fallen behind but what I didn't realise was the science teacher had to sign a form that enabled me to get my grant. The trouble was, as I'd rarely turned up for his class, he refused to sign it.

My mum kept asking me, 'When's that money coming?'

'It's on its way, Mum, just another few days to get it sorted out. Just a bit of red tape at college.'

The truth was, I had no idea when it was coming or if it was coming at all, and I started to stress out big time. In the end, this teacher agreed that if I turned up for ten lessons, he'd sign the form and I could get my grant. I decided to knuckle down. It wasn't as if I was doing anything exceptional; I was supposed to be there anyway. As far as I was concerned, though, I was doing him a favour and going out of my way. At the end of the tenth lesson, I felt a huge sense of relief, but I had a shock coming to me.

'I'm not signing it,' the teacher said.

'What? But I've done everything you asked.' I couldn't believe what I was hearing.

'I'm not signing it,' he said.

I can clearly recall the feeling that came over me: absolute fury from head to toe. I thought, *I'm going to kill this prick right here in the classroom. I'm going to do him in.* In hindsight, not murdering my science teacher was the right call – I'd have had to change the title of this book from *My Lifey* to *Doing Lifey*!

My mum kept asking me where the money from the grant was, and by now I was sick with worry. In the end, I went to someone more senior in the college, a bloke named Ted Heath, who'd taken a bit of a shine to me and some of the other rough diamonds in our little group. I explained to Ted what had happened, and eventually he signed the form, which enabled me to get the grant and give my mum the money she needed.

Unfortunately, the anxiety and stress of it all had already taken its toll on my body. I'd been suffering with bad stomach pains for a while, for which the doctor had prescribed medication, but they were getting worse. I had no idea they were being caused by stress. As it turned out, I'd actually developed a stomach ulcer, which is quite rare in someone so young. Financial stress is the worst, and not knowing where the next pound is coming from is an awful feeling. I think that's what still drives me on to work and earn money – it doesn't come from greed or always wanting more, it comes from knowing what it's like to have nothing. Christine sometimes tells me I'm working too hard or doing too many things at once but I want our kids to have the things I didn't have and I certainly don't want them to feel the money pressures I did when I was a teenager.

Despite the stomach pains, I was still living this mad life with the boys. In the day, we'd be racing around the streets on mountain bikes 'we'd found, your honour' and sprayed up a totally different colour. It wasn't like we were pulling wraps of coke out of our pockets and selling them, but we were always on the lookout for ways to make a few quid. We'd stay out all night, hanging around on the streets and sleeping in cars. We always knew where the cars and vans that had been abandoned were, and once we were in them, we'd rip the carpets out of the footwell and put them over us, like blankets. Myself and Del did that one night in a Volkswagen Scirocco, very snug. I had a home to go to, we all did, but for some reason this seemed normal. We were a gang and we were on the streets, and that's how it was. Our lives revolved around girls, computer games and having the best trainers we could get our hands on.

One afternoon, Del needed a new coat and it seemed like the only way he could get one would be by robbing a coat out of a

C&A. It didn't feel like it would be the crime of the century. I'm not condoning any kind of criminal activity, but my mindset at the time was if it was a big shop like C&A then it didn't seem bad, not like burgling someone's house and stealing their belongings, which was completely unacceptable. In any event, nothing at all happened. Out of the blue, I was doubled up in pain in the middle of the shop.

'Are you all right?' Del asked.

'No, I think I need to go home,' I told him, and staggered out on to the street.

I could barely straighten up as I walked home, and soon as I got there, I collapsed on the bed in agony.

Mum panicked and got the doctor out. He examined me, gave me some tablets and left. My mum was old school so whatever a doctor said was taken as gospel. Luckily, my dad called round soon after and saw how much pain I was in. He called an ambulance straight away. The ulcer, which the doctor totally missed, had now burst. In fact, if my dad hadn't called the ambulance when he did, I'd have died. No sooner had I arrived at the hospital, I was under the knife. I woke up wondering what the fuck was going on. I mean, three hours ago I'd been in C&A, contemplating whether to help get a security tag off a coat, and now I was flat on my back with a scar on my belly and a tube up my nose.

I spent the following week in hospital and the worst of it was I couldn't eat solid food due to the operation. The bloke in the bed facing me was ordering bacon on toast for his breakfast every morning while I had the delights of 10ml of water every three hours.

I couldn't wait to eat some food again and I had my sights set on that bacon butty. The day eventually came. The nurse removed the tube from my nose and told me I could now try solid food.

'Bacon on toast, please!'

My mouth was watering as they put it in front of me – the smell was heavenly. Just as I was about to take my first bite, a nurse popped up and whipped it out of my hand.

'That's far too salty and heavy to be eating, we're going to do you some wet porridge instead.'

Great.

* * *

My mum had no idea that the stress I was experiencing had led to me developing an ulcer. To be fair, she never really knew what was going on in my life once I went through our front door. I didn't share much about what I'd done at college or work and she never really asked me much about it either. Even though there were no parents evenings attended, or interest in what college courses I should do when I left school, I knew I could always rely on her to be there for me whenever I needed it. She had put her life on hold to bring me up, and I loved her more than anything. Her main concern in life was whether we had food on the table and the rent was paid. The cause of my burst ulcer was undoubtedly due to the financial stress I was under at that time. Trying to juggle college, two jobs and keeping my mum happy proved too much.

My dad never really knew what I got up to either. He was so lenient and chilled out, I could have got away with murder. My mum always said, 'If you'd have lived with your dad, you'd have ended up in jail,' and I think she was right. I could stay out for days on end and my dad wouldn't bat an eyelid, whereas Mum would worry herself to death. Still, on this occasion, I suppose you could say that my dad saved my life – well, him and the surgeon.

Once I'd recovered, I was straight back to Del's flat. It was in an area called School Hill, which was rougher than a sandpaper enema. When we discovered a repossessed flat on the same block, I decided it would be the ideal place to live, rent free.

We managed to get in through a window and get the bolts off the front door. We got ourselves a leccy card and I put a mattress on the floor to kip on – luxury. There were a couple of stools in the living room, a telly and a Sega Mega Drive, which to us were far more essential than couches or food. I remember going out for supplies one evening and coming back with a packet of pork sausages, not the brightest of ideas as half the lads were Muslim. Still, with me on Wall's skinless sausage butties and a couple of the others tucking into a tin of peas, we were living the life. Never mind the bills and demands coming through the door with someone else's name on – this was our place. We certainly never thought of it as squatting, we didn't even see it as illegal. Most of the lads around were doing what they were doing to get by: ducking and diving, maybe nicking the odd thing.

At weekends, we had our own little hang-out spot in the Bolton Market Place, which was a decent-sized indoor shopping centre. We'd sit, talk and laugh while trying our best to attract the attention of passing girls. This was also where we made plans for what we were going to get up to that evening, pooling any money we had for a night out. The town centre seemed so vibrant; there was always so much going on. We never felt bored or short of things to do. I class myself lucky, growing up in the eighties and nineties. True, we didn't have many of the advantages and all the tech that kids have now, but we also didn't have the pressure of social media, or the need to be as good or successful or attractive as everyone else. For us, dating wasn't swipe left or right, it was begging the bar staff for a pen so you could write someone's phone number on the back of a fag packet. I never thought I'd say you don't know you're born but young people today really don't. All the hard yards you had to put in to get a girl's number. Now a shag is just the swipe of a phone screen away.

Back then, if we did manage to find enough money to get into a club of a Saturday night, we knew we had to look our best. You were getting in nowhere wearing trainers, so you had to buy a nice shirt, smart trousers and, as was fashionable round our way at the time, shoes that looked likes spats. There was also a craze for coloured contact lenses, which we not only wore to the clubs but to college as well. One of the lads, Paul, was black and wore the brightest blue contact lenses ever. This particular day he'd run out of contact lens solution so decided to use washing-up liquid instead. I mean, it gets the plates clean enough and I'd been bathing in it for the first 14 years of my life, why not? When I got to his house to walk to college, he told me his vision was crystal clear, he couldn't believe how clean his lenses were. During our first lesson, I heard this agonising cry, and looked round to find Paul unable to open his eyes, with tears streaming down his cheeks. With it being a science lab, there was always eyewash on hand, but by the time the teacher got to him the bloody things had almost melted on to his eyes. In fact, he was lucky he wasn't blinded. The rest of the class, meanwhile, were in hysterics. One of the lads, Olly, had to walk Paul home because he couldn't see. Back then, everything in life was a learning curve.

Most of my mates were good dancers, so almost the entire evening in a club was spent on the dance floor, which is how we got chatting to girls – the blokes who stood around the dance floor holding their pints and trying their best to look hard never stood a chance. We didn't always stay in Bolton either. Sometimes we'd venture to Blackburn or Preston, where there was a fantastic hip-hop club. Those nights were brilliant fun – proper little adventures.

It was around that time I drove my first car. I was 17, had no licence, no insurance and the car had no MOT. I did have a tax disc though. Yes, it'd been taken out of somebody else's car, but once rubbed with a bit of brake fluid to get the ink off, you could write your own details on it. All of us did it. None of us had a licence but we all drove. I'd driven my dad's car from when I was around 11. He used to give me lessons on a big wide road called Beaumont Road.

I loved driving. As soon as you could get behind the wheel, legal or not, you'd do it. The way we got around not having insurance was to ring up an insurance company and get a cover note. If we ever got stopped, we could just say, 'Yes, I'm insured, but I'm waiting for it to go through, and here's my cover note.'

I didn't think about how stupid and dangerous it all was, but now the thought that I could have hurt or even killed someone makes me feel sick. You hear about these dickhead drivers crashing with no insurance and it makes my blood boil, but back in my teenage years those kind of thoughts didn't enter my head. I was oblivious to it all at that age. I got arrested once for siphoning petrol out of a car that had seemingly been dumped outside the Farmer's Arms pub on Daubhill. I was 13 or 14 at the time. We had found a mini motorbike in the back yard of a derelict house and we weren't sure if it worked or not so we needed some petrol to find out. When we opened the car's petrol cap, instead of a screw cap we were greeted with an old pair of knickers stuffed in it – not dainty ones, either, these were proper apple-catchers. We decided that the car had most definitely been abandoned. While I was in the middle of siphoning the petrol, a policeman on a motorbike clocked us and stopped. The next thing I knew, I was in the holding cells at Bolton Police Station.

The cells weren't particularly scary but the thought of my mum finding out shit the living daylights out of me. After I was released, due to the bloke using a pair of knickers as a petrol cap not pressing charges, I had to go back to the station a few days later. I was stood in the sergeant's room, on the receiving end of a bollocking from this police officer. In the middle of this telling-off, I heard my mum break down in tears behind me. My heart sank. That's when it hit home how fucking stupid I was being. It wasn't being arrested, or being put in a cell, or the bollocking I got from the sergeant. It was hearing my mum cry that drove the point home. That woman had done her best for me in life, and I was breaking her heart. I knew that she was seeing what might happen: the boy who was always in trouble turning into a man who's a criminal. I guess that was the moment things changed for me. Don't get me wrong, I was still up to all sorts with the lads, but I never went too far. I knew when to stop and say no. Not long after that arrest, I jumped into the back of a car that my mate was driving. A few minutes later I clocked a screwdriver stuck in the ignition.

'Is this yours?' I said to my mate who shall rename nameless.

'Nah, I nicked it today.'

I told him to pull over and let me out. I wasn't scared of getting arrested or even my mate's dangerous driving, I just couldn't bear the thought of seeing my mum cry again. I couldn't put her through it. If your mum's crying and upset, you feel like shit, I don't care who you are. That was the last time I ever got into a stolen car.

THE FICKLE FINGER
OF FATE

Fate is a strange thing, and if I hadn't been the wayward kid I was, skipping college and hanging about on the streets, I probably wouldn't have bumped into Peter Kay again one afternoon, and the whole trajectory of my life might have been very different.

I'd known Peter for as long as I could remember. In fact, our lives had been intertwined from when we were toddlers, albeit unknowingly. We were both at the Alexandra Street Nursery on Daubhill, although our mums didn't know one another and neither of us has any recollection of each other. Eventually, we ended up at secondary school together.

This is when we became friends, but our friendship blossomed more outside of school than it did inside the school gates. As students, we were polar opposites. I was more into playing football, messing about, climbing on rooves and general tomfoolery kind of kid and Peter was more of a going home for his dinner and staying in the classroom type. Outside of school, however, we found a common ground and were two peas in a pod. We liked the same things, got on brilliantly, and our sense of humour was totally in sync. I loved going to his house, talking about films, music and telly. I loved it because secretly that's what I really enjoyed doing more than anything – and it was definitely more fun than getting arrested.

Peter had an endless supply of ideas and stories he'd scribbled down on notepads. We'd perform mini movie montages to songs – one of our favourites at the time was a Marillion track called 'Assassing'. I'd stand in front of the mirror in Peter's bedroom, he would whack 'Assassing' on the record player (yes, it was that long ago) and then he'd direct the action. We both had vivid imaginations and were never short of things to talk about. We'd howl with laughter listening to the likes of Billy Connolly and Jasper Carrott, and watch films like *Stir Crazy*, *Trading Places*, *Silver Streak* and *Young Frankenstein* on his dad's VCR – all copies, of course. Another thing Peter used to do was if I hadn't seen a film he'd talk me through it, start to finish. I honestly preferred this to actually watching the film myself. In fact, he still does that to this day. If he's seen a film or programme before me, I'll just get him to describe it. Those wonderful innocent times will stay with me forever.

Anyway, on that chance meeting I bumped into Peter on Manchester Road, which ran right past the front of our college. I was hanging out with Stotty and Del and I spotted him doing a bit of filming with a camcorder.

'Oi, Kay, fuckin' hell!' I was buzzing to see him. We'd spent all that time together making pop videos in his bedroom and watching films but we'd lost touch after leaving school.

CHAPTER 4

'What you doing, Kay, making porn?' asked Stotty. Quick one: at school everyone called Peter 'Kay', do you follow?

As it turned out, he was also studying at Bolton College, doing some kind of theatrical production course or something like that. Even though I loved all the stories and stuff we used to do together at school, the idea of doing a course like that just didn't appeal to me. I mean, how was learning to perform onstage going to provide for a family? (Fast-forward to me typing these words in my fancy home office.) In fact, that was exactly the kind of course I should've done. It would have been much more interesting and made me so much happier. It's amazing how social conditioning works. Here I was, a lad who loved telly and films and the idea of making them – but I would never have dreamed of pursuing a career in that world. It was deemed a bit poncey and something I wouldn't have mentioned to anyone for fear of being ridiculed. It's at times like this when I can totally relate to Billy Elliot. That lad knows what I'm talking about.

Anyhow, back to that chance meeting and the fickle finger of fate.

'I'm filming something for a college project,' Peter said, brandishing his camcorder.

'Go on, film us, Kay,' I said.

We all started larking about on a digger at the side of the road while Peter filmed us. Camcorders were still a bit of a novelty, and the idea of seeing ourselves 'on telly' was fantastic. It was like one of those programmes you see on National Geographic: we were some hidden tribe that had been discovered in the jungle. When Peter played the footage, witchcraft! In fact, he's still got the video we made that day.

After that day, Peter and I reconnected again, which might not have happened if I hadn't been wagging a lesson. Fate and truancy brought us back together.

Over the next year or so, I re-took my GCSEs, twice, at Bolton College, mainly because the grants kept coming in and at school they never seemed important to me. I'm not sure how it is now but at my school the kids who were deemed naughty or not interested just never got the time put in with them by the teachers. I had no aspirations whatsoever, which is quite sad really, although at the time it didn't feel that way. When I eventually left college, that was when things felt a bit scarier. College for me was just like school without the uniform, apart from not getting free dinners any more.

As it turned out, my dreams of a career in science were not to be. I lasted a day in a dental laboratory. It was the most horrendously monotonous job I could imagine, and despite there being hundreds of different jobs within the various fields of science, it put me right off and I decided it wasn't for me. Not only was it monotonous, the lab was slap bang next to a factory that made dog chews. There's a smell I'll never forget! Boiled pig skin. It made my Saturday job at Warburtons feel like the Ritz! Still, I've got fond memories of my Bolton College days, Del's flat and our little gang. And despite being under financial pressure, most of it felt like one long adventure.

I'm still good friends with most of the boys now. Del moved to London but we reconnected recently and for as long as I can remember I've taken Stotty, Niggi and Bully out for a Christmas meal and piss-up every year. If you can't treat your mates, what's the point? I've never understood tight-fisted people. One of the things that motivates me is being in a position where you can help others – that always gives me a nice feeling.

So, with a couple of years' worth of science studies in the locker I left college with all my qualifications and within the space of a few days I was working on a building site, that hotbed of science and technology. When you're young you live in the moment, and pensions, job security and mortgages are just boring things adults speak about. The fact that I'd been to college for a couple of years didn't feel like a waste of time because I'd had so much fun and made some lifelong friends. Also, my mum and dad weren't on my back about getting a career; no one was pushing or guiding me into anything really.

My old school pal and best mate to this day is a lad called Francis Tobin, and it's safe to say I love him to bits. I've always looked at Franny as family. In fact I look at all of his family as mine too. I see him as a brother more than a mate. Franny, along with his two older brothers Taz and Anton, who I'm also great pals with, worked as floor screeders. Screed is a mixture of sand and cement and it's pretty much in most floors you've walked on. We're all football mad so I'd go with Fran and his brothers to play footy on the local parks and playing fields in Bolton. Franny, and he'll dine out on this, was a magician with the ball, a real natural talent. At school there'd be four or five of us around him trying to get the ball off him but it was like it was superglued to his feet. I'm convinced he could've gone on to play professionally but most of us back then weren't really pushed, guided and supported. You need someone to really invest in you as a youngster. Even though we were all loved and happy, I never saw that kind of help growing up. Fran's brothers could play and his dad 'Tucker' was decent too, so I could see where he got it from.

Anyway, missed callings aside, Fran was now working with Taz and Anton as a labourer so I asked him if he could get me on. The answer was an immediate yes and I soon knew why. You see, it's impossible to get sacked from screeding. The job was that physically demanding that stopping lads from quitting was the biggest part of it! One lad, Jay, even chose prison over screeding. He'd got in trouble for not paying a fine and was given the option of paying the fine or going to prison. Anton offered to pay his fine in return for Jay working on the screed. Jay opted for prison! Much to his objections, Anton still paid the fine. I remember working with Jay and he'd be moaning about how he could've been in a nice comfy cell instead of this!

The job was made even harder by the fact Taz and Anton never had any decent tools. Some jobs would require you to fill buckets up with screed and carry them up flights of stairs because the machine pumps couldn't reach that high. This was real labour and if that wasn't hard enough they didn't even have proper buckets! Instead we used old industrial three-gallon paint pots which had no handles, due to them being snapped off under the weight of the screed. By the time they were filled up they weighed around 35kg each, made even worse by the heavy-duty string used as make-shift handles. By the time you'd picked them up and put them back down, your hands were nigh on cut in half. The buckets were filled that much that you'd have to dig your knuckles into the top of the screed just to be able to grab hold of the string handles. To add insult to injury, even the shovels we used to fill them were goosed! The edges were usually snapped off and they'd be coated in layers of old dried cement that'd built up over time.

Franny laid the floors and I was his labourer. We travelled all over the UK doing jobs together and we did a lot of laughing. Working with your best mate has its advantages and disadvantages. We messed about that much, it was more or less guaranteed we'd never get a job finished while it was still daylight. We worked on this one job in Manchester, a high-rise building, which meant bucketing up 12 storeys, yes, 12. I'd have to stop every three or four floors just to get the circulation back to my fingers where the string was cutting the blood supply off. One day we'd decided to stop for a bit of dinner, which we ate sat on the side of some scaffolding around 100 foot in the air. You'd never see that these days, two young lads, no hi-vis vests, helmets or safety harnesses, just sat with their feet dangling off the edge eating sarnies. Back then the main source of entertainment for us was the knacky mag and the *Sunday Sport*, staples for the young upwardly mobile builder – we'd always have copies in the van. From where we were sat, I spotted a paper shop below.

'Shall we get a *Razzle*?' I asked.

'Yeah, but I'm not getting it!' said Franny.

Here lay our usual dilemma. We both enjoyed an adult magazine but neither of us had the balls to buy one. Especially if it was a little old lady behind the counter, that'd be mortifying! It always ended up in an argument about who went in last time and whose turn it was this time. Anyhow, mid-argument Fran said he'd go in for it if I smoked a cigarette. He was smoking at the time and although I'd been surrounded by smokers all my life, I'd never liked it and the thought turned my stomach. On the other hand, I really liked looking at breasts, so of course I agreed.

We sat on that scaffolding, me coughing and spluttering.

'She's fit!' (cough, cough) 'Look at the size of those!' (splutter, cough).

He'd given me a Lambert & Butler red – it nearly blew my head off! That kind of behaviour was typical for us, though, always trying to get one over on each other. Another time we were on a wheelbarrow job together. I'd shovel the pre-mixed screed into the barrow and wheel it in for Franny to lay. We'd had some bacon butties for our dinner and there were some of those little sachets of brown and red sauce left over. What Fran decided to do, in all his wisdom, was squeeze them under the handles of my wheelbarrow. This went on all afternoon and by the end of the day my hands were sticky, stinking and stinging.

It was now my turn to exact some well-earned revenge. Fran's Achilles' heel is he's a clean freak: he was using hand sanitiser long before Covid reared its ugly head. I've never known a hairy-arsed builder to be so particular about cleanliness. On our way home from the job, we stopped to fill the van up with diesel. While Franny was filling up I noticed he'd left his sandwiches exposed on the seat beside me, a massive schoolboy error. The one thing you never did with that group of mates was leave any food or drink lying about. I've been on sportsmen's dinners where if you needed to nip to the loo you'd put your knife and fork in your top pocket, pick your plate up and take it all with you. Taking your dinner plate into a public toilet was a better and more hygienic option than leaving it on the table with all the lads there.

I spotted Fran's egg mayo baguette and then noticed the van ashtray was overflowing with cigarette ends. I took the most horrendous, yellow, nicotine-stained one I could find and pushed it deep down into his egg mayo, then carefully wrapped it back up in the clingfilm. That was the trickiest part – everyone was that paranoid about leaving food and drink about that if even the slightest sign of tampering was seen the baguette would end up in the bin, uneaten, even if nothing had been done to it.

Patience was key to this working. If I asked him why he wasn't eating his sarnie then that would immediately arouse suspicion and the whole thing would topple like an egg-mayo-filled-with-fag-end house of cards.

We'd been on the road for an hour or so, chatting away, before he picked up his baguette and started to unwrap it. *Here we go!* I thought. My jaw was aching trying not to laugh as he took his first big bite. I watched him intently out of the corner of my eye. He swallowed it down and hungrily took a second bite – down that went without any issues. Now we were getting ready for bite number three. This was ground zero, no turning back now. He took another big old bite and started chewing. How I stopped myself from laughing was anyone's guess. My stomach was tensed as I watched him slowly discover what hidden delight was in his egg mayo baguette. The thing with a cigarette butt is it's quite squishy so Franny was chewing away, oblivious, until he did that classic, slow, something isn't right in here movement. I couldn't hold on any longer and burst into hysterics, a proper doubled-over, can't-breathe job. He knew something was definitely not right now and immediately stopped chewing. The sight of him pulling that festering cigarette butt out of his mouth was priceless. Even more so as it was then followed by a bit of retching, absolute gold.

* * *

Another job I worked on was the rebuilding of Manchester's Strangeways prison. In the early nineties there'd been a riot and rooftop protest there so major work was needed. Myself, Franny and his brother Anton ended up laying all the floors in solitary confinement and most of the other prison cells. In fact, if you're an inmate in Strangeways and you're reading this, firstly good choice, secondly if you think you've got it bad you want to try bucketing in all that screed! On a sidenote, if you're thinking of rioting again, spare a thought for me and my mates – we sweated our bollocks off putting that in. The rebuilding of Strangeways was a great job because it was so big. This meant we had steady work only a 25-minute drive from Bolton and, more importantly, they had catering on site. We'd rock up in the morning and make our way straight to the portacabin that was doing the breakfasts. This one particular morning we noticed quite a bit of commotion outside the cabin. There were a group of builders trying to get in.

'Bloody hell, they must be doing a two for one on brekkies,' I said.

When we got nearer it became apparent why: there was a stripper performing in there. Bit random to see at the best of times but 7.30 in the morning during a breakfast serving was a bit mad. This didn't deter us, though, so we made our way around the back of the breakfast cabin and opened the fire door – bingo, front-row seats! It turns out one of the other builders was getting married and this had been arranged by his mates. So there we were, first thing in the morning, enjoying a cup of tea and a bacon butty, watching some bloke on his knees, covered in squirty cream, being whipped by a naked stripper while a load of builders whooped and cheered.

Myself and Franny were very competitive back in the day. We still are now. One time we were driving to, funnily enough, another prison job, this time in Lancaster. We were on the motorway, Franny's window was slightly down and it was winter so he started to close it, to which I said, 'Pussy.' That was all it needed. He immediately wound his window all the way down in a display of 'I'm not cold.' At the time he just had a T-shirt on and I was wearing my work coat. Normally we were in a van but today he was driving a car so my seat was in the fully reclined position – any chance to get a bit more sleep.

'Oh, you're not cold then?' I asked.

'No, I'm not,' he said.

'OK, you won't mind if I put my window down as well then.'

So we're now driving up the motorway, first thing in the morning, middle of winter with both windows down. Franny, in an extra show of stubbornness, even had his arm up on the side of the door, and the wind was that extreme his entire T-shirt was flapping about. His arm started turning blue so I decided to open the back windows as well. We're now doing about 70mph with all the windows down in what was essentially a freezer on wheels. Fran then went one better: he opened the sunroof and switched all the blowers in the car full on and to cold. When we finally got to the prison it was like that scene from *Dumb and Dumber* where they're both frozen together. Franny's arms were purple and my face was bright red with wind burn. The foreman came up to the car and asked if we were OK. 'We're fine, thanks, pal.' Well, apart from mild symptoms of hypothermia! We then wound up every window in the car and put the heaters on top whack. We sat there for a good hour thawing out, which again set us back on the job and meant another late finish. That's how quickly things could escalate, all from a little jibe.

One evening Taz, Franny's oldest brother, was throwing a house party and said make sure you bring a bottle or some beers. Being skint, I came up with a genius idea. I toured round a few local pubs and asked if they had any empty vodka bottles. I managed to get my hands on one, took it straight home and filled it with water. The bottle was still fresh so you got a nice waft of vodka once you removed the lid – that'll do nicely. I then bought the cheapest four-pack of beer I could find in the supermarket. It was called Askers, I'd never heard of it before and I've never heard of it since but it was cheap and alcoholic. Taz and the rest of the lads knew I was a careful Christian when it came to shelling out money so when I arrived at the party and held up my Askers I was met with a barrage of abuse. It was then I played my ace in the hole and whipped out my water-filled bottle of vodders! Taz couldn't believe his eyes.

'I've brought the good stuff, Taz!' I said.

Quick as a flash I went straight to the kitchen, stuck my bottle of water at the back of everyone else's drinks, placed my Askers in the fridge and tucked into some Buds that were nicely chilled. Trawling those pubs for empty bottles had really got me a thirst on.

Now, what I didn't take into account was that all the lads were complete piss pots and to say they enjoyed a drink was an understatement. No sooner had the beer touched my lips when I heard my mate Andy C exclaim, 'Who the fuck's brought this?'

Luckily for me Taz was out of earshot so I decided to style it out by looking equally perplexed.

'Brought what, C?'

'This vodka, it tastes like water!'

Due to the party being in full swing, not many people had got on to Andy's protest. I jumped up and made my way over to calm down the situation before the entire house heard him. I was a bit like a low-rent UN peacekeeper in the middle of a potential war zone.

'Water?' I said, putting my best acting confused face on. 'Are you sure?'

Of course he was sure. Andy C could've put Oliver Reed to shame! If there was one thing C knew about it was alcohol. I then went through the motions of sniffing it and exclaiming that it smelt like vodka and maybe he'd got it wrong? This is what's known in the trade as grasping at straws and lying through your teeth. By now a small mob had formed behind me.

64

'What's going on?' someone asked.

Here we go, I thought, *this is where it'll all kick off.* I desperately tried to change the subject.

'Fran, have we still got those wank mags in the van?'

Just as I tried to change their train of thought, Taz appeared. Oh, for fuck's sake, that was all I needed.

'Paddy brought that vodka! Give it here, let me have a taste,' he said, eyeballing me.

That was it, the game was well and truly up. It's a fair cop, guv. If Andy C was Oliver Reed, Taz was George Best, Richard Harris and Ernest Hemingway combined. Even though I was now bang to rights, I still tried one last roll of the dice. Sometimes in these kind of situations, a great little trick is to be equally disgusted and upset.

'Water!' I said. 'The robbing bastard at the off licence has ripped me off! I can't believe it!' And funnily enough neither did they. The rest of the evening was an onslaught of barracking from the lads and to be fair to them I admire their commitment because even now, some 27 or so years later, it still gets brought out whenever we have an argument. Like most of my mates from back in the day, nothing's really changed. Myself, Franny and the lads still go on holiday together every year – we call ourselves the Hateful Eight and we even have tattoos to prove it. Franny, Taz and Anton will be laying the drive of my house soon and I might even do the buckets for them! Lifelong mates – and here's to many more years of laughter and watered-down vodka.

CHAPTER 5

WONDER WOMEN AND A FEW SUPER MEN

Most of the strength, influence and protection in my life has come from strong women – girl power. My mum, Angie, aunties, cousins, my wife, and many more within the entertainment industry. I've always felt that women have been the guiding light in my life. There was one man, however, who had a huge part in shaping me, and that was my mum's brother, Tony. My uncle Tony was the person who taught me how to be a man. I've never told him, but I love him very much. Although I rarely see him these days, I think about him a lot and the formative years I spent in his company. He did more for me than he'll ever know.

My uncle Tony was one of those blokes who encouraged his kids to do what they loved. He'd be there at football practice, swimming, running – you name it, he'd get right behind them. As much as I loved spending time with my dad, I never had that kind of relationship with him. He took me to a few kung fu classes when I was younger but that was about as far as it went. We laughed a lot and I always looked forward to him picking me up at the weekend but it wasn't a very supportive relationship. After he dropped me back off home, that was it until the following weekend. There was certainly no interest in my schooling or sports days, well, not that I was aware of. So Uncle Tony stepped in and filled the gap. I never knew him growing up and didn't have much to do with him until my late teens. I'd left college with my BTEC in Science and had been working with my best mate Franny, labouring on various building sites up and down the UK.

It was during this time that my uncle Tony threw me a career lifeline. I had a lot of good times working on building sites but it was going nowhere and wasn't something I wanted to do for the rest of my life. Tony was a skilled engineer and I think my mum had given him a call to see if he had any work for me. At the time he was working for a company called Vibroplant, a huge supplier of plant machinery you'd find on a building site: diggers, compressors, dump trucks, steam rollers, etc. A vacancy had come available for the position of Yard Man. This was the nineties, so the word 'Man' was used a lot in job titles. Basically, I was a semi-skilled apprentice fitter. My job required me to repair pneumatic drills, from hand-held ones to the big heavy breakers you see digging the roads up. My uncle Tony taught me how to do this, which was way below his pay grade but he wanted me to learn properly and from the best. He was a brilliant and well-respected engineer so I made sure I listened. He only ever showed me anything once, twice at a push, so I knew I had to concentrate. Tony did so much for me and really encouraged me to do well. He even forfeited his dinner hour to give me driving lessons in the works van to get me through my driving test.

Along with the skilled side of things, the job of Yard Man came with all the other bits and bobs an apprentice is required to do – basically all the shitty jobs like cleaning machines and engines for the engineers to work on, keeping the workshops and yard tidy, cleaning the toilets, changing all the towel driers, wax on, wax off, you get the picture. One of the trickiest jobs was brewing up and taking the butty orders.

Making cups of tea for hairy-arsed, roll-up-smoking engineers was a whole new world of pressure. Every single bloke wanted their brews made a different way. Some strong, some milky, some with sugar, some without. One bloke used to have eight sugars. Eight! He was a big Scotsman called Ken and he only had one tooth, probably due to the eight sugars in his tea. Ken mainly ate soup, for obvious reasons. All the engineers had their own individual mugs, which were stained brown, with more rings than a redwood, due to them never being washed.

One day I bleached all the mugs – that was a mistake. I soaked them all morning in red-hot water and nigh on half a bottle of bleach. Once I'd rinsed them off they were sparkling, and I stood in the brew room proud as punch waiting for the blokes to come in and pat me on the back. I thought they'd be over the moon. Turns out I was wrong. The amount of abuse I got from them! 'Who the fuck's washed my cup?' Talk about set in their ways! Cholera aside, apparently tea tastes nicer out of a dirty cup. Sometimes you can't do right for doing wrong.

Eventually I got very proficient at tending to their needs. Yes, there was the odd bump in the road like when I put one bloke's trifle in the oven with a load of pies by mistake. It took me two days to get the melted plastic and burnt cream cleaned up. The longer I worked there, the more I got used to all their quirks and traits, so much so that doing the butty run became the highlight of my day. The boss, Geoff, let me drive his car, a red Astra, to pick up the food orders. I'd just passed my test, due to Tony and an incredibly tight pair of blue silk shorts that the lady examiner seemed to enjoy, and I was desperate to drive. I'd go round the workshop in the morning and write down all the blokes' food orders in my little notepad. I'd put the oven in the canteen on low, set up all the various cups of teas and coffees, ring the order through to the shop then off I'd go in Geoff's car. The reason I got this routine so precise was the more on the ball I was, the longer I could spend out driving Geoff's Astra. Which meant picking my girlfriend up for a little morning treat. All the shops and cafes knew me, so as soon as I phoned through with my orders, they'd get them ready. I knew the exact time it would take me to collect all the various bit and pieces so I could get back and make the brews in time for the morning butty break. All this meticulous planning gave me a spare 50 minutes, which was enough time for a quick shag in Geoff's Astra, ever the gent.

My girlfriend was studying at a local college at the time, which was a five-minute drive from Vibroplant. Once in the car I'd whizz straight down to the college. She'd be stood outside waiting for me with a big smile on her face. It was like all my Christmases had come at once. This is what being young was all about, having a good time without a care in the world. If it was a Tuesday we'd drive to my house because I knew my mum was shopping on Bolton

Market. Any other day it was the local supermarket car park. The supermarket was called Normid and it overlooked Burnden Park, which at the time was home to the mighty Bolton Wanderers. For a young lad, it didn't get much better than this. Getting paid for having sex while overlooking my team's football pitch – well, I was living the dream. Don't get me wrong, it wasn't exactly candles and Barry White but to me it was the best thing ever. It was so exciting – soon as we parked up it was 12 minutes of sweet, sweet loving. And when we were done I'd drop my girlfriend back at college, pick the butties up and get back into work with no one any the wiser. None of the blokes, nor the boss, and not even my uncle Tony, knew about it. I'd just come right back to work and start grafting. Christ, these days, if I had sex in the morning I'd have to lie down for an hour, never mind completing a full shift at work.

The mobile loving wasn't just consigned to Geoff's Astra either. I was eventually allowed to take home the small flatbed pick-up trucks at night, as long as I promised not to drive it around outside work. Of course, Geoff, I'll go straight home and that'll be that, which is where I came a cropper. Obviously I was straight round to my girlfriend's and off we went for more vehicle-based gymnastics. We were parked up in a well-known spot that was frequented by other people doing the exact same thing. Unfortunately we had the seats back, mid-bonk, when the area manager drove straight past us. How's your luck! I got into a bit of trouble for that, and I was off driving duties for a while. What I should have asked was, what the fuck was the area manager doing up there on his own? This was in the days before dogging: he was ahead of his time, that fella. When

I was eventually allowed back on driving duties they gave me the sales rep's blue Peugeot to do the butty run in. Happy days – there was a bit more room in that for me and my girlfriend.

I loved my time at Vibroplant, apart from the winters, which were brutal. Outside in the freezing cold, washing mud off a 22-ton dump truck or being on the spanners in an equally as cold workshop was horrendous. In the big main workshop there was a huge heater set up during the colder months, which helped thaw out your blue fingers and toes but also eventually led to my uncle Tony getting the sack. You see, the thing about Tony was he had a bit of a fiery temper, although he had mellowed with age and to me he was always happy and positive. He was the nicest bloke in the world but wouldn't think twice about smacking someone in the mouth if he thought they were taking the piss. He was only five foot two but when he went off he went off big style. I knew he'd been sacked in the past for whacking one of the area managers over the head with an iron bar, as you do, but I hadn't seen that side of him. I've worked in lots of different shop-floor-style jobs and one thing that always remains consistent is the workforce's hatred of management.

So we're all in the main workshop, it's the middle of winter and the lads had the heater on full pelt. The heater was right at the side of my uncle Tony's workbench, so if you had to turn it on or off you'd have to walk past him. On this occasion the area manager walked into the workshop – he'd just got out of his company car and he was in full shirt-and-tie management dress. (This is the kind of thing that got disapproving looks off those hardened engineers.) Without saying anything to anybody, he strode down the middle of the workshop to the heater and turned it off while saying how hot it was and how the blokes shouldn't have it on. This is the kind of dick move that causes problems in the workplace, none more so than for that particular area manager, who hadn't banked on dealing with Bolton's answer to Joe Pesci in *Goodfellas*. Before you could say 'Funny how? Like a clown?' my uncle set about this manager and that was the end of Tony's employment at Vibroplant.

I was absolutely gutted. Tony was the one who looked out for me at work and made sure all the older blokes didn't take the piss out of me too much. Having said that he'd always help himself to the butties my Mum had made me! Every dinner hour I'd spend at his workbench talking and laughing with him. He used to encourage me with the stuff I did outside work. I loved karate and was training a lot, so much so that I got a request to try out for the national team. When I told Tony, he was so made up for me you'd swear blind he'd got the letter, that's how passionate he was. He'd served in the army so he brought his old kit bag in for me to use as a punch bag, filled it with sawdust and hung it on a hook that was used for lifting engines. Every dinner hour I'd train on the bag while Tony encouraged me from his workbench. He never knew anything about martial arts but he'd sit there and take the time out to support me. Looking back, having a male role model in my life was great. I could speak differently to what I was used to with my mum. For a kick off, I could swear, something I didn't dare do in front of her.

Once I'd been accepted by the blokes in the workshop, life at Vibroplant got easier, even without my uncle Tony. Geoff gave me a bit more licence to get on with things and use my own initiative, and I mentioned that the canteen could do with a lick of paint so he gave me some money out of petty cash. The smell of paint fumes meant we couldn't use the canteen for a few days so I was asked to set up a portacabin to use as a makeshift place to eat our dinner. I hooked it up and plonked it right outside the workshops. Now back in the day, like most male-dominated workshops, there was always a few pictures of topless ladies knocking about, whether it was Page 3 or a calendar, and in this particular portacabin there were a couple of *Razzles* (knacky mags). In my infinite wisdom, knowing how all the blokes there enjoyed a pair of breasts, I decided to give the portacabin a 60-minute makeover. That morning, I wall-papered the entire portacabin with pictures from *Razzle*. The walls, door and ceiling were completely covered – Carol Smillie would've been proud. I never mentioned what I was doing to the blokes cos I wanted to see their reactions when they first walked in. This was in the days before *Changing Rooms*. I was ahead of my time.

As dinner hour approached, I couldn't wait for the lads to see it. When they did, I couldn't have hoped for a better reaction. As they entered the room a cheer went up.

'Fucking superb!'

'Pat's played a blinder!'

I was now a fully fledged member of Team Man. Alas, the saying 'you can have too much of a good thing' rang true. Eating a cottage pie with Sharon from Disley spreadeagled at the side of you got a bit much. After a week in Peter Stringfellow's portacabin, a few of the blokes had hit the wall.

'I can't eat my wife's crumble looking at that! Get 'em all down, Pat.'

Two bin liners I filled, getting rid of it all. The bin men must have thought Vibroplant meant something totally different.

Another of my many tasks there was cleaning the toilets. This entailed changing the hand towel and toilet rolls, filling the soap dispensers with Swarfega and cleaning turd marks off the toilet – still more enjoyable than that Saturday job I had at Warburtons. My uncle Tony had insisted on showing me how to do the job right. This was a time-served engineer showing me how to use a toilet brush. Tony had a saying: 'If it'll do then it's not right and if it's not right then it won't do.' All that aside, for some reason known only to him, Tony always kept the toilet door open while he was on the loo. I discovered this, to my horror, when I walked into the bogs to find my mother's brother sat having a shit in full view. This blew my mind and my nostrils! I lock the toilet door at home, even if there's nobody else in the house – doing your paperwork with the door open just doesn't compute. I've witnessed a few mad things in my life but seeing a grown man having a shite, with the door open, bold as brass, will stay with me forever.

'You all right, Patrick?' he says, with a wave.

'Fuck me, Tony, what are you doing?' I ask.

'I'm knitting a jumper, what does it look like? Can I not have a crap in peace?'

Probably be a lot more peaceful with the door shut, I thought.

Blokes there didn't give a monkey's. If one-tooth, eight-sugars Ken had been in there, the smell would strip paint. Ken came out of a cubicle one day and the stench can only be described as hell on earth. I was retching. Ken looked at me and in his broad Glaswegian accent said, 'Fuck's wrong with you? Do you want me to drink a bottle of perfume first?'

Despite all this, I enjoyed working at Vibroplant. Getting to drive all those great big bits of machinery around was like having access to my own giant Meccano set. Having sex in the boss's car, fixing pneumatic drills, punching my uncle Tony's sawdust-filled army kit bag, walking the few miles home on a summer's evening, tired but satisfied at having done a hard day's work – life was good. My mum would have my tea ready when I got in, then it'd be a bath and straight out again. I still remember fondly everyone who worked at the mighty Vibroplant, so to Brian (stores), Simmi (driver), Paul (Geoff's deputy), Bob (fitter), Sheila (admin), Liz (admin), Gary (manager), Glenn (sales rep), John Senior (driver), John Junior (driver), Charlie (fitter), Ian (fitter), Ray (fitter), Alan (fitter), Terry (fitter), Pie'O (tight-fisted fitter), Ken (he's here!), Stewart (driver), Colin (fitter), Geoff (shopfloor manager) and of course Geoff's car (passion wagon), thank you, lads, I learned a lot.

ALL THAT GLITTERS IS NOT GOLD

Although I was happy at Vibroplant, one particular day I had one of those Road to Damascus moments and decided it was time to move on. It was winter and working in that kind of job when it's freezing wasn't very pleasant. Building a fire under a frozen water drum so you can get enough water to then start cleaning the mud off a machine while it's snowing was never any fun. I was getting over fixing those heavy pneumatic drills and trying to keep my hands warm, my ears constantly ringing with the sound of heavy machinery. Anyhow, I was on my dinner break and I was glancing through the paper when this job advert leapt off the page at me.

It's not all sex, sex, sex.
There's a bit of sun and sea as well.

It was for Club 18–30 and they were looking for holiday reps. I'm sat there in my overalls, wet through, looking around the room at

76

all these dejected old engineers. Did I want to be here in another 30 years? Did I balls! That night I posted my details to the address on the ad and a week later got my reply. I'd got an interview. I was buzzing, I could already smell the Piz Buin. Going for an interview for Club 18–30 wasn't a suit and tie, what makes you think you're a suitable candidate for a job type of thing. It was more so they could see your personality and how you worked in a group. My first interview was at a hotel in Manchester. I didn't have a car at the time so I asked Franny to give me a lift. On the way over, Franny told me a joke, the one about the centipede going shopping, you know the one? If not here it is:

A bloke walks into a pet shop and asks for the most amazing pet they've got.

Pet shop owner: 'We've got a talking centipede, sir, I think you'll be very impressed.'

Bloke: 'A talking centipede?'

Up pops the centipede.

Centipede: 'Hello there, my name's Dave the talking centipede.'

The bloke is taken aback and immediately pays £100 for the talking centipede. A week or so goes by and the bloke and Dave the talking centipede are now getting on like a house on fire. They talk about everything from football to politics, day in, day out, talking. One day the bloke goes to the fridge and finds that he's no milk left.

Bloke: 'I'll have to go to the shop.'

Centipede: 'Don't worry, I'll go for it.'

Bloke: 'Are you sure you'll be OK carrying it back?'

Centipede: 'Not a problem, I'll just get ready, leave the money on the side.'

An hour goes by and the bloke notices the money is still on the side. Then another hour passes, and another, and another. Eventually the bloke shouts up the stairs to Dave.

Bloke: 'Dave, are you going for this milk or what?'

Centipede: 'Give me chance, I'm still tying my shoelaces.'

It's a classic but I'd never heard it before and I laughed a lot. When I got to the interview it turned out to be more of an open audition. They split us into groups of eight and sat each group around a table with a team leader to ask us questions and see how we interacted with each other. It was a bit awkward at first, no one was really speaking, so the team leader asked if anyone knew any good jokes. Bingo, I was in! Out came the talking centipede, freshly baked from the joke oven. It went down very well at the table and this gave me a real boost.

They had us doing various other things on the day, one of them being asked to sell a watch to the group. That was a bit random, not sure what that had to do with being a holiday rep but here we were. At the end of the day they sent us all home and said they'd be in touch with the candidates they wanted to come back for a second interview.

A week or so went by and I got a call to say I'd been successful. Well done, you're going to boot camp – well, Blackpool, to be precise. It was in a big hotel on the seafront and Club 18–30 had booked the entire place out for what was a two-day final interview. There were easily over a hundred of us there all wanting to become holiday reps, along with senior and club management from Club 18–30. There was a buzz in the air and it felt really exciting to be there.

We all had rooms at the hotel but we had to share. This meant spending two nights with a total stranger who was essentially going for the same job. Being an only child growing up, this was a bit odd for me but I thought, *OK, let's make a good first impression.* I knocked on the door and my new roommate let me in. I walked in with a big smile and extended my hand.

'Hi, I'm Paddy, pleased to meet you.'

To which he then lifted up an empty sleeve because he only had one arm. Now this was awkward, so I'm stood there with my hand extended waiting for the ground to swallow me up and he's stood there holding up an empty sleeve looking right back at me. This whole thing happened in about ten seconds but it felt like hours. He then smiled at me and said, 'Don't worry, it happens all the time. I've still got another hand you can shake.'

I mean, it was definitely an ice breaker and from thereon in we just got on with the job in hand (no pun intended).

I can't remember too much from those two days but the gist of it was we were put into groups of ten or so and given our own Club 18–30 team leader. Each group had to come up with a show to perform onstage in the hotel on the second night. For me the natural reaction was to look around at everyone else and worry about not being as good or as confident as them. There were singers and dancers there, all kinds of performers, and me, an ex-labourer from Bolton. I sucked it up and got stuck in best I could. I always find if you're not very confident but you can pretend you are, that usually does the trick – it's not the easiest thing to master but it's got me through a lot of TV shows and tours over the years. During our little performance, my part of the show was a solo piece. Oasis were massive at the time so I had to walk onstage like a cod Liam Gallagher and do a minute or two of jokes in my best Manchester accent. Racked with nerves, I put the fake confidence on and the fact that I was acting the part of someone who is a natural front-man helped a lot. My memory is a little vague after that but it was around two weeks later when I got the call to say I'd been successful and got the job – next stop, Kavos!

* * *

My time working for Club 18–30 was brief – I'm not cut out for going months on end without seeing my friends and family, especially my mum. I said goodbye to her outside the Pike View pub, the place where it felt like I'd spent most of my childhood. We were both crying and the realisation kicked in that this was actually happening. I'd only ever been abroad once before, a week in Majorca with my cousin Kathryn and her family, and I was now off to work in a place I'd never been to before. I landed in Corfu and was met in the airport by one of the Club 18–30 reps, who whisked me off to Kavos.

The first five days or so were great. They put all the new reps in the same apartment building while they gave us our training and for me it was so good meeting all these people from different parts of the British Isles – up till then I'd only ever socialised with my mates in Bolton. Some, like me, would regularly be stood at the payphone outside to call home and tell their families how they were getting on (no one had a mobile phone back then). Euros weren't even a thing yet, so it was a pocketful of drachmas to use the payphones. Other reps were a bit more hardened and very rarely called home – each to their own, I suppose. It felt good hearing my mum's voice and it definitely kept my spirits up.

All the trainees bonded really well. We'd go out together in the evenings and generally just have a good time. A part of the training was learning the scripts we'd have to reel off to holidaymakers in order to sell them excursions, T-shirts and reunion party tickets for when they were back home. I never thought about this much, I was too busy trying to learn and remember the spiel to really think about what it entailed. The minute we'd finished our training it all became apparent very quickly what life as a rep for Club 18–30 was all about: sales! That advert I'd applied to in the back of our local newsapaper – 'It's not all sex, sex, sex' – should've been 'It's all sales, sales, sales!'

The shine of being a holiday rep quickly disappeared. Every other day the bosses would get us all together for a meeting to find out how many sales we'd made. It was really pressurised and definitely not what I'd signed up for. I thought it was all about entertaining the holidaymakers, putting on shows, getting thrown in the pool and generally just being there for them. Instead we were just a glorified sales force in shorts and T-shirts. As the days went on I could feel my mood getting lower and lower; even the sun got to me. It's OK when you're lying at the side of a pool chilling, but when you're dressed and lugging about a holdall full of paperwork and sales documents that beautiful sunshine felt like the flames from a crematorium oven. Waking up on a cloudy day actually used to pep me up – although I'd have to pretend I was gutted for the holidaymakers.

There'd be allocated days where you used to have to get a load of 18–30 T-shirts together, sling them over your shoulder and knock on every door in the hotels and apartments to sell them, it was mad. Even food became scarce. Most of the reps would be skint so we had to gorge down any food that was left over at the buffets on the excursions. One of my favourite nights was a Christmas-themed excursion in this big old venue where there'd be a full Chrimmy dinner laid on (even though I had to eat it stood up with my fingers). After a few weeks of pressurised sales work, cheap sambuca and indigestion, I was getting close to breaking point. I rang my mum and she was in tears down the other end of the phone. I hadn't told her what it was like out there but she just knew from my tone of voice.

I got pals with a Welsh lad who was also a newbie rep. He'd had enough and ended up working for another company in the resort – I can't remember if it was First Choice or Thomas Cook but they were definitely more family orientated. This was more what we'd signed up for, no hard sales, just making sure all the holidaymakers were having a good time and sending them home happy. I could see the weight had lifted off his shoulders and even though I wasn't being myself I was still doing a good enough job for his new bosses to ask me to work for them. I was seriously thinking about it. Even having sex had lost its appeal to me – that's saying something for a lad in his twenties! I was so tired and run down I remember one night hiding in my room with the lights off because there was a girl trying to get in. It took me back to when I was a kid when my mum would turn all the lights off and hide us behind the couch whenever the rent man was due. Only this time I wasn't avoiding paying money, I was avoiding sex!

The day came that really made my mind up for me. Whenever new holidaymakers arrived you had to get them all together for a welcome meeting. What you've got to remember is this is Club 18–30 so pretty much everyone was young, skint and often on their first holiday that they'd saved up for. We'd have to knock on all their doors in the morning, round them up and do the welcome meeting. That was a pain in the arse itself. I mean, who wants to be woken up first thing in the morning, on holiday, to be told about a bloody Christmas night or tickets they can buy for a Big Reunion night in the UK? Let them enjoy their holiday first!

On this particular day we'd done our pitch, explained what was on offer and given out some free sambucas – this was purely to keep them there so we could get some money off them. I'll never forget, I had three young girls sat together and my boss told me to get some sales out of them. I was already under pressure from him because he'd allowed me to finish early the night before. A couple of girls had asked me to go to their apartment because they wanted to buy some tickets and T-shirts off me. That was genuinely what I thought until I got there … and they just more or less threw me onto the bed for a threesome, woe is me. The next thing I know it's six in the morning and I'm walking back to my hotel, bleary-eyed, with no sales – but I've got to be honest, I've had worse nights. But my boss wasn't pleased with me and my protestation of it all being a trap to lure me there wasn't washing – to be honest I wouldn't have believed it either. Those kind of things only happen in the pages of *Razzle*.

Anyway, he's torn me a strip off and told me I'd have to get all three girls to buy excursions, T-shirts and Big Reunion tickets. I'd been sat with them for about an hour and two of them had agreed to buy everything but the third girl didn't want any of it. She now not only had me pestering her to buy something but her two mates were also pressurising her as well. They were all young girls who'd just qualified as nurses and clearly didn't have a pot to piss in. All of a sudden this girl burst into tears and I instantly snapped out of what I'd been told to do. What had I become? I've never been a fan of sales reps and there's nothing worse than being chased around a shop by some pushy salesperson asking you to try something on. That's exactly what I'd turned into and it was a million miles away from the kind of person I really was. I calmed the girl down, apologised to her and her mates and eventually got them smiling again. I told them not to worry about being hassled again and that they should go and enjoy their holiday. We hugged and that was the last I saw of them. I got up, walked across the road to my boss's office and told him to stick his job and his sales right up his arse.

Due to the conditions out there, reps were dropping like flies. There was always someone quitting, and even though we'd all gone through that interview process in Blackpool, the bosses were constantly out in the bars trying to recruit anyone who was interested. If you quit they'd literally have you on the next flight home because they didn't want anyone bad-mouthing the company to holidaymakers. Now this is where it gets interesting. My boss told me to get my case packed because I was being put on a flight that evening. *Fair enough,* I thought, *that suits me.*

I'd formed a good relationship with a few of the locals out there who owned bars, restaurants and shops. Even though I'd only been there for a few weeks I'd picked up a bit of broken dialect and they'd help me along with it. In return I'd always make sure I recommended their businesses to the tourists. I made my way around to say my goodbyes. There was one old bloke who owned a little supermarket and used to call me Patrayzio. He had tears in his eyes and gave me a big hug and wished me well in life – I'll never forget him.

The coach arrived to take me to the airport but there was a problem. My passport was in the hotel safe and my boss couldn't trace the hotel owner to open it up. The coach came and went and the following day I was woken by a knock at the door. One of the senior reps who'd already done a couple of seasons there gave me my passport.

'You lucky bastard!'

I was a little confused. 'Why?'

He explained how there wasn't a flight back to the UK for another four days and the bosses were that keen to get rid of me they'd paid to have me moved to another resort, in a five-star hotel, all expenses paid. What a result!

I'd never been in a fancy hotel before and suddenly here I was, at the side of a pool, food and drink on tap, all at the expense of Club 18–30. All of a sudden the sunshine was my friend again! It got even better when a topless girl approached me. I know people go topless all the time on holiday but back then I wasn't used to it, there were breasts everywhere. I didn't know where to look but she sat on the end of my sun lounger and started chatting to me. She was from the UK and out there with some friends. We hit it off and spent the next couple of days or so in each other's beds. Oh, those innocent, fun days of youth, I do miss them.

I landed back in the UK relaxed, tanned and happy to see my mum again. The one thing that had completely slipped my mind was that Franny and the rest of the Hateful Eight had all agreed to come out to Kavos to see me. I was sat in our front room when the phone rang. It was Franny.

'Where the fuck are you?' he said.

'Well, you're phoning me at my mum's so no prizes there.'

'We're in Kavos looking for you!'

Back then communication wasn't as easy as it is now so Franny and the lads had no idea that I was back home. Our planes must have flown past each other on our separate journeys. Still, they all had a good time – of course they did, it was Kavos in the nineties!

 CHAPTER 7

TAKE CHANCES, MAKE MISTAKES AND LEARN!

Sometimes the best thing you can give someone is a chance.

After college I lost touch with Peter Kay until another chance meeting, this time at a petrol station in Bolton. To refresh my memory, I asked him about this and he reckons it was the petrol station he was working at on Daubhill. I'm saying it was at the bottom of Beaumont Road. All totally irrelevant unless you live in Bolton. Anyway, I spotted him with the bonnet up on his little red Ford Fiesta.

'Pete, what's up?'

He was basically pouring water over his engine.

'I'm overheating.'

When it comes to comedy, writing, acting, voices, making TV, editing and directing, Pete's a genius. Anything above and beyond that, the man's a show-up! He's by far the worst driver I've ever seen, and I've nearly been killed by Freddie Flintoff in a hearse.

CHAPTER 7

Anything hands on, forget about it. When he told me about *Car Share* my first thought was *Who'll be driving?*

Anyway, back to the petrol station on Daubhill/Beaumont Road.

'Pete! You're gonna piss your spark plugs through! Get out the way, I'll sort it.' My anxiety goes through the roof if I have to watch Pete attempting anything practical. I get that off my uncle Tony.

Not having any real cash flow, most maintenance on my own cars was done by myself. I'd change things like spark plugs, dizzy caps, oil and water, wiper blades, stereos – I even changed the alternator on a Vauxhall Cavalier during my lunch break at Vibroplant once. Anything more technical than that, there was always a mate who knew a decent enough mechanic who'd sort it for cash in hand.

Anyway, I topped his radiator up and checked his oil, and once it was sorted I asked him what he was up to. He'd started doing stand-up comedy and told me about a gig he had in Manchester and asked if I fancied coming along. So one night soon after, we drove over to a comedy club in Manchester called the Frog and Bucket. I'd never been to any live shows up until that point. I'd never even been to a zoo, let alone a comedy gig.

That night was certainly an eye-opener for me. I was sat there watching my mate from school standing onstage telling funny stories to a roomful of strangers. It amazed me that people knew who he was! Pete wasn't on TV at that point but he was getting a good following in the comedy clubs. I don't remember any of the other acts that night but I do remember laughing at his routine. He finished his act, I sank a few pints and it was time to head off home.

'Hang on, Paddy, I'm just going to get my money.'

When we got in the car I asked what he got paid. It was around 80 quid. I couldn't believe it!

'No way! Eighty quid? You were only onstage for twenty minutes!'

I didn't earn that putting in a full shift at work, so it seemed like easy money to me and definitely piqued my interest. It's a bit of a cliché but the more I watched other people do stand-up, the more I thought, *I can do better than that.* I still had no inclination to pursue a career in entertainment but from a work-rate-to-earnings perspective it seemed like money for old rope. I'd always had the ability to get laughs socially, whether it be in a work canteen or out with friends, but the tricky part is transferring that to the stage. I know a lot of very funny people, I've got mates who can make me cry with laughter, but stick a microphone in their hand and put them onstage in front of strangers and it's a different story. That's the thing with stand-up comedy – unless you've given it a go you can't really understand it, that feeling of fear, the knot in your stomach, shaking with adrenaline, and then the sheer elation and relief when it's done and the punters have laughed.

All the fear, stress and anxiety aside, I couldn't see past the earning potential, so I thought, *Balls to it, I'll give it a go.* My first ever stand-up gig was at a student union bar in Lancaster University, part of a thing called the Newcastle Brown Ale Comedy Circuit. You got the chance to do five minutes onstage as part of an open mic spot, 'open mic' meaning nobody has ever heard of you so you're not getting paid. The night was hosted by Hovis Presley, a poet and a bit of a legend on the northern comedy circuit. This quiet man was a genius and could have had an amazing TV career but he preferred writing poetry, doing a bit of teaching and performing stand-up comedy.

I hadn't done that much prep for my set; I didn't have much idea of what to do. Peter told me to write about something I could relate to. So my first five-minute stand-up routine was pretty much written around how Escort and Fiesta were not just cars, they were also porn mags. I wasn't exactly sure how to do 'the comedy' – getting the rhythm and the stories to flow right – but what I did know was that I could make people laugh, and that had to be a good start.

Before I stepped onstage, I dashed off for a nervous wee and noticed the urinal was stupidly high up on the wall. So, coming out onstage, nerves taking over, I just blurted out, 'Lancaster University, the only place in the UK where you need a stepladder to take a piss.' This got a really good laugh from the audience and gave me my first experience of ad-libbing and the power of observational comedy. It also gave me that first laughter fix – what a high that was – but like with most drugs, you're always chasing it. The rest of the set was OK but I didn't get any laughs as big as the ad lib at the beginning.

Hovis Presley then came onstage and I'll never forget what he said.

'Patrick McGuinness there, he *claims* it's his first time …'

That was a great compliment to hear, yet despite that, once I was offstage, I had absolutely no desire to do it again for a very long time. I'd never felt as sick and nervous doing anything. Although stand-up seemed like easy money, it most certainly wasn't.

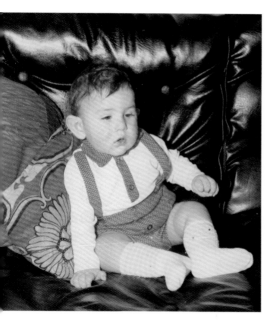

◄ Baby me – can a picture be any more seventies?

▼ The sun was in my eyes.

▲ Our front room, with my cousin Kathryn.

▼ Back in the days when phones used to be plugged into the wall.

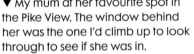

▼ My mum at her favourite spot in the Pike View. The window behind her was the one I'd climb up to look through to see if she was in.

▲ The only evidence I have of my Mum and Dad ever showing each other affection.

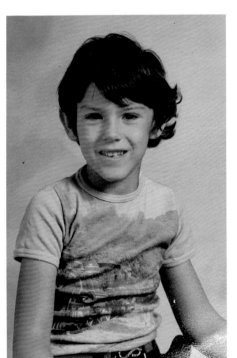

▲ Butter wouldn't melt.

► My confirmation day. Here I am having my picture taken in a neighbour's house because they had nicer furniture.

◀ School photo from Mount St Joseph's.

▶ Me cocking up Stotty's passport photo.

▲ My big sister, Angie.

▲ At Angie's house with Ian, her husband, and Rebecca, their daughter.

◀ Getting ready for bed at Angie's. Look at those pyjamas and the state of my shins. I was always out climbing and playing on my bike.

▲ Fully committed to having my ears on show.

▲ My first ever suit. I wore this to my leavers' do at school. I thought I looked fantastic. On reflection, I was wrong.

◄▼ My first foray into martial arts. I loved Bruce Lee. Some of my Karate trophies on a shelf behind my bed. Angie bought me that radio in the middle.

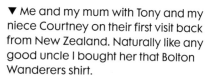

▼ Me and my mum with Tony and my niece Courtney on their first visit back from New Zealand. Naturally like any good uncle I bought her that Bolton Wanderers shirt.

▲ The only photo from my childhood with me and Tony in it, together with my Mum. You can also just make out the side of Angie's hair.

▼ Me and our kid in the kitchen of my house on my 40th. Just 30 minutes after this photo was taken I was in an alcohol-induced coma. Christine had to put me to bed.

▲ Me, Tony and my mum in a rare picture together.

▲ My uncle Tommy, the only relative of my dad's I knew growing up. I used to love visiting him in Lytham St Annes.

▲ Me and my dad at the Queen's Hotel, Blackpool.

▼ Me and my dad on my wedding day.

▼ Me and my mum in 1974, outside my auntie Maureen's. Their windowsill was always nicely painted.

▲ Me, my cousin Lorraine and my Mum. 1975, what a year for interior design.

▲ Me and my cousin Dominic. He was like a little brother to me growing up.

▲ Me, Lorraine and my Auntie Maureen at my cousin Dominic's 21st.

◀ Leah, my mum's dog.

▼ Christine and I on our first holiday together in Majorca.

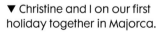

▲ Our last holiday before the children were born. Christine was six months pregnant in this picture.

◀ Our first Twinkle Ball, which we organised to raise funds for the National Autistic Society.

▲ Dressed to impress on a rare night out together.

◀ A day out feeding the ducks. Whenever we find something all the kids like doing it's the best feeling.

▼ Asleep with my boy, Leo, both exhausted at bedtime.

◀ They are growing up so fast. Leo and Penelope taking Felicity for her first day at school.

A few months later, I was playing football with my mates at a new five-a-side football centre in Bolton. The manager had heard that I'd done a bit of comedy and asked if I fancied doing some stand-up at an awards ceremony he was planning. The anxiety from Lancaster Uni was still with me, but this time real money was thrown into the mix.

'We'll give you two hundred quid.'

'Where do I sign?'

At the time an established comedian performing at the Comedy Store wouldn't get £200 so I couldn't believe my luck.

I knew it was a risk so I said to the owner, 'If it doesn't go well, I'll just take a hundred off you.'

'You're on,' he said, and with that my second stand-up gig was booked.

The big night arrived and the conditions couldn't have been worse. Still broad daylight, curtains open, tables and chairs just dotted about randomly, lads in football kit walking in and out of the bar due to the pitches still being open, and to cap it all off, no microphone. If I do any gigs these days, I make sure in advance everything is sorted out down to the last detail. Back then I didn't have a clue. All I knew was there was 200 quid to be made for 20 minutes' work. I had long curly hair at the time so I walked onstage (end of the bar) to chants of 'There's only one Kevin Keegan!' That was as good as the gig went. I died on my arse in a roomful of lads who didn't even know I was on. I'm stood there like some random nutter shouting about Escorts in the hope someone might just hear me. In over 20 years, performing on- and offstage, I can honestly say

I've never died like I did that night, but even though those gigs are a nightmare, they stand you in good stead going forward. I finished my set and walked over to the owner.

'That'll be a hundred quid then,' he said.

'Yep,' I said, and took the money.

It had been a tough, hostile, horrendous gig but I was still going home with 100 quid in my pocket. That's the thing with stand-up comedy. Some people try it once and never do it again. There's those who don't do well but carry on regardless and after hundreds of unpaid gigs eventually craft a routine and start getting laughs. Then there's people like me who can get laughs but don't give it the time and respect it deserves. I did stand-up for the wrong reason: to make money. I was prepared to put myself through that horrendous gig to earn a few quid. Don't get me wrong, it's a lovely feeling being onstage and making people laugh, but doing it just to make money is not the right way to approach it. The older I get, the more I understand it, and I will definitely tour again, global pandemics aside.

* * *

Anyway, more on touring and stand-up comedy later, back to the early days with Peter. After watching that first gig I'd travel around the country with him, just for the crack, really. It was exciting and a million miles away from anything I'd ever known. Like I said, theatre, panto, gigs were all things I'd never experienced in my neck of the woods. One of the many delights that came from travelling around the UK was the digs. Most of the hotels and B&Bs we stayed in were, to put it politely, shitholes. Neither of us had any money so we always shared a room, and by room I mean bed. We'd check into some dodgy B&B, only to be told there was only one bed in the room. 'Yeah, we know.' Cue the awkward pause and 'they must be gay' looks before being given the key. We'd been mates from school so jumping into bed together was never an issue for us. We were just saving money and if it was good enough for Morecambe and Wise it was good enough for us. Honestly, some of the best laughs I've had with Peter over the years were in those early days. We'd cry with laughter talking about anyone or anything. Even when Peter started earning decent money, we still carried on sharing a room. In fact, when the going got good, we slept together in some of the finest hotels on earth.

The best times were when Peter got booked for a corporate gig – that meant free food and more importantly a free minibar. We flew out to Geneva for a gig once – I couldn't believe it. I think we did three nights there in a five-star hotel and we dined in a restaurant right in the middle of Lake Geneva, which had a picture on the wall of Bill Clinton eating there! I managed to take every freebie from that hotel, which seemed like a good idea at the time until I got on the flight home. What it cost me in luggage excess, it would've been cheaper to buy the frigging towels and dressing gowns.

In one hotel we stayed in I ordered some extra towels to the room. When they arrived I popped them straight into my case, fresh as daisies. I couldn't wait to get home and show my mum – all our towels were mismatched or threadbare. It was a nice feeling seeing my mum sat there in a plush dressing gown, with the name of whichever hotel I'd nicked it from on the front.

I remember one corporate gig Peter got booked for was for a well-known and often disliked businessman. The bloke shall remain nameless but the image he cultivated was pretty much spot on. Peter had been booked to entertain this bloke's family in a castle. Talk about court jester. I remember being sat in our room having something to eat when the unnamed individual walked in. His opening gambit was, 'Hi, I'm blank or blanks, and I've just sold my business for 85 million pounds.' To which I replied, 'Is that all?'

The gig was horrendous for Peter but I laughed my pippins off. You see, I know how good Peter is at stand-up, but sometimes you fall victim to the room and the conditions. The gig was basically Peter stood in the corner of a dining room with a shitty little microphone and speaker. Half of the people at the dining table had their backs to him and the ones facing him weren't in the slightest bit interested. This is why I found it hilarious – it wasn't his material, it was the fact that everything about the gig was wrong. The more his jokes fell flat, the more I laughed. Seeing that happen to a mate is hilarious, especially when he's laughing along as well because he knows exactly why I'm laughing.

The very last time I remember spending the night with Peter (even typing that seems mad), the roles were actually reversed. For years I'd plundered his rooms for towels and free drinks, and it was finally time for him to decimate mine. It happened totally by chance. I was working in London at the time and I always stayed at the Soho Hotel, which back in the day was practically a second home for me. This particular night I was lying on my bed and Peter called me out of the blue.

Peter: 'Hiya, what you up to?'

Me: 'I'm working, son.'

Peter: 'So am I, whereabouts are you?'

Me: 'London.'

Peter: 'So am I. Where are you staying?'

Me: 'Soho Hotel.'

Peter: 'No way, so am I! What room are you in?'

Me: 'Eighty.'

Peter: 'So am I!'

Me: 'What do you mean?'

With that I heard a knock on the internal door that connected the rooms and Peter was only staying slap bang next to me. We got giddy, like two big kids; it was unplanned and a bit of a treat because we hadn't seen each other for a while. It was all great fun until Peter swanned into my room starkers, only for the door to lock behind him.

Peter: 'Fuck me, the door's locked, I can't get back in my room.'

Me: 'I'm not spending the night looking at that! I'll get you a dressing gown.'

Firstly, that's when I knew I was doing well – I'd not packed the dressing gown into my suitcase. Secondly, the dressing gown was too small for him, there was no way it would close at the front. I'd have to call down to reception to send someone up to unlock the door. I mean, how do you explain that one?

Reception: 'Good evening, Mr McGuinness, how can I help?'

Me: 'I've got one of the nation's best-loved comedians in my room with his cock out. Can you let him back into his own room, please.'

The manager knew who we both were but to be fair just opened up the locked door and left. That was the good thing about the Soho Hotel, it was discreet. If that'd been anywhere else we'd have probably ended up on the front page of the *Daily Star*!

I loved those early days travelling around with Pete, especially when he started getting TV gigs. He'd do lots of daytime quiz shows back then and that was really enjoyable. He did a show called *Night Fever* on Channel 5 and I'd buzz off meeting all these people I'd seen on the telly. Before I'd done any TV work, I met a lot of showbiz folk through Peter and I remember how they treated me. I was just a mate tagging along for the journey but it made me conscious of how to treat people who are just starting out. Comedians like Jason Byrne, Andrew Maxwell, Milton Jones, Smug Roberts and Johnny Vegas didn't ignore me just because I wasn't known. They won't even remember those times but I do. I remember Shaun Williamson (Barry from *EastEnders*) inviting us to the pub to watch the footy – it was a Chelsea game but I won't hold that against him – and Paul Ross taking us out for a curry. Probably no big deal to them, but for me it meant a lot to feel welcomed and not just like a spare part. I try my best to be like that myself now because it really matters to that person.

Before Rob Beckett was making telly he was doing warm-up on various TV shows. This one time he happened to be on warm-up duties for a show I was hosting and he was struggling with the audience – it happens, it's just one of those things. Warm-up for

TV can be a tough and thankless job, and I always clock how they do because to me they're an integral part of making that show. I had a word with Rob after the show just to say not to worry and keep up the good work. I'd forgotten about this but years later Rob reminded me of it and thanked me for the kind words. I was glad he told me because it really brought it home how much treating someone with a bit of respect stays with them. There were a few knobheads along the way who wouldn't give me the time of day, but again that stayed with me and most of them didn't last very long within the industry.

CHAPTER 8

BOLTON LEISURE SERVICES

Let's slip on the red trunks, put a whistle around our necks and head to Horwich Leisure Centre. A council leisure centre can be a weird place, and Horwich Leisure Centre in the late nineties had to be one of the weirdest. There was all sorts going on behind the scenes of this seemingly ordinary civic building. In my early days there, my main concern was finding ways to make a quick pound, and I was nothing if not enterprising. At weekends, I would scour all the bargain shops in Bolton, buying T-shirts, sportswear and trainers, then take them into work and sell them at double the price. I always had my pitch rehearsed. For instance, a pair of trainers which I sold as being from some European designer had actually come from Shoe Market. I didn't mind who I sold to either, the lads I knocked around with or the blokes who worked at the leisure centre. The way I looked at it was, if they'd have got off their arses and gone down to the shops themselves, they'd see that the trainers they'd bought for 20 quid were actually only a tenner. I was doing all the donkey work so they had to pay premium. Around the same time, I had a regular car-boot stall on a Sunday, selling toilet rolls, bleach, cans of pop, soap, badminton rackets and anything I could lay my hands on. Everything was a laugh or a blag. I had the gift of the gab and I suppose I saw myself as a Del Boy type: slightly dodgy dealings, but always with a glint in the eye.

My career (I use that term loosely) in leisure services started with a phone call from my cousin, Lorraine, who was one of the managers at Horwich Leisure Centre in Bolton. I'd put Club 18–30 behind me and was on the lookout for something new to do. The job title was dry recreation attendant, or dry rec as it was known. It was a zero-hours contract but it got my foot in the door and I was up for a new challenge. Working in a leisure centre with a load of lifeguards, I had visions of *Baywatch*, red swimsuits and suntans. That fantasy quickly disappeared on my first shift at Horwich: a 6am cleaning shift ... with my uncle Tony! What was an engineer with a penchant for thumping middle management doing mopping changing room floors? Alongside a 20-year-old semi-skilled fitter with a penchant for wallpapering portacabins with pornographic magazines? Turned out Uncle Tony had agreed to do it for a bit of extra pocket money and to get him out of the house. He'd be in his sixties at the time and was more or less retired, but he was still very active.

I used to watch people walk past him while he mopped those floors and think, *They've no idea that this old fella cleaning is actually an ex-military, highly qualified mechanical and electrical engineer.* That used to drive me mad. I always told everyone how well qualified and intelligent he was – I felt I needed to because this was a man who deserved respect, and the preconception that anyone cleaning is somehow beneath the rest of us is a load of old bollocks. Anyway, here we both were, on the early-morning dry rec shift, cleaning the leisure centre. Back then my ambition drove me on – yes, I'd sweep up because I knew I'd eventually move up to the heady heights of lifeguard.

Eventually I got put on a course and became a casual lifeguard. 'Casual' was the name given to a zero-hours contract back in the day. There'd be shifts available that the full-time staff weren't up for doing, like the late swim on a Tuesday night. That shift was 9pm till 10.45pm, which was a ball ache because I lived around five miles from the leisure centre and didn't have a car at the time. The management would put a sheet up in the staffroom with all the shite hours nobody wanted to do. I made sure I put my name down for every single one: the more I worked there, the more experience I'd get and the quicker I'd get promoted. If you showed willing and worked hard, leisure services would pay for you to go on courses to improve yourself.

Life then was a million miles away from the health-and-safety-obsessed world we're in now. I mean, there was a fully licensed bar and function room for a kick off. One evening one of my mates was on shift as step-up duty manager, and I was on the late swim shift. We're still mates to this day. He actually still works in leisure as a manager, which is why he shall remain nameless. It's fair to say that most of the lads I know are quite competitive and he was no differ-ent. During the shift we were sat in the manager's office. My mate was in his uniform, black trousers, green polo shirt, and I was in mine, red shorts, yellow T-shirt. Eventually we got to talking about drinking and who could do the most, which culminated in a £5 bet on who could finish the top shelf behind the leisure centre bar. Now we're talking about a council facility in Bolton here, so the top shelf wasn't Grey Goose and XO Cognacs. It was more Bell's whisky and Aftershocks! To be fair, he necked just under half a pint of every cheap, nasty spirit there was on that top shelf. He then ran out of the building and jumped in his wife's car, wanting to get home before the dizziness and spewing kicked in, good plan. I on the other hand didn't have a wife and car to pick me up. I was on a BMX. I rode home with no lights, no helmet, pissed up, in a pair of small red shorts. Not a good look. I still don't know how we managed to lock the leisure centre up that night.

* * *

In my time working at Horwich Leisure Centre I pretty much did every job going there: cleaner, bar staff, sauna attendant, fitness instructor, all-weather pitch attendant, receptionist, outdoor services, boxercise instructor and step-up duty manager. All valuable experience and fantastic memories. It's mad when I think about it now. I hated early mornings, still do, so if I was on an early shift in the gym, which was a 6.30am start, I had a little routine. My mum would wake me up and give me my breakfast, always sausage butties and always Wall's Skinless. She'd leave them at the side of my bed with a cup of tea and I'd pretend I was getting up. Soon as she left my bedroom, I'd have my head straight back on the pillow. I figured out that I had roughly 25 minutes to eat my butties and drink the tea before my mum came to check I wasn't back in bed. I never drank a hot cup of tea or enjoyed the sausages because they'd be cold by the time she shouted at me to see if I was ready. Soon as I heard her approaching I'd jump out of bed, ram the sausage butties into my mouth and down the tea in a oner. By the time she opened my bedroom door I'd be stood bolt upright as though I'd been up and getting ready from the get-go. Then I'd drive to work in my Nissan Sunny – at least I had a car by this point – still in my PJs.

Early morning in the gym you always had your regulars and there was a cracking bloke called John. He'd lost around ten stone and he was there at 6.30 on the dot every morning. When you get chatting to blokes it becomes apparent within the first minute if they're sound or not. I knew straight away that John was one of the lads so he ended up being a valued part of my unofficial leisure centre team. I'd walk in, grab the keys for the gym and throw them to big John. He'd then unlock the gym for me, flick on all the tread-mills, turn on the TVs and crank up the music. To this day I think the rest of the morning regulars thought he worked there. While John got the gym opened and ready for customers, I'd be in the sauna and steam rooms. They didn't open till ten in the morning so I'd go in there, crash out on one of the loungers and catch up on a bit more sleep for an hour. Then I'd jump in the jacuzzi, put on the telly and watch *The Big Breakfast*, which Kelly Brook used to host at the time, a lovely little morning pep-up before my shift. I'd be sat there like a pound-shop Scarface. After half an hour of Brook and bubbles, it was shower time, uniform on and venture down to the gym at around quarter to ten. John had usually left by then but he'd sometimes leave a little handover note on my desk. 'Everything OK, filled the water cooler with cups and put fresh paper towels in the gym, see you tomorrow morning.' Fantastic routine, thanks, John. I'd then walk up to the staffroom around 10.30am and have a bite to eat. No one questioned this break because I'd been on shift since 6.30am, wink, wink.

I remember a bloke turning up for a fitness programme on 9/11. We had all the TVs on in the gym and everyone had stopped what they were doing, transfixed. I was trying to explain to this bloke that something really bad was happening, but he was having none of it. I remember vividly talking him through abdominal crunches as the second plane flew into the Twin Towers – he didn't bat an eyelid. The world was shifting on its axis but this chap was more interested in getting a six-pack.

If my cousin Lorraine (Reeny) was manager while I was on shift, I'd join her for a cup of tea in her office. She'd be smoking a fag and I'd have my feet up on the other side of her desk. I was always careful not to do it in front of the other staff, though, and I always made sure my jobs were done, otherwise I'd have just got someone grassing on me for taking the piss.

Honestly, some of the things that went on back then were unbelievable. Part of my job as a fitness instructor was working in the sauna and steam rooms, or as I liked to call them, my apartment. There were set days for same sex and other days for mixed. Most of the staff hated working in the sauna due to a small clique of older men who would complain about everything and give the staff a really hard time. The heads of the sauna mafia were Gordon,

George and Sid, all retired and all very opinionated. I'd never met any of them but I'd heard of them from other staff. I've always been a people person and having previously worked on building sites and at Vibroplant, I'd had my fair share of dealing with older, awkward buggers.

When I started that first shift in the sauna I knew I had to get these blokes on my side if I was going to have any kind of peace in there. A lot of their complaints were about the lack of cups for water and the floors being wet through. Knowing how much older blokes like seeing someone get stuck in and not answer back, I got my head down and made sure the floors were bone dry and there were enough plastic cups to give Greta Thunberg a stroke. I let on to the Steam Room Cosa Nostra – 'Morning, lads, anything I can get you just let me know' – and that was it, simple as that, really. They were like a pride of lions so I knew not to get in their faces too much. They accepted me and that's when, like the gym, life in the sauna became another job that worked for me. In the end I became great pals with them all and they even invited me out on curry nights.

Gordon was an ex-builder who looked just like Ernie Wise, and although there was a big age difference, we became close. I'd go over to Gordon and his wife Joan's house with my girlfriend for meals – this went on for years until he sadly passed away with cancer. I even let the old boys bring a few drinks in if I was on shift – the sauna became Bolton's answer to the Bada Bing! club. I'd sit playing draughts with Gordon while George and the rest of the old blokes enjoyed a brandy or two. It was a bit like the prison scene in *Goodfellas*. They were all away from their wives, getting pissed and

putting the world to rights. I'd been brought up in and around a
lot of boozers in Bolton so a few drinks in the sauna were nothing
to worry about for me. They were having a great time and, to be
honest, so was I. These old blokes liked me being there because I
made them laugh and I listened to them.

One of the oldest members, Sid, would even bring me in his
Viagras to sell for him. Back then, Viagra was a new thing, a miracle
pill that you could only get from the doctor. I started buying Viagra
off Sid for a quid each, then I'd go upstairs to the staffroom and
sell them to the other lads who worked in leisure services (oh, the
irony) for a fiver each. Consequently, I was making money hand
over fist. The only trouble was demand got so high, I was constantly
badgering poor old Sid.

'Can you get us some more, Sid?'

'I've already had thirty this month, Pat!' he'd say. 'The doctor
thinks I'm shagging morning, noon and night. I'm eighty-one, for
fuck's sake!'

You couldn't write it. John, my unofficial gym opener upper,
would also bring in knock-off T-shirts for me to sell. In between
selling Viagra and fake Nike T-shirts I was writing fitness programmes
for pensioners who'd been sent to us by their GPs. It was a weird
balancing act that I found quite easy.

I must've been the only person at HLC who actually looked
forward to working in the sauna. Being in the company of those
older blokes and the stories they'd come out with was great. All
that was achieved by letting a few things slide, not being cocky
and showing a bit of willing. Whenever I was on duty, the sauna

and steam rooms were packed – the regulars all knew the place was going to be jumping when young Pat was on duty.

There was even a period when the HLC sauna was advertised as a cottaging spot in an adult magazine. Might I add, not by Bolton Council. I remember being in the middle of a tense game of draughts with Gordon when one of the regulars informed me there were two blokes at it in the steam room.

Without looking up from the draughts board, Gordon said, 'I'm on for a double jump myself here.'

It wasn't all geared up for retired men; the leisure centre also did ladies' nights. This consisted of a comedian, male strippers and a disco. Myself and a few of the boys would work behind the bar on those nights. We were all topless, apart from a bow tie, and wore either a kilt or black trousers, weather dependent. We made a fortune in tips, and witnessing what those ladies got up to on the male stripper nights was definitely something to behold. I'd finish my shifts with claw marks all over me.

Horwich Leisure Centre, like most of the buildings from my past, has been knocked down now. A shiny new, sanitised, health-and-safety-conscious one has been built instead, minus the stripper nights, sauna drinking club, unofficial staff, smoking and illicit sexual get-togethers, which is a bit of a shame but there you go. All those fantastic memories have now been reduced to a car park.

CHAPTER 9

GIVING IT A WHIRL

Failure is fine, if you learn.
Not trying, though, that's just boring.

My first taste of being in front of the camera myself came when I was working at HLC, and by the time I left I'd been part of five different TV shows. This one morning I walked into the staffroom and something on the noticeboard caught my eye.

INDIVIDUALS WITH A SPORTING BACKGROUND
WANTED FOR NEW NATIONAL LOTTERY
TV GAME SHOW

Ooh, I thought, *telly! That'd be good!* At the time I was competing in various karate tournaments around the UK and I'd just been selected to be part of the Federation of English Karate Organisations squad, so I definitely ticked the sporty box. I applied, along with a few other people from the leisure centre, and went for an open fitness test/audition. This consisted of a mini indoor triathlon in a gym: treadmill, rowing machine and bike. I was the only one who got selected after that round and next up I was taken down to an army barracks in Aldershot. I think it was where the Paras trained. They really put us through our paces there – the minimum requirements were the ability to do 10 straight-arm pull-ups, 50 sit-ups and at least level ten on the bleep test. *Jesus,* I thought, *what kind of show is this?* Anyhow, after spending the day being beasted by the PTs, culminating in scaling a massive indoor climbing wall, I got selected to be on the show and was flown to Amsterdam to film the pilot episode.

It wasn't the smoothest of starts – from getting off the plane in Amsterdam to walking into the airport I managed to lose my passport. The company had sent a young researcher by the name of Suzy Lamb to pick me up. (I want you to remember that name because later in life Suzy became a massive part of my career in TV.) So I'm stood in Schiphol Airport shouting to Suzy from the other side of passport control that I'd lost my passport.

'You've only just walked off the plane!'

That was the first time I'd stressed her out but it certainly wouldn't be the last. Anyway, I found my passport – it was in my back pocket – and off we went to the Endemol TV studios. (Endemol have made shows like *Big Brother, Wipeout, Deal or No Deal* and *Fear Factor* but back then those shows had yet to hit British TV.) They had Europe's biggest TV set and that's why the pilot episode was to be filmed there. It was full of weird and wonderful games, massive 360 swings, climbing walls, giant bookshelves and zip lines. There was one game where we had to climb into this giant pinball machine and load it full of balls for our celebrity partners to catch. I was lying in this giant pink pinball machine thinking, *Those fitness tests the Paras put us through may have been a touch unnecessary.* Each contestant was paired up with a sports personality. This will give you an idea of how long ago it was: they were tennis player Annabel Croft, swimmer Nick Gillingham, athlete Tessa Sanderson and rugby player Victor Ubogu. I was paired up with Annabel. The hosts were Gaby Roslin and Patrick Kielty, who both treated me really well.

We finished that pilot episode and the show got commissioned to be made in the UK. Such is the world of telly, a few things changed. Gaby Roslin was replaced with Anthea Turner and the sports stars got replaced with celebrities. This time my partner was eighties pop star Sonia from Liverpool. I had a lot of fun and picked up a few trade secrets, namely that the executive producer, a lovely fella by the name of Tony Wolfe, made a few changes so the celebrities had a slightly easier time. We got knocked out in the semis due to my giant revolving swing being made slightly slower than my celebrity opponent's – swines! All enjoyable stuff, though, and I got some good first-hand experience of being in a TV studio.

After filming, I shared a car with Anthea on the way to my hotel. It dropped her at home first, so I asked if I could use her toilet. This was my only chance to see inside a celebrity's house, well, aside from watching *Through the Keyhole.* Anthea very kindly agreed, and in I went. She showed me where the loo was and I remember thinking, *Bloody hell, this is posh, a bog on the ground floor?*

CHAPTER 9

Her home looked and smelt great, even after I'd used the toilet. I remember sitting in that downstairs toilet, just soaking it up. I couldn't wait to tell my mates. *I've just had a shit in Anthea Turner's house – living the dream!*

* * *

My next TV appearance was on a dating show called *God's Gift*. Again, like the lottery show, a notice was put up on the staff noticeboard:

LIFEGUARDS WANTED FOR DATING SHOW!

That sounds like a bit of fun, I thought. So myself and one of the lads I worked with in the gym, Stewart, went for an audition together. This consisted of sitting in a room with two researchers asking you things like, 'If you were a Gladiator what would your name be?' All highbrow stuff. Anyhow, after an hour of cringey questions, I got through and Stew didn't. At the time I thought what a great result, especially as Stew was a good-looking bodybuilder type. Yes, it was all harmless fun till years later when one of the lads off *Phoenix Nights*, Steve Edge, dug out the clip and gave it to his mate for one of those before-they-were-famous type programmes. Ten years later there I am back on national TV, dancing in a pair of silk boxer shorts. Nice one, Edgey! *God's Gift* was originally hosted by Davina McCall, and then a relatively unknown Claudia Winkleman took over. It definitely wasn't a family show; it was on around midnight, and what made matters worse was the voting on the show was done by the girls in the studio audience. If they liked what you did in a round, they'd all stand near your podium. I came up with a master stroke. I asked a load of the girls who worked at HLC to come down to the filming and help me out with the podium votes – genius! The only trouble being they filmed two shows a day and my lot turned up for the wrong show! That could only happen to me. Years later I've co-hosted shows with both Claudia and Davina, and I even re-enacted *God's Gift* with Davina for one of her chat shows. At the time, I could never have conceived of something like that happening.

The annoying thing about that clip is every now and again they'll play it on a show I'm a guest on and I've got to fake that I've never seen it before! 'Oh no, where did you find that?' I was on *The Jonathan Ross Show* and they showed it as a big surprise. I didn't have the heart to tell them it had already been played on numerous shows beforehand.

What was really interesting and helpful about *God's Gift* was being a contestant. When I was hosting *Take Me Out* and the single men got nervous or self-conscious, I had in my locker the fact that I knew exactly what they were going through and I lived to tell the tale. On *TMO* we had runners (runners are young whippers starting off in the industry who have to do a lot of the skivvying, pretty much like all apprentices) and I would always make sure they looked after the contestants. 'Keep them relaxed, get them a coffee.' I can remember what a big deal it was for me, back in the day, coming in off the street to take part in a TV show, and the frantic pace of a studio floor, with everyone running around dressed in black, talking on headsets. It can be quite daunting if you've never witnessed it before. I never wanted the *TMO* contestants to feel like living props. I wanted them to enjoy the experience and tell their friends and family how good it was. My first telly experience, on *The National Lottery Big Ticket*, was made all the better because the presenters, Patrick Kielty, Gaby Roslin and Anthea Turner, were really lovely to us, and I learned from them how to treat people on a studio floor. Of course, I've also been on sets when I've seen people treated like shit, and in those situations I've jumped in and pulled people up on their behaviour. It's the easiest thing in the world to bite someone's head off but that will stay with them for a long time.

Anyway, I didn't lift the *God's Gift* trophy but I did get the ultimate prize – I went on to host the world's most successful dating show, and I'll gladly take that. It's only now thinking back I realise how important working at HLC was during my formative TV years. Whether it be *God's Gift*, *Phoenix Nights*, or my first proper acting gig on *The Services*, I was working for Bolton Council at the same time and I was still very grateful to have a job to fall back on.

The Services was Peter's first show of his own. At the time Channel 4 were running a series of shows called *Comedy Lab*. These were essentially 15-minute pilot episodes showcasing up-and-coming writers and performers and they helped launch the careers of people like PeterKay, Ricky Gervais, Mitchell and Webb, Olivia Lee, Jimmy Carr, Jack Whitehall and Karl Pilkington. *The Services*, set in a Bolton service station, was Peter's TV writing debut, with him playing several characters, something that he carried on very successfully with *That Peter Kay Thing* and *Phoenix Nights*. My character's name was Terry. Peter always had faith I could do it and I suppose it was also good to have a trusted face around for an honest opinion. Terry was a service station employee and I had one or two lines, most notably:

'Who's that dick?'

Also in *The Services* was Sian Gibson (then Foulkes), who I later had my first and only TV kiss with in *Phoenix Nights*. Sian went on to co-star with Peter in *Car Share* and I'm made up for her. She's one of the loveliest people I've ever met and it's nice when the good ones do well. Playing Terry was a bit of fun – I didn't get paid for it but I was glad to be filming something with my clothes on! Anyhow, that came and went and I carried on working at HLC. Then, in 1999, along came *That Peter Kay Thing*, a series of stand-alone spoof documentaries, also set in Bolton. The first episode was called 'In the Club' and was set in a fictional working men's club called the Neptune. It followed the grand finale of an annual talent show competition, and that episode turned out to be the unofficial pilot of *Phoenix Nights*. It featured all those familiar characters: Brian Potter, Les Alanos, Ray Von, Kenny Senior, Jerry St Clair, Holy Mary, Young Kenny and of course Max and Paddy.

Pete asked if I fancied getting involved. It was a no-brainer. Of course I wanted to be involved. I'd got the TV bug now, and maybe this time I'd get paid! There was one sticky point, though – this time I had to audition.

'Why?' I asked Pete. 'We're mates and it's your show! What about the old school ties? Bolton floodlights and all that?'

Back then Pete wasn't a household name and he certainly didn't have the influence to dish out a part to a mate that worked in a local leisure centre. This was proper telly, and I had to go through the process like everyone else. It actually turned out to be two auditions, one in London and a second in Manchester. I didn't have a clue what an audition consisted of, and with zero experience it was round to Pete's for a bit of guidance. He still lived with his mum, as did I, at the age of 25, and his room was exactly the same as when we were kids, full of LPs and videotapes. You couldn't see an inch of the walls or ceiling for movie posters. (Come to think of it, maybe his bedroom was subconsciously the inspiration for the Vibroplant staffroom decoration!) There we were, back in the same room where we'd acted out all those music videos, the same room we used to laugh and tell stories in when we were kids. This time there was a bit more riding on it. This time I had it all mapped out: I was going to be famous! I was gonna get the girls, I was gonna get recognised, I was gonna be somebody and I was hopefully gonna get paid.

There was no thought about who the character was or how I was going to play him. My main concern was remembering the lines. Pete was on the bed and I'd be stood in the doorway playing the part of this doorman. Until I started writing this book I'd totally forgotten about those times, and it's mad now to think how it all started. So after a night of practising, it was time for the first audition in London. That in itself was a massive deal – I'd never been to London for a casting and to this day it's all a bit of a blur. I couldn't tell you how I even got there! I vaguely remember waiting outside the audition room, shitting bangers, wondering what was going to happen.

I got called in and there was Pete sat behind a desk with the director and a casting agent. I've only ever done a few auditions over the years and I've hated them all. I'm fine playing an arena in front of 10,000 people, with all the atmosphere and laughter, but put me in front of ten or in this case three people and I'm all over the place. Still, I got through it and went back to Bolton slightly traumatised but relieved. The following week, Peter phoned me.

'Paddy, they like you but they want you to do another audition. This time it's in Manchester.' *Are you taking the piss?* Although Peter wanted me to get the part, Channel 4 needed a bit more convincing. Back round to his little back bedroom. This time he had the audition tapes so I could watch my first go at a casting. Not only did this give me a chance to see what I'd done right and wrong, I also got to see all the other actors auditioning for the same part, Paddy O'Shea. I could now see what had to be done. I mentally copied and pasted their good bits and popped them into my second audition.

The fact that it was going to be in Manchester made me feel a bit better. Just going down to London was a big enough ordeal for me, let alone auditioning in front of three strangers in an old office suite. I now had to do it all again but with a bit of extra confidence. Some people are just good at auditions, Steve Edge (one half of Les Alanos) being one of them. If you had to go for an audition and Edgey was sat waiting to go in, you may as well just go home, it was obvious he'd get the part. I was too self-conscious and nervous at auditions; I don't even like auditioning people myself, never mind the other way around. I auditioned for a Daz advert once. I had to sit there with no shirt on, pretending to drive a car. With the best will in the world there's not a lot you can do with that, unless you're Steve Edge – he probably got the job. Anyhow, I did the second audition and not long after, Pete rang me to say I'd got the part. The lad had done his best to give me a shot and it had paid off!

* * *

The next problem I had was a set of massive ears. I had long curly hair at the time, those were the days, so you couldn't really see that they stuck out. Laurence Llewelyn-Bowen aside, I knew I needed to cut my hair if I wanted to properly make a go of it. A doorman wouldn't have long curly hair, would he? No, he'd have a skinhead, or at the very least short hair. So I decided I'd get my ears pinned back. I've definitely lost the focus and determination I had back then. When I was younger, if I wanted something badly then I'd move heaven and earth to get it.

I'd enquired with my GP about getting my ears done many years before and been put on a waiting list to see a surgeon at the hospital. Around two years later, I received a letter for a hospital appointment. I felt so embarrassed – the thought of going to see this surgeon filled me with dread – but I somehow managed to pluck up the confidence to go. The surgeon was very blunt and to the point.

'Unfortunately we can no longer do the procedure. You've been on the waiting list for so long you're now too old to get it done on the NHS.'

I was around 15 at the time.

I was totally crushed.

He then said, 'Don't vote for the current government because they're the ones who stopped it.'

'Vote for the current government? I'm not old enough to vote, you prick!' is what I should have said, but being so insecure and shy I just got up and left. That was that. I hadn't told my mum or family about any of these appointments, so nobody had any clue what had happened or how shitty it made me feel.

Fast-forward around ten years, I had more confidence and determination to get it done. Cosmetic surgery was becoming more acceptable then but was still fairly new to the mainstream. The stupid things you do when you're young: I did zero research, had no advice and got no recommendations. I literally picked my surgeon at random out of a magazine because they had the nicest, glossiest-looking advert. The thought of chatting about it made me very anxious but I called the number on the advert and made an appointment. They had this private hospital facility in Preston. I was met by a very persuasive salesperson who talked that much my ears were naturally getting smaller! Anyway, the upshot of all this was the procedure was going to cost £5,000. Even though I'd always worked from leaving school, there was no way on God's green earth I had access to that sort of money. My bank account always had a minus sign next to it and no one I knew was any better off. So I went to the bank for a loan, but not with one of the big high-street banks – this was a relatively unknown set-up. Again I thought this would be better. Again I was wrong!

'What's the loan for, Mr McGuinness?' the bank manager asked me.

'A car,' I said.

I had a few mates who had taken out loans and they advised me that cars could be always be repossessed if you didn't make the payment, so a bank was more likely to lend you the money for one. Repossessing a pair of ears would be a little more tricky, although I suppose that was down to who you borrowed the money from. My mates were right and the bank gave me the cash for a car. What no one explained was the amount of interest and APR they'd be putting on the loan – I was absolutely shafted! I think the monthly repayments were around 200 quid at the time and out of that only around 30 quid was paid off the loan, the rest was interest.

Anyway, I got the loan and I was straight on to the cosmetic surgery place. It was finally time to get my ears pinned back. Stardom beckoned!

Straight from the off I didn't like my surgeon. Something wasn't right but the tunnel vision took over. After the humiliation at the hospital, I just wanted the procedure doing. Dr Herbert was an abrupt posh bloke, the type who looked down his nose at everyone. Every time I asked a question he'd just cut me down in a very dismissive way. He made me feel like a thick, useless, working-class oik who he clearly had no time for. Although I was confident among my peers at the leisure centre, this was a different gravy. I never questioned anything and just went back to my usual shy self. If it'd been now I'd have let him have it both barrels, but back then he definitely had the upper hand. I kept my mouth shut because he was so dismissive and vile. I thought, *Just get it done and I won't have to deal with this prick again.*

The procedure itself was a speedy, cold, silent affair. This charmer of a surgeon pulled my head back and forth and did what he needed to do without a word of encouragement or comfort. He never even spoke to or made eye contact with me. I felt like a piece of meat on his horrendous production line. It was so quick, I reckon he was done in around 20 minutes and then off he went. The nurses bandaged my head and that was that. Due to no one knowing what I was having done, I think I told my mum I was staying at a mate's for a week. I was actually booked into a B&B in Bolton. That was a very long week. I'd put my hood up and leave to collect painkillers from the chemist and then head back to this grotty little room. It was only a tenner a night and no one bothered me so that suited me fine. I couldn't go home and see my mum or any of my mates until it was all healed, or at least until I could take the bandages off – I looked like a Poundland invisible man.

After three days I had a look at Dr Herbert's handiwork. My ears were black and blue, pinned flat to my head, which I'd specifi-cally asked him not to do, and full of dried blood. Not what I'd been expecting at all. Luckily, my hair was still long so I was able to cover up the mess. I did another two nights on my own then decided to go home – five nights of being on my own, feeling like shit and eating aspirins like Smarties was enough. Also, I'd promised my dad I'd pick him up from a holiday he was having in Blackpool.

As the wounds healed, my ears didn't look right. There was this weird line running through both of them that clearly shouldn't have been there and they were pinned back much too tight to my head, making them a bit pointy – something my fellow *Top*

Gear host Chris Harris takes great delight in! He often refers to me as Spock, along with other names that aren't for the pages of this book. It turned out Dr Herbert/Crippen had botched me, and there'd been zero duty of care from the cosmetic surgery. They'd had my money and that was that. The maddest thing was that not long after, I was sat at home watching a programme called *World in Action*, which used to be ITV's version of *Panorama*, when I heard the announcer say, 'Tonight on *World in Action* … rogue surgeons.' I couldn't believe my eyes! There on the telly was Dr Herbert, who wasn't even qualified to do any of the procedures he'd been doing! He was a fraud who had been struck off years before. The entire programme was an exposé dedicated solely to him. Fuck me rigid! What were the odds of picking up a magazine and out of all those adverts choosing a dodgy surgeon? It could only happen to me! I'm not sure if Herbert is still alive or performing surgery in hell. If he is still drawing breath and I bumped into him, I'd take great delight in booting him straight in the stones.

That said, although my ears were botched, at least they didn't stick out any more. The weird thing is my mum never mentioned it to me. It was so clear to see, especially when I walked in our house for the first time with short hair, but she never said a word. I think she knew how uncomfortable I'd be talking about it so she never did, and nor did any of my family or friends, for that matter. In fact, the only person who did mention it was Claire, my first girlfriend, who I bumped into not long after having my hair cut.

So after auditions in London and Manchester, rehearsals at Peter's mum's and some botched cosmetic surgery, the part of Paddy

O'Shea was mine. Also, a little factoid for you, the first person to appear on-screen in that series? Me!

I loved playing Paddy in 'In the Club' but as soon as it finished, it was back to the day job like none of it had ever happened. Was that it? Where was the money, the showbiz parties, the girls? Turns out it doesn't work like that. Despite dipping my toe into the world of television, I was back at Horwich Leisure Centre … but at least I had a few decent stories to impress my mates.

THE FIRST STEP ON THE SHOWBIZ LADDER

We laughed, we drank, we laughed some more.

The world of show business was a distant memory and in the 12 months that had passed since 'In the Club' I'd done a couple of courses and ended up working in the gym as a fitness instructor. This was a step up from being a lifeguard and although I still did that as well, I now had an official contract. Out of the blue Pete called me up and told me the news about *Phoenix Nights* being made into a series.

'*Phoenix Nights*, what's that?' I asked.

'It's from the "In the Club" episode in *That Peter Kay Thing*, Paddy. Channel 4 have given it a series!'

What a result! I'd totally forgotten about all the telly stuff so this was a complete surprise.

'Please tell me I don't have to do another audition.'

'No, everyone who was in "In the Club" will be cast in *Phoenix Nights*.'

I agreed to do it without any thought of my job at HLC.

'So when do we start, Pete?'

'Well, it's not been written yet.'

So my plans for a fancy celebrity lifestyle had to be put on hold again. The series was written by Peter along with Neil Fitzmaurice and Dave Spikey in a small office on an industrial estate called Bolton Enterprise Centre. Peter likes getting other people's opinions on things, so he'd talk me through ideas to see what I thought. Eventually he invited me down to the writing room, which was a great learning curve for me. I'd drive over on my dinner hour or if I had a day off, usually armed with a few pies and cakes. Pete would be sat behind his laptop with Dave and Neil either side of him. I felt Dave and Neil didn't want me there. Who was I? No experience, no comedy background, and turning up in my leisure centre uniform probably wasn't a good look. The main thing was that Pete wanted me there, and he gave me confidence and made me feel valued, always listening to my ideas and thoughts. So much so that I eventually got an 'additional material' credit in the titles. He was very good at drawing things out of me, and the fact that we both found the same things funny helped. He told me if I had any ideas to write them down and if they were good enough they'd be used in *Phoenix Nights*. I was in no way, shape or form a writer, and back then I wouldn't have had a clue how to put a script together. The one thing I was confident of was making people laugh, so I sat there and watched how the writing process worked.

One of my proudest achievements was writing a scene that fans of *Phoenix Nights* know and quote to this day: the drunken dwarf fight scene. I was on a late shift in HLC at the time. The gym was practically empty in the evening so I got out a few of sheets of Lifestyles-headed A4 (Lifestyles was the name of the gym) and decided to write something while I was sat on reception. I only had a red biro but it had plenty of ink in it so off I went. The following day I went down to see Pete at the Enterprise Centre and gave him these few sheets of paper full of writing and scribbles in red ink. He was quiet at first and then he started to laugh – that was a big relief. It's mad to think that entire scene was filmed exactly how I wrote it on that Lifestyles paper while I was on shift in the gym. 'We're Bolton, we're barmy, we're on the piss tonight!', 'Who you calling tattoo, yer long streak of piss?' and of course 'How far away are they?' All still quoted to this day, which gives me a massive sense of pride.

Even though I was chipping in with ideas and writing little bits for Peter, I still felt Dave and Neil didn't want me there. I get it but it was upsetting. I found myself walking a fine line, contributing just enough but not too much. I didn't want to step on anyone's toes, and to me it was just exciting to be a small part of it. One of the times I'll never forget, because it made me feel like shit, was turning up one day to discover that Peter wasn't there, it was just Dave and Neil. I sat down in my usual seat and asked them if they fancied a pie or a pasty, always a good move in my eyes.

'No, we're fine.'

'Is Pete coming in today?'

'No, he's not in today.'

And that was that. I sat there in silence. I felt like they'd totally blanked me, proper cold-shoulder stuff. They made me feel like a spare part and after about half an hour of them muttering to each other and not even acknowledging my presence, I just got up and left. As the door shut, paranoid me knew they'd be slagging me off. Again, one part of me can see why they were so frosty towards me, but on the other hand I would never want anyone to feel like that. Over the years I became good pals with Neil, we'd often go out for a beer, but with Dave it was more of a working relationship. He didn't really come out with us on many nights out, but we all got on and there was always a good atmosphere on set. I've not forgotten how uncomfortable and unwanted I felt that day, but I've never held that against them. I've had some fantastic nights with Neil, nights where we've howled with laughter, and whenever he's asked me to help him out with anything I've always been there – that day is all water under the bridge for me.

* * *

Skip forward a few months and here we all were on the set of *Phoenix Nights*. None of us had any real telly experience, apart from Dave, who used to host a quiz show on daytime TV, and Neil, who had done some acting. Luckily everyone got on, and because we were all more or less in the same boat, in at the deep end, it was just so much fun. The core cast was made up of Peter, myself, Archie Kelly (Kenny Senior), Neil (Ray Von), Justin Moorhouse (Young Kenny), Dave (Jerry), Janice Connolly (Holy Mary), Toby Foster (Les), Steve Edge (Alan) and Ted Robbins (Den Perry). Out of that group, myself, Edgey, Neil, Justin and Archie would regularly go out on the piss. Toby would join us now and again, but he lived in Sheffield so it wasn't as straightforward for him. Dave never came out at all, and I can't blame him really. He was a good few years older than the rest of us, married, and also had a proper job with the NHS.

The only night we all went out for a big session was in London. Channel 4 had invited us down to their annual get-together to showcase new shows they had coming out. The first series of *Phoenix Nights* had already been on and although not a massive success it had a bit of a cult following. We were all very excited about going, even more so when we found out it was going to be a free bar! We started drinking on the train and got a game of cards going. We were playing for money, the only trouble being that every time we went through a tunnel, the carriage would be in complete darkness, and once we'd come out of the other side half the money on the table would have disappeared! We never did find out who the culprit was but I'd put my mortgage on Archie Kelly.

When we got to our hotel and found out we had to share rooms, we all started arguing about who was going to share with Justin. This was nothing to do with his character, it was due to the fact he snored like a Siberian freight train! So in the hotel reception we drew straws for who was going to share with him and I ended up drawing the short straw. Luckily I found a legal loophole to get out of this situation. At the time Justin and Edgey smoked, so I put it out there that surely the smokers would be better sharing a room? It worked, justice prevailed and I ended up sharing with Archie.

Once we'd freshened up, and by that I mean emptied our mini-bars, off we went to Channel 4. We were put in a room with a big screen and they played clips of all the new shows they had coming up. One of those shows was *Bo' Selecta!* I remember standing with the lads, thinking, *What the fuck is this madness and who's this guy with the masks?* No one knew how successful that show would become and that myself and Leigh (Keith Lemon) would end up with our own series on ITV nigh on 20 years later. After a few speeches from the commissioners and heads of Channel 4, talk got on to where we should go next. The free drinks were still flowing and we were knocking them back. Iain Morris, who ended up commissioning *Max and Paddy* and went on to write *The Inbetweeners*, mentioned going to the wrap party of another Channel 4 show.

'Is it still free drinks?' we asked.

'Yes,' said Iain.

'What's the show, pal?'

'It's called *Model Behaviour*, it's a show about finding the next top models.'

So Ian had invited us to a bar in Soho that was serving free drinks and would be full of beautiful women. It took us a nanosecond to decide.

'YES!!!!'

None of us could believe it – we ended up in this bar grabbing free drinks four at a time just in case they stopped serving, all the while surrounded by drop-dead gorgeous models! There were also a few male models in the room, one being Jamie Dornan – yes, him of *Fifty Shades of Grey* and *The Fall* fame. Could this first introduction to show business get any better? Yes, it could. Randomly, and unbeknown to the rest of us, Justin had found out that Peter Stringfellow was a fan of the show and had contacted the clubland lothario to let him know the cast of *Phoenix Nights* were in town. As soon as he mentioned this to us it was like lighting the blue touchpaper – *If I'm dreaming I don't want to wake up!* Even Dave had a spring in his step. What a night this was turning out to be. So we all made our way across town to the mecca of lap dancing. The place where film stars, TV personalities, rock stars and models went to party. We were living the dream.

On our way over we had a bet among ourselves: whoever could get a strand of Stringfellow's hair would be the winner. It seemed like a good idea, probably because we'd all been drinking since nine o'clock that morning. We got there with no names on the guest list and none of the door staff having a clue who we were, and Stringfellow himself was nowhere to be seen. After a bit of blagging from Justin, we were eventually let in. I went straight to the bar with Neil, where we got the biggest culture shock ever: London prices!

'Fuck this, we're going,' we said to the rest of the lads.

'Whoa, whoa, we've only just got here. What's the problem?' said Toby.

'We've just been charged thirty quid for a glass of Coke and a pint of lager!'

None of us were used to London prices and looking at Toby and the rest of the lads' faces, we'd have to get the gas and air out at this rate.

Just as we turned to leave, on cue Peter Stringfellow appeared, grabbed Toby and Edgey in a headlock and shouted, 'It's the best backing band in clubland!' We were in! There he was in all his splendour, long peroxide blond locks, silk shirt opened to the navel, big glistening smile.

'Where are you going? I've invited you as my guests. I want you to stay.'

'Sorry, Peter, not at these prices.'

'Nonsense, it's on the house! Drinks are free, as are the dances off my girls.'

With that he whisked us all off to his ultra VIP room. We definitely weren't VIPs but I think because Stringfellow's roots were in northern working men's clubs, *Phoenix Nights* totally resonated with him and he wanted us all to have a great night – and that we did! Cut to a Channel 4 assistant swinging around a pole and the boys sat around this big round table with me on Peter Stringfellow's personal throne! Edgey said he looked over at me and I had two semi-naked girls on my lap, a third popping grapes and champagne into my mouth and a fourth massaging my shoulders. He said he'd never seen a man happier in his life. We had a group picture with Stringy; he must have wondered what was going on. His head must have been tugged backwards in all directions because everyone had their hands in his hair, trying to rip bits out. I, for one, had my arm around him, with a strand of his hair wrapped around my finger, trying to yank it out of his head. I wish I could get my hands on that photo.

We had the best night ever, apart from Dave. For some reason the girl who danced for him wanted payment. One of the funniest, most surreal things of that night was watching Stringfellow arguing with Dave over payment for a lap dance.

'She's one of my best girls, Dave.'

'Yes, but I thought it was all free. No one else is being asked to pay.'

Whenever I look at Dave I just see Jerry St Clair, so it really tickled me to see him arguing the toss with Peter Stringfellow.

I can't remember how that argument finished, probably because I had four topless women gyrating all over me at the time and the free drinks were still flowing. If this was show business, we were doing it properly. Despite the plethora of exotic dancers, I ended up dancing with the Channel 4 assistant on the pole. We were having a good laugh, so much so that I ended up back at her apartment. I woke up wondering where I was.

'You'll have to get up and go soon, my cleaner will be here in minute,' she told me.

Cleaner?! Where had I spent the night, Sandringham Palace?

My mum was a cleaner but she cleaned bingo halls and pubs. I had no idea people had cleaners in their houses. Welcome to London!

I made my way back to the hotel we were booked into. Edgey wasn't best pleased as he'd spent the night in Justin's room and didn't get a wink of sleep due to the incessant snoring, a room he didn't even have to stay in. I don't think my argument of 'Well, I didn't get much sleep either, Edgey' went down too well. Archie then added insult to injury by saying he didn't sleep because his room was too quiet to nod off. While all this was going on I found a few strands of Stringy's hair in my pocket, happy days!

* * *

We had some fantastic nights out back in the *Phoenix Nights* days, especially around Manchester. The first series of *Phoenix Nights* was one big stag do, really. We'd laugh and mess about all day on set and pretty much do the same on an evening. I didn't really take it all in and soak up what I was a part of. I wasn't tuned in to what was happening around me during the filming of the show, or in any of my early TV performances. I was all about having a good time, thinking more about what opportunities and perks might come out of me being on the telly rather than learning the ropes and enjoying the experience of being around talented, creative people.

The piss-taking and wind-ups were brutal. There'd be this little portacabin/green room we'd all congregate in during the first series and Toby used to sit near the window, where there was a blind which had a piece of string hanging down from it. While we laughed and took the piss out of each other, Toby constantly chewed on the end of this string. One day Archie Kelly decided to cover the end of it in red-hot Tabasco sauce. We all sat there as Toby, totally unaware, popped the string into his mouth. His blood pressure was through the roof at the best of times, but now his head was purple and his eyes were bloodshot. We absolutely pissed our sides and Toby knew instantly it was Archie.

'You little prick!!'

Archie Kelly is a proper little wind-up. He used to be a schoolteacher and he's fluent in five different languages, Spanish being one of them. While we were filming we had this old-fashioned double-decker bus that had been turned into a mobile canteen for us to have our dinner in. One day it came up about Archie speaking all these different languages, so I asked him to prove it. I was tucking into a sponge pudding at the time.

'How do you say "this pudding is a bit sweet" in Spanish?'

'*El pudino mucho sweeto.*'

The entire bus went up with laughter. Archie Kelly is the living embodiment of his character Kenny Senior. I remember arguing with him once about a cup of tea. I was round at his house and he made me a cuppa. I took a sip and gagged.

'What the fuck's all this in my tea, Archie?'

'Tea leaves.'

'Tea leaves? Who still uses tea leaves these days?'

'Well, it's the bleach, you see.'

'Bleach?'

He then went on to tell me that he doesn't use teabags because they're full of bleach.

'I don't think there's bleach in teabags, Archie.'

This argument is still raging to this day, 20 years later. My point is that whenever he's in my house or whenever we're gigging or in a restaurant he has no problem drinking bleach-filled teabags, but if you go to his house you spend the best part of an hour fishing tea leaves out of your mug. He doesn't even use a tea strainer. It's amazing how bleach only affects the teabags if he's paying for them.

Honestly, I could write a book just on *Phoenix Nights*, the things we got up to. I needed a decent car and my mate from the leisure centre (he of top-shelf drinking fame) was selling his Ford XR3i. His dad worked at a Ford dealership in Bolton called Gordons so all of his cars came from there. It was an absolute beauty but he wanted 800 quid for it and I didn't have that kind of money. Pete stepped in and offered to buy it for me, which absolutely blew me away. To this day I'm still scratching my head as to why he offered. I love him and he's the one who opened the door for me into the world of teledom, but when it comes to money he's tighter than cramp. I've had arguments in chippies with Pete over who was gonna pay. This sudden and unannounced show of generosity properly threw me. While writing this I gave him a call to ask why he actually bought me that XR3i. He said at the time it was a thank you for helping him with *Phoenix Nights* – he also reminded me that I'd agreed to pay him the money back. I don't recall that but it's something I would have definitely said in good faith, even though I never did.

Anyway, that XR3i went on to make a cameo appearance in *Phoenix Nights*. I was talking to one of the crew on set and he told me how they had to pay to use cars on-screen. It all seems pretty reasonable now but back then I didn't have a clue about things like that. Straight away I could smell a pound note, so I had a word with the bloke who sorted all the vehicles on set and managed to get my motor on the show. I drove it into shot with the song 'Tarzan Boy' blaring out of the speakers. The fee for the car worked out to more than what I was actually getting paid per day for appearing in *Phoenix Nights*. Having said that, the mighty XR3i put in one hell of a performance.

* * *

The club we filmed *Phoenix Nights* in, St Gregory's, was still open for business. There was a separate billiards room (the Tony Knowles Suite) where the regulars would have a pint and play snooker.

Certainly during the first series no one had a clue who any of us were, and in those days there was no social media and selfies to be had, so we used to play snooker in between takes. It got that competitive, filming actually became a hindrance. Obviously none of the lads could be trusted not to move any of the balls, so even if you were winning a frame, the game had to be replayed if you were called in for filming. One of the assistant directors called me in for a scene once while I was on a 26 break – broke my heart having to void that game. Filming *Phoenix Nights* put a stop to a lot of promising young snooker careers.

Along with the regulars having a pint, we also had to contend with functions – weddings, christenings, birthday parties, even funerals were booked in during filming. One of the most surreal things I've ever witnessed, and trust me I've witnessed a few, was a wake having to be stopped. There was a roomful of mourners, all dressed in black, weeping over the loss of a loved one, and the assistant director walked in and shouted, 'Quiet, please, we're going for a take.' It's someone's funeral, for fuck's sake!

Across from the club was a car body shop business, J&S Autos. The blokes who owned it, John and Stu, let us use their forecourt for our catering trucks, wardrobes, portacabins and so on. They were paid for this but we'd also let them get a bit of dinner from our catering team. I became good mates with them and they'd look after me if I needed any bumps and scratches sorting out on my car. Long after *Phoenix Nights* finished I'd still go up for a brew and a catch-up. This one particular day Pete turned up on set after having a bit of a bump in his car. It was nothing major, just some superficial damage to the bodywork. Peter was obviously a bit pissed off, no one wants to see their motor pranged, and he was fretting about his insurance premiums, so I told him I'd have a word with the lads at J&S to see if they could sort it. This was during the first series so no one knew who Max and Paddy, Brian Potter or any of the characters in *Phoenix Nights* were. We'd just finished our dinner on the catering truck so I told Pete to whip his car over and I'd get John and Stu to have a look at it. Archie was there as well and we were all dressed as our characters. So I'm there in my doorman outfit, Archie's dressed as Kenny Senior and Pete's in full Brian Potter get-up. We're all stood there as Stu's looking at the damage on the car.

'Can you sort it, Stu?' I said.

'Yeah, no problem, just tell that fat (bleep) I want a part in his series,' Stu said.

He didn't have a clue it was Peter dressed as Brian Potter. Pete just shook his head and walked off. Anyhow, I got Pete's car fixed and Stu got his five minutes of fame sat in the back of shot in one of the bar scenes.

I was still working at the leisure centre when I was filming *Phoenix Nights* – in fact I carried on working there right up to filming *Max and Paddy*. I'd get my filming schedule through and manage to wangle it around my shifts at HLC. I wasn't required on set every day, so it was just a case of getting a few shifts covered and using my holidays for the rest. Some days, I would finish filming on *Phoenix Nights* and drive up to the leisure centre to do a late shift in the gym. I had to keep my job on because I wasn't sure if *Phoenix Nights* would be a one-off. In the early days, before the XR3i came along, I still had my old Nissan Sunny and that little rascal got me backwards and forwards between work and work very nicely. Both uses of the word 'work' I use very loosely.

 CHAPTER 11

GAMBLE OR TAKE THE MONEY

At the end of a TV series there's usually a wrap party to celebrate, like the *Model Behaviour* one we gatecrashed in London. We couldn't afford a night in London so we held our wrap party at the Phoenix Club. One of the producers on series one, a guy called Henry Klejdys, decided to hold an impromptu awards evening, but instead of giving out awards he randomly gave out dildos. It got even more bizarre when his niece, who worked on the show, accepted one onstage. As the awards ceremony and speeches went on, Toby won 100 quid in pound coins on the fruit machine – the noise of it paying out took a bit of a shine off proceedings, especially as he was collecting them into the bottom of his jumper, which he'd now fashioned into some kind of carrier bag.

No sooner had we finished the first series of *Phoenix Nights*, my life more or less went back to normal. I'd had a taste of the good life, enjoyed the nights out and paid off all my debts. I had a car and was able to give my mum a bit of extra money every week for my keep. I still kept in touch with the rest of the cast, but all the excitement of making a TV show slowly dissipated with time. Close friendships and intense relationships form during filming, which all seem so meaningful, but once you walk back out into the real world it all changes and the intensity of it all disperses.

Another thing I discovered back in the day was TV shows don't necessarily appear on our screens straight away. After filming finished on *Phoenix Nights*, it didn't actually air on Channel 4 until well over a year later. When you're young, a year feels like an eternity, especially when all my colleagues at the leisure centre kept asking me if this show was ever going to be on the telly. I couldn't wait for everyone to see it, especially my mum, so it was very frustrating. The one good thing was I now had the ability to pay off my botched ear surgery debt. My fee for the first series of *Phoenix Nights* was around £4,000, equally liberating and soul-destroying at the same time. Yes, I had finally got rid of the crippling debt, but also every last penny I'd earned from *Phoenix Nights* was now gone. What a kick in the balls!

Channel 4 eventually aired the series and it came and went. The viewing figures weren't all that great and back then there was no catch-up TV or on-demand services, so if you missed it that was it, unless someone you knew had taped it and could lend you a copy on VHS (google it). So I was back to square one, with no money, working at Horwich Leisure Centre. I was racking my brains how to capitalise on the fleeting passing of *Phoenix Nights*. I knew if you did a bit of coaching at the leisure centre you got more money than if you worked as a lifeguard or fitness instructor – I think they got paid around £9 an hour at the time. The management were quite good at putting you on courses if you could show you'd make money and bring people in. I sold my idea to the manager at the time, a fella called Chris Jackson, and he agreed to pay for a course.

A couple of weeks later, I became a qualified boxersize instructor. I'd get more money in my wage packet and hopefully be able to cash in on the minuscule amount of celebrity I'd gained playing Paddy the bouncer. Our local paper, the *Bolton Evening News*, did a piece advertising the class, and people came along because it was 'him off that show on the telly'. That was good enough for me and the classes started to gather momentum and became very popular. I was happy, Chris was happy and most importantly the punters were happy. I had people telling me how much weight they'd lost compared to other classes they'd tried and this really pepped me up. I even forgot about earning the extra few quid in my wage and got stuck into making the class as good as I could. My sessions were always booked up weeks in advance, and I got a real kick out of seeing people slowly changing shape as they got fit.

When I think about working at Horwich Leisure Centre during both series of *Phoenix Nights*, it's totally bonkers that it even happened. I mean, finishing a shift in the gym or on the pool then jumping into my car to film a television show for the rest of the day is a bit of a stretch. Crazy to think that after being a part of two successful comedy series I was working in a leisure centre and still living with my mum in our little bungalow. There's no way that'd work in this day and age – if Instagram, Twitter and *Mail Online* were around then, I'd have been forced to keep up some kind of faux celebrity lifestyle or labelled as a failure for still doing a 'normal' job. I feel for a lot of the younger generation coming into this business now, especially those involved in reality TV. Keeping up the façade of living their best life 24/7 must be horrendous. I didn't have a pot to piss in after *Phoenix Nights* but I didn't have the pressure of pretending I was more than what I actually was, a young lad still living at home with his mum who worked in a leisure centre. I'm not sure how I'd have managed the whole social media thing back then. Selfies in the shower with a disability chair stuck to the wall or pictures of me with all the old blokes in the sauna isn't exactly influencer material, is it? If someone off *Love Island* or *EastEnders* was spotted working in a local supermarket, someone would take a picture, post it online and they'd instantly be trolled. I'm so glad I started out when those kind of external pressures didn't exist. Knowing how I am for trying to impress people, I've no doubt I'd have had a bad time.

I still fancied a career in the media but it didn't keep me awake at night. What did keep me awake was this strange need to impress people, constantly wanting everyone to think that I was doing well. I'm still not sure where this need came from. I wasn't really like that as a kid. Maybe it's down to not having much that I felt the need to show off a bit more? When I think about it, I probably wouldn't have done half the things I did if I hadn't been looking for approval from others. It might be something I need to talk through with a therapist one day; maybe I harboured some deep-seated need to be liked.

Whatever it was, I think a lot of my decisions back then were clouded by this quirk in my nature. One of the most ridiculous things I ever did was buy a car to impress a girl. I happened to get talking to her about cars one day (ever the romantic). At the time I owned a perfectly decent motor, an S-type Jag, which I loved. It was black, proper murdered-up spec. I thought she'd be impressed but it turns out she really liked the Subaru Impreza WRX STi. My agent at the time, Phil McIntyre, happened to own one – ding! Light-bulb moment. I rang Phil up and asked if he'd sell it me.

'You've already got a Jag, Paddy. Why do you want my Subaru?' he asked.

'Well, I was talking to this girl who really likes them, Phil, and I reckon there might be a chance,' I explained.

A week later I'd sold my Jag and was now the proud owner of a bright blue Scooby with gold wheels. I drove up to where she worked, asked her to come outside and … ta-da! The big reveal. I took her for a spin and the following week we had the seats back for an impromptu session of car aerobics. Job done. Everyone was happy apart from me – I was now stuck with a car I didn't need and couldn't really afford to run. At the time, however, lads' mags were extremely popular. *Loaded, FHM, Zoo* and *Nuts* were a staple for the young man who didn't have the courage to buy a proper adult magazine. I had a brainwave. I came up with the novel idea of trading in on my new-found fame and called up *Zoo* magazine.

'All right, I work on *Phoenix Nights* and if I do you an exclusive interview and a photo shoot at the Phoenix Club, will you sell my car for me as part of the article?'

Sure enough, it worked. They sent one of their team down to the Phoenix Club, along with a photographer. I sat on a bonnet of the car, did the interview, had my picture taken and in went the story the following week. In the space of another week or two someone had got in touch and offered to buy the car. I actually got more than I paid for it, which was a big relief. All that for the sake of impressing someone I didn't know from Adam. Having said that, the sex was a very welcome bonus.

* * *

Time went by and *Phoenix Nights* had now become very popular due to the boom in DVD players. DVDs became all the rage and sales went through the roof. To Peter's testament, he had seen what was happening and released both series just at the right time. He crammed them full of outtakes, unseen footage and some really good commentary from the cast and crew. They sold a shitload and it went to number one in the charts. I'm not sure how it all worked but the cast got a little bonus from that, around £10,000, and to say we were happy was an understatement. The morning we got the money, myself, Archie, Justin and Edgey all met up for a brew at a cafe in Manchester. We were so giddy at the time – this was more money than any of us had ever earned. I'm not sure what Peter, Dave and Neil got but we were happy just to get a taste. It was a really good period for us all back then and I was enjoying the whole experience, living in the moment.

With the DVDs' success, the two doormen from the Phoenix, Max and Paddy, became very popular with the viewers. That's when Pete had the idea to do a spin-off, *Max and Paddy's Road to Nowhere*. When he asked me if I fancied it, obviously it was an immediate yes. He then asked me to co-write it with him, which really blew me away – what an opportunity this was. I'd just been asked to write and star in my very own series with one of my mates, who was fast becoming one of the biggest names in comedy – and on top of all that I was going to get paid for the privilege.

I'm not sure what happened between Peter, Neil and Dave but I know he also asked them to help write it. They wanted to do more *Phoenix Nights*, though, and I don't think the idea of writing *Max and Paddy* really appealed to them. This was a really big moment for me – unlike on *Phoenix Nights*, I was no longer going to be in the odd scene while enjoying a game of snooker with the lads; now my name was going to be above the door.

Even though this amazing opportunity had been offered to me I still wasn't ready to give up the security of a proper job. I went into Horwich Leisure Centre and told Chris Jackson that I was going to need some time off. *Max and Paddy* was going to be a big commitment, so I asked if I could take unpaid leave. Chris basically told me he couldn't do that. He then gave me the spiel about how I already had a good job and how this telly game may not work out for me and that I'd be much better off working at a leisure centre in the long run.

The following day I went round to Pete's. He'd now bought his first house and this is where we would end up writing *Max and Paddy*. It wasn't a particularly fancy house but compared to where we were brought up it was a palace. This to me was proper success – one of the things I'd always dreamed of was a nice house for myself and my mum. Seeing Pete's new gaff gave me a real sense of how achievable it was.

I told him the dilemma I was in. Obviously he was a lot further down the line than me when it came to working on the telly, but I knew he could totally relate to how I was feeling – we're both from similar backgrounds and we both love a pound note. Pete was always good at pushing me out of my comfort zone and giving me the confidence to try something new. We had a good long chat and among other things he said I'd have to leave work, otherwise I'd never commit to treating this as an actual career.

'Fucking hell, Pete, I don't know if I can risk it,' I said. 'I mean, what am I going to tell my mum? I've got to pay her rent every week and all that ...'

'You're going to have to trust me on this,' he said. 'You won't be able to juggle the two things this time. Just give it a go. You'll be right, I'm telling you.'

I knew he was right. *Phoenix Nights* was an ensemble cast whereas *Max and Paddy* was going to be just the two of us. When I look back now, I can't believe how long I actually took to make my mind up. This fantastic opportunity was being handed to me on a plate, and all I'm thinking about is if I'll still be able to give my mum 50 quid a week and what about my boxercise class? There was a truly defining moment, though, that made me leave leisure services for good and go full-time with this comedy lark.

We were doing GP referrals in the gym at the time. This was aimed at people with various physical and mental conditions where it was deemed by their doctors that exercise would be beneficial for them. I enjoyed the referral scheme – it was made up of folk who hadn't been to a gym before and it was nice to show them the ropes and make them feel welcome. On that day my client was a fella called Terry. He was in a wheelchair and had turned up with his carer. Wheelchair aside, he was totally capable of doing most things in the gym, so I set him up with a nice programme of exercises to get him started. He was soon happily working out on the rowing machine and his carer was on hand should he need anything. I was sat at my desk – of dwarf fight scene fame – when I heard a cry of 'Oh, Terry!'

From the tone of Terry's carer's voice I knew something wasn't right and I wasn't wrong. Unbeknown to me, Terry had a catheter fitted and his urine bag had exploded due to his furious rowing. To be fair, Terry didn't seem fazed by it. I, on the other hand, now had a gym carpet covered in piss. This wasn't my first rodeo. Working at a leisure centre you get used to cleaning and mopping all sorts up – let's not forget some of the things I'd seen in the sauna. This was different, though. It absolutely reeked. I ran to the store cupboard to grab a metal bucket full of bicarbonate of soda and an old wooden scrubbing brush. I spent the next hour on my hands and knees scrubbing the piss up out of the carpet. Just as I couldn't feel any worse, one of the old boys from the sauna, Miles, a lovely Irish chap with a wicked sense of humour, walked past me and shouted:

'Patrick! When you're done down there, can you go upstairs? Someone's had a shit in reception.'

Everyone burst out laughing, apart from me, knelt in piss, fingers stinging off the bicarb and eyes watering from the smell. That was the moment my life changed forever. Thanks to Terry's stale urine and Miles's sense of humour, my career in leisure services was now over.

That night I went home and phoned Pete to tell him I was in. The following day, I went straight up to Chris Jackson's office.

'Are you sure about this, Pat?' The tone of his voice was full of foreboding. 'You've got a good job here. Secure pay and prospects. I mean, telly? Do you *really* think that's going to lead to anything?'

It was a big moment for me but my days of scrubbing piss and fishing turds out of the kids' pool were over. In went my notice and off I went to start my new career. Fast-forward ten years or so after I left Horwich Leisure Centre and I've popped to a retail park in Bolton. I'd started doing quite well for myself around that time and I was driving a beautiful all-black Bentley GT. As I parked up I noticed a bloke looking at the car – nothing new there, that's what we do if we spot a nice motor. I got out and the look on the bloke's face was priceless. It was Chris Jackson, my old boss who had told me I was making the wrong decision wanting to leave.

'Mr Jackson!' I said with a big smile on my face.

'I think you made the right decision, Pat.'

ON THE RAZZ!

There was a place in Manchester called the Press Club, a members-only bar tucked away down a narrow side street, just off Deansgate. Its clientele consisted of people from the world of entertainment, journalists, lawyers and local badboys – an eclectic mix but it worked. If you weren't part of that world, you would never know the Press Club existed. It didn't look anything special from the outside. In fact, you wouldn't have known it was there if you walked past it during the day. There was no sign or smart foyer, there wasn't even windows! It was just a single doorway that opened to the top of a staircase where an elderly lady called June sat. If June didn't know you or like you then you weren't getting in, simple as that. The only drinks I remember being served in there were cans of Red Stripe and Aftershocks. The Press Club was essentially an after-hours club. No one went there till at least 11 o'clock at night and most left when it was daylight.

Honestly, this place was so difficult to get in. I used to imagine what it was like inside. Cool seating booths, champagne bottles with fireworks stuck in the tops, ice buckets, glamorous cocktail waitresses, funky décor – I could see it all. Whenever I passed it, there was always a long queue of people trying their luck to get in. Before June, the first line of defence to get through were the doormen. The head honcho was a guy called H. Much like June, if H liked you or knew you then he'd probably let you in, but it was never guaranteed; it was always 50/50. He wasn't a big, burly bloke, but you just knew he wasn't to be messed with. I got on well with H and we'd have the odd chat but nothing more than that, just enough to keep on his good side.

My first taste of the club came on a night out in Manchester with all the *Phoenix Nights* lads – well, apart from Dave Spikey, but as I said earlier he wasn't one for going out. We were drinking in the bar at the Comedy Store when someone, I think it was Justin Moorhouse or Edgey, said we could get in the Press Club that night. My ears pricked right up. This was a big deal.

'Are you sure we can get in?' I asked.

'Yeah, June said we'll be OK to come down,' said someone.

We finished our drinks and marched down Deansgate to the club. I remember buzzing with excitement. This place was legendary – if you could get in the Press Club you'd made it. We got there and the old butterflies were going in my stomach.

H was on the door along with another couple of ominous, stab-vest-wearing associates. Justin or Edgey went to the front of the queue and chatted to him and he pointed for them to go in and see June. I couldn't stand the anticipation: was I actually going to get in the legendary Press Club? One of them appeared again at the door.

'We're in!'

I couldn't believe it. I made my way through those steel doors, trying my best to look cool and nonchalant as you like. This was it … I made my way down the stairs to this wonderous underground club. Here we go!

'What the fuck is this?' I said.

I couldn't believe my eyes. All this time I'd been waiting to get in this place and what I was confronted with was less Studio 54 and more Rovers Return. Where was the lit-up dance floor and the booth seating? It was sticky carpets, a few old leather Chesterfield couches dotted about and that was it. It wasn't even busy.

It only took me another hour or so to realise why people were so desperate to get in there. Slowly, the magic of the place starts to get into your bones. Before I knew it, the room was packed and the atmosphere was jumping, and that's when the karaoke started. Not the kind of karaoke you're used to though. There was a little stage with velvet curtains at the back of it and on there appeared Press Club stalwarts Charlie and Martin. They ran the karaoke but there was one thing missing: the lyrics. That's the whole idea of karaoke, isn't it? You get up and sing along to the lyrics on-screen? Not in the Press Club. Here you were given the microphone and you were expected to know the lyrics. Consequently, everybody could only sing the bits they knew, so you'd have people getting up on the stage, half pissed, mumbling through bits and pieces of a song before belting out the chorus.

One night the girl behind the bar just lifted her top up and showed me her breasts.

'What do you think?' she asked.

'Lovely. Three cans of Red Stripe and an Aftershock, please,' I said.

Stuff like that used to happen in there all the time, it was the most random club ever. I even saw folk bonking (dear God, there's an old reference for sex) in there once, and no one batted an eyelid. That was the unwritten rule of the Press Club: what happened in there stayed in there. This was at a time when camera phones were just coming out but there was a zero photos policy in there as well. It gave the *Phoenix Nights* cast the opportunity to just be young and stupid and enjoy the moment. If it was nowadays, I don't think we'd have half the fun. You put one foot out of place now and it's everywhere instantly.

Christmastime was always buzzing in the Press Club because the panto casts would finish their shows and go there to party after. One night I got chatting to a bloke called Colin, who was playing one of Snow White's dwarves at the Manchester Opera House. He was a great bloke and he liked a drink, which was good enough for me. People were singing, dancing and spewing up in the toilets – it was a classic Press Club night. It got to about four or five in the morning and I'd hit the wall, time to go home. I made my way out and while I stood waiting for a taxi this rather attractive girl walked over, put her arms around me and started to snog me. *Merry Christmas,* I thought. This kind of thing wasn't that unusual at Christmastime, you couldn't move for mistletoe. So I'm stood there, enjoying a festive smooch, when I felt someone grab my arm. I looked down. It was Colin.

'Daddy, can we go home now?' he said.

The girl recoiled, looking very confused.

'Oh my God! Wait, you're with your kid?' she said.

'No, no, you've got it wrong. He's one of Snow White's dwarves.'

'What?'

Colin then started yanking on my arm again.

'Come on, Daddy, I want to go.'

'Colin, fuc—'

The girl interrupted me mid-curse. 'I'm off.'

And that was the last I saw of her. God knows what she told her mates the following day. Colin was in hysterics and although he had stitched me up, I couldn't help but laugh myself.

Along with most of the lads from *Phoenix Nights*, I was getting my first real taste of fame – well, an after-hours club in Manchester – but it was a start and we all loved being a part of it.

CHAPTER 13

A BROKEN HEART

I was 29 when my mum passed away and the grief from that kind of loss never leaves you. You learn to live with it and somehow manage to carry on with your life, even though the pain is still there. I'd recently left Horwich Leisure Centre and was very much looking forward to starting work on *Max and Paddy's Road to Nowhere*. It was me and my mum living in our little Housing Association bungalow, 8 Queens Road, and that was all I needed.

Even though it hurts thinking about it, one slight comfort for me was being at home with her when she died. I still to this day don't know half of the ailments my mum had. She didn't talk about things like that, and although the side of her bed and cupboards resembled a Lloyds pharmacy, I never really thought too much about it. Having said that, I was constantly worried about something happening to her. My mum was everything to me and the only person in my life who I knew was always there for me through thick and thin. Our bedrooms were right next door to each other and I'd lie in bed listening out to hear her breathing, worried sick in case anything happened to her. Some mornings I'd wake up and the house would be really quiet. This used to put me on edge, but then I'd hear her pottering about or find a note to say she'd gone to shop, and instantly I'd feel better. I'm not sure if anyone else has those kind of morbid thoughts, but for me the worry of losing my mum kept me awake at night.

The day my life changed forever was just like any other. My mum had gone to our local supermarket, which was a Netto at the time, to pick up a few bits. It was only round the corner from where we lived so I never gave it much thought. When she came home, she was carrying two big bags full of groceries.

'I thought you were only getting a few bits, Mum. I could've picked you up.' I was a bit annoyed because I wouldn't let her do stuff like that normally and I didn't like the fact that she'd walked home with heavy bags. That's the old-school mentality, though, they just get on with it.

She looked tired so I made us a cup of tea and put the shopping away. The rest of the day is a bit blurry, but nothing out of the ordinary happened. We watched a bit of telly, I may have popped out for a few hours, just a normal day. I had a girlfriend at the time called Kathryn. She lived by herself in her mum's house so I'd stay over there the odd night or two. Thankfully I didn't this day – she and I were going through a bit of a rocky patch so that might have been why I was at home that night. My mum always used to leave her bedroom door open till she was ready to go to sleep, and even then she would never fully shut it as she didn't like feeling locked in. She'd normally ask me to close her door slightly when I went to bed. She'd never close it until I was home, though. This proved to be a bit of a pain over the years, especially if I was sneaking home late or with a girlfriend. She'd never fully relax until I was home and although it felt annoying at the time, I'd give anything to have her waiting up and watching out for me now.

This particular evening she told me she felt tired and was looking forward to a good sleep. We used to like a cup of tea before bed so I took one in and placed it on her bedside table. My mum's room was only small – her bed was right up against the wall and at the other side there was just enough room to open the door without catching her bedside table. That little table was always full of medication, along with newspapers with half-completed cross-word puzzles and wordsearches – she loved anything like that. So I squeezed the cup of tea on a spare bit of table, told her I loved her and wished her goodnight. That was the last time I would ever do that. Even writing this now I'm in bits, it hurts so much.

I got in bed myself and I remember quite clearly something happening to me that I've never been able to explain. I was lying with the lights off, watching my little portable telly. I wasn't particularly tired so I was just staring at the screen and thinking about stuff I was going to do the following day. Normally if I had my telly on at night and it got late my mum would shout through to me to turn it off and get some sleep. So I'm lying there, looking at the screen, when suddenly I feel this wave wash over me. I can't describe what it was or why it happened, but it's like it controlled me to sit up, turn the TV off and instantly fall asleep. I'm convinced that was the moment my mum passed away. It was as though her spirit was checking in on me for one last time, making sure I was safe

▼ The one picture I have from the yard at Vibroplant. That's Simmy, one of the drivers.

▲ Having a beer with Ian Benyon , the only person my age at Vibroplant. Not sure whose thumb that is.

▲ Form a queue, ladies.

▶ Some of the lads I used to work with in Kavos, at Club 18–30.

◀ My first holiday abroad, in Santa Ponsa. The heat (and alcohol) did me in.

▼ Santa Ponsa with two Dutch lads I met there.

▼ Meeting back up with my original Sensei Tom Scott.

▼ Competition time. I used to love sparring and competing in Karate tournaments.

▶ Our annual boys' trip to Alton Towers. Left to right: Bully, me, Rick, Niggi, Tansy, Bitch Lips, Coco and Michael.

▼ Another trip to Alton Towers, this time with the Horwich Leisure Centre lot.

◀ I vaguely remember having a six pack.

▼ On duty as a fitness instructor at Lifestyles Gym in Horwich Leisure Centre. The same gym I wrote the *Phoenix Nights* sketch in.

▲ Me and some of my workmates from the leisure centre days.

◄▼ Ladies' night at HLC. We'd be covered in scratch marks at the end of those shifts.

▼ Winning things at HLC. The lady is Karen Whitman, I used to have such a laugh working with her.

◄ Me, Danny Short (yellow top) and Dave in the duty manager's office at HLC. Danny could've easily had a career as a professional drummer – very talented lad.

▼ Another boozy HLC night out.

◀ Danny and Daddy Short from HLC days.

▶ A night out at FuFu Lamars in Manchester with the HLC lot.

◀ Me and Del with his family. I was godfather at his son's christening. Del's brother Ian, in the lime-green shirt, ended up being a contestant on *Take Me Out*.

▶ The day I bumped into Taz, the bloke who taught me how to shave, after more than twenty years of not seeing him. Ironically we both had stubble.

▼ See what I mean?

▶ Bobby B Bad, Bernard, me, Zola Budd and Mr Angry on my wedding day.

◀ The Hateful Eight on one of our trips to Portugal. Left to right: Dick Fingers, me, Knock Knee, Buscemi, Gazza, Fauntleroy, Palance and Ruprecht.

◀ The Hateful Eight in that fancy villa. My best mate Franny facing me with his cap on, to stop the light bouncing off his head.

▼ Me, Stotty, Niggi and Bully on our annual night out. We ended up at a hip hop club that night.

▲ The years hadn't been kind to the cast of *Baywatch*. Left to right: Bernard, me, Mr Angry, Zola Budd.

and tucked up in bed. I've never told anyone that because it's the kind of thing no one would believe, but it happened and it's never happened again since.

When I woke in the morning it was the first thing I thought about. As I lay there thinking about the strange feeling, I became aware of how silent the house was. I knew what had happened. I didn't want to believe it but I did. I shouted out to my mum, hoping she'd answer back.

'Morning, Mum.'

'Mum, can you hear me?'

That gut feeling when you know something isn't right washed over me as I walked out of my room and pushed open my mum's bedroom door. She was all snuggled up in her blankets with her little sleep mask on.

'Mum,' I said again. 'Mum, please wake up.'

It took me all my courage to touch her face because I didn't want to feel whether she was cold or not. This was a face that I'd kissed and snuggled into from being a child. When you kiss your mum's face and feel that soft cheek, it always makes you feel safe and loved. That had now gone; she was cold and still. I completely lost it. I was screaming and shouting at her to wake up.

'Mum, please!' I was in floods of tears. That moment I never wanted to experience had now happened, and there wasn't a single thing I could do about it. I was ringing everyone to help me. I needed someone with me, I felt so vulnerable and lost. I rang my cousins Kathryn and Lorraine. I rang my uncle Tony, Peter, my best mate Franny and my girlfriend, Kathryn. I'm not sure if I rang the doctor or someone else did but he turned up to officially pronounce her dead. He'd been our family doctor since I was born and although I had never particularly warmed to him before, this time was different. He came in and without even looking at my mum he just wrapped his arms around me and gave me the biggest hug. The professional side went out the window and his human side came through. I certainly needed it and from that day on, up until his retirement, I looked at him in a completely different light.

It was horrendous when they came to take my mum away. I didn't want anyone taking her out of our house. I didn't want her to leave. The next couple of days are a complete blank to me and I can't remember much about anything during that period. Lorraine and Kathryn were more like aunties to me than cousins, and I know they stayed with me because I couldn't be alone in that bungalow.

* * *

My mum was taken to our local funeral directors and I was told I could go and see her. I really struggled with this. I didn't want to see her in a coffin, lifeless. I was scared. Eventually I built up the courage to go and it was very traumatic. Firstly, she didn't even look like my mum to me. I'd never been in that situation before and I didn't know what to expect. The other thing that drove me mad was knowing how claustrophobic she was. Even though my mum wasn't tall, her coffin was too small for her and her feet were turned in at the bottom. I went straight up to the office and in no uncertain terms let them know that they better get a bigger coffin and make my mum look a bit more like the pictures they had of her. I also let them know that if this didn't happen I was gonna pull down the building brick by brick, with them in it. It wasn't a nice thing to do but I wasn't thinking straight. I was so racked with pain, I didn't care. The one person in my life who I loved more than anything wasn't getting the treatment she deserved. I went back the following day and although she still didn't look quite the same, they'd now given her a bigger coffin and she wasn't as crammed in.

For me, my mum was my world. Writing this chapter has taken a while because I have to keep stopping due to the tears running down my face. If anyone walked in now they'd find me in front of the computer surrounded by lots of used tissues, never a good look for a bloke. It took me over a month to spend a night in my mum's bungalow alone. The place I called home, that bastion of love and security, had turned into a place I couldn't step foot in alone. I'm not sure why I couldn't be in there on my own but it just didn't sit easy with me. The one thing I needed more than anything was support and although I wanted out of the relationship I was in at the time, Kathryn actually helped a lot. We'd been together a while so she knew my mum and family well. I was so thankful she was around to get me through that horrendous time.

We held my mum's wake in the Pike View, the pub she used to work in, where I'd climbed up onto the windowsills to see if she was in there when I was a kid. All those characters I remembered from my childhood had turned up to pay their respects. It was quite sad seeing a lot of them again. When I was a kid, these people were all larger-than-life characters. They were intimidating, loud and funny. Now they all looked small and vulnerable, most of them pensioners. That era of pub people has slowly died away, along with all the little locals they used to frequent. Those pubs and bingo halls my mum used to clean and work in are still physically there on Daubhill but now they're phone shops, dentists and takeaways.

It's been 19 years since my mum passed. I've had a good cry on my own today but I've also smiled a lot thinking about her and her sense of humour – she was very quick-witted and I definitely get that from her. She once rang Horwich Leisure Centre for me and the receptionist said, 'I'm not sure where he is in the building.' My mum replied, 'Try the biggest mirror, he'll be in front of that.'

I love you, Mum, I miss you, and when it's my turn to leave this world I'll be happy because I know you'll be waiting for me.

 CHAPTER 14

MAX AND PADDY

It had now been a few months since my mum had passed away, and although still racked with grief, I was managing to function again on my own. I was slowly getting my head around doing things like paying bills and generally looking after myself, basically everything my mum used to do for me. I was focusing on starting work on *Max and Paddy* – it was the one positive thing I had to look forward to – but even that was short-lived.

Pete rang me one day and said he had something he wanted to discuss with me. He was over at his mum's at the time, round the corner from Queens Road, so he picked me up and drove me round there. He said he wanted to talk about *Max and Paddy*, the upshot being that he didn't want to do it at the moment. My heart sank. I'd not long lost my mum and was now being told the only thing I was looking forward to wasn't happening. Working with Peter in the past, the one thing I know about him is he'll do everything in his own time and it's as simple as that. I knew no matter what I said or how I was feeling wasn't going to make him change his mind so I just went with the flow.

I can't remember much about the period in between that conversation and when we started on *Max and Paddy* but the main thing is we did eventually start. I absolutely loved the writing process, just me and Pete spending days together laughing and putting the world to rights. I'd ring him up to find out what time we'd be starting writing that day, and although I was usually late I'd always bring the pies and cakes. That little glimmer of the writing process on *Phoenix Nights* gave me the bug and I was now sitting down in pole position. I've always enjoyed writing: the thrill of hearing the words you've written being spoken by somebody else is a good little buzz. Somedays I'd forget we were writing a comedy series for Channel 4 because it was such a laidback process. It didn't feel like a big deal and I suppose that's due to the way myself and Peter look at the world.

Those days spent writing *Max and Paddy* at Pete's house were more enjoyable than the actual filming. Don't get me wrong, I thoroughly enjoyed making it, but when it was just the two of us in a room laughing, well, that can't be beaten. The only trouble for me, as I sit here writing about that series, is I can hardly remember anything from that time. Honestly, my mind is a complete blank – it was with *Phoenix Nights* but I rang the people up who appeared in it and they refreshed my memory. Problem is, I've no one to ask about *Max and Paddy* to refresh my memory and I'm not going to be ringing Pete every two minutes. I mean, there's the odd bits I can remember around that time but it was all outside of filming. For instance, we got invited onstage by the legends that are Queen to sing the theme tune to *Max and Paddy* live at the Manchester

Arena! That was surreal to say the least. We both loved Queen so were there purely to enjoy the concert. When they asked us up onstage I couldn't believe it – singing a song we'd both written in an afternoon with one of the world's biggest bands providing our backing track. I was looking around trying to take it all in – Roger Taylor was drumming away and Brian May gave me a wink, absolute madness!

During that time we were both being represented by Phil McIntyre, who had partnered up with Queen, Ben Elton and randomly Robert De Niro to put on the musical *We Will Rock You* in the West End. We went to the opening night and after the show we went out for something to eat. There was myself, Pete, Craig Cash, Phil and Robert De Niro sat round a table. I was nudging Pete's leg and whispering, 'It's Robert DeNiro. We're out with Raging Bull, son.'

We'd often have those fangirl moments. Another time we were filming our workout DVD (yes, really), *Max & Paddy's The Power of Two*, at Granada Studios in Manchester. They used to have a big canteen there where everyone had their lunch. You'd often spot people from *Corrie* or Matthew Kelly because that's where they recorded *Stars in Their Eyes*. So you'd get used to seeing people you recognised, but every now and again you'd spot a really big hitter. One day we were sat at a long dining table eating our lunch and chatting when this fella plonks himself down at the side of us. We both looked up and couldn't believe our eyes. It was Richard Harris. *A Man Called Horse*! We were kicking each other under the table like naughty kids. That was the beauty of Granada – it was proper old school. On one table you'd have Jeremy Kyle, on the other an absolute icon of the movie industry. Turns out he was recording some bits for Harry Potter that day and we lucked out by being in the right place at the right time. Robert De Niro and Richard Harris, not a bad couple of dinner guests.

I've met a lot of folk over the years through Peter. I've had a Findus crispy pancake with J. K. Rowling and enjoyed a Chinese with the League of Gentlemen, but the one person who really resonated with me, not for the right reasons, was Steve Coogan. I loved him and had followed his career from the get-go. He was a real inspiration and I'd go and see him live whenever I got the chance. I loved everything he did, including his lesser-known characters. Pete had been asked to do a sketch with Coogan for Comic Relief in which he'd play the part of a boxing trainer and Coogan would be Alan Partridge. I'd done a bit of boxing so Pete asked if I wanted to be part of the sketch. I leapt at the chance – I couldn't believe I'd be working with the mighty Steve Coogan.

On our way to filming in Manchester I was nervous but excited. I was going to meet him, and not only that, he was going to be playing Alan Partridge! This was dream-come-true stuff for me, but within five minutes of meeting him all that excitement and joy disappeared. We hadn't filmed *Phoenix Nights* at the time so I was a complete unknown and Coogan made me feel like a spare part. Even though I was with Peter, he completely blanked me – he never even looked at me, never mind spoke to me. I'd never treat anyone like that, famous or not. What I thought was going to be one of the best days of my life turned out to be one of the most disappointing. The saying 'never meet your heroes' isn't necessarily true because I've met a lot of fantastic people, but in this instance those words rang very true.

Years later I found myself in a room with him again. It was Phil McIntyre's stag do and we all had a meal together. Myself, Pete, Ben Elton, Lenny Henry, David Walliams and a few others Phil represented were there along with Coogan. Again he was only interested in speaking with the 'famous faces' in the room, which I most certainly was not. I've never forgotten those moments and even though I'm still blown away by his talent and a huge fan of his work – my favourite programme at the minute is *This Time with Alan Partridge* – I still think he's a deeply unpleasant chap. Having said that, he inadvertently taught me a valuable lesson about respect and decency. I try to encourage people and I'd never blank anyone like that, especially young people making a go of it.

Another memory from *Max and Paddy* was meeting Brendan O'Carroll. He was brought in to play Gypsy Joe because Peter knew him from *Mrs Brown's Boys*. Back then I'd never heard of it or him. Pete would tell me about this character and how massive he was in Ireland, but like always with me, I take people on face value, and Brendan didn't disappoint. What a lovely fella he was and I instantly felt comfortable in his presence. Obviously now he's uber well known, everyone knows Mrs Brown and his shows on BBC1 consistently bring in millions of viewers, along with his sell-out world tours. Every credit to him, it's great when the good people do well. I recently met his son, Danny, at Soccer Aid, and you can see he's cut from the same cloth as his dad, a thoroughly decent lad.

I got a well-known face in the series too – well known to me, that is – my older brother, Tony. He played one of Raymond the Bastard's henchmen in the prison episode. In fact, I got our kid in a few things over the years, namely because he's not shy to get his kit off. He's a big lad with a bald head, so in pretty much everything I've featured him in he's either naked or in some kind of thong, which always gets a laugh. He even made it on to the front cover of the *Max and Paddy* DVD.

At one point I got him a job driving Pete, which lasted all of a week. I had them both ringing me up, each slagging the other off.

Peter: 'He's never on time.'

Tony: 'I won't be spoken to like that.'

Peter: 'He's not got a clue.'

Tony: 'I'm a grown man.'

This back-and-forth went on for about a day. Eventually my ears stopped bleeding and they parted ways. Never the twain shall meet and all that, but they're back on speaking terms now, I think.

Max and Paddy did well with the audience – it was the highest-rating Channel 4 comedy at the time – and although it wasn't well received by the TV critics, Mr and Mrs Public really enjoyed it. Seeing my name at the side of Pete's in that opening shot, I knew from there on in I had a chance of bigger and better things. It's been nigh on 17 years since it aired on TV and to this day I get asked if there will be any more. It's lovely to hear, though, because it shows how loved *Max and Paddy* was, and even though I can't remember much about it there's a lot of fans who do. We always spoke about doing another series, so we've got lots of stuff already written, but as old Father Time ticks on I don't think it'll ever see the light of day and neither will a new series of *Phoenix Nights*. I'd love to be wrong but in my heart of hearts I know it won't happen. Weirdly, I think I'd just enjoy sitting with Peter and writing, regardless of anything ever getting made or not. I know it'd be a few months of laughter and sharing precious moments together that no one but us will ever have. Those are the moments I cherish: sometimes once that process finishes and it's out there for everyone to enjoy, it loses its appeal to me. Which is totally the wrong attitude to have because if that was the case I'd never earn a bloody living.

CHAPTER 15

TOURING

If you want the rainbow,
you gotta put up with the rain.
Dolly Parton

Both *Phoenix Nights* and *Max and Paddy* finishing was my trigger to get out and create my own body of work – that way I wouldn't be waiting on anyone else to pick the phone up and ring me.

Touring is a very lucrative business and for someone like me, who was paranoid about not having a proper job any more, the lure of making money was too hard to resist, no matter what I'd be putting myself through. Listen, there's worse jobs out there, but standing up in a roomful of strangers trying to make them laugh can be quite stressful. Having said that, it can also be quite seductive; money aside, there's no better feeling than getting lots of people laughing, especially when they're calling for more. The thrill and buzz you get in that moment is euphoric but luckily for me I never had a problem switching it off. Soon as I walk offstage, it's more a sense of relief than any kind of buzz. *Phew, they liked it, another one done, off to the next town or city.* There's no punching the air as I go back to my dressing room. Job done, simple as that, really.

Looking back, though, it took me a while to learn the difference between simply making people laugh and delivering good comedy. My first big solo tour was called The Dark Side and it sold out everywhere. *Max and Paddy* had been on the telly by this point and people wanted to see me live. I'd get a call from my promoter at the time, a guy called Nigel, who was Phil McIntyre's younger brother, a lovely fella too. He'd tell me another one had sold out and ask if I was interested in putting another night on sale. Of course I said yes because at the time all I was thinking about was the money. It didn't really occur to me that I hadn't actually got an act as such. I was more swept along by the success of the ticket sales. I didn't have the respect for comedy or for the craft behind it, which sounds a bit of a wanky thing to say but you have to learn as you go along.

A lot of very successful stand-up comedians, who you've probably never heard of unless you follow the live comedy circuit, have been going for years, honing and developing their material, and they make a very good living out of it. It wasn't because I was arrogant, it's just that I didn't understand how things worked back then. I was young, gullible and easily sold on something. With Phil and Nigel behind me, I felt like I could do anything, even a 180-night national tour. Phil McIntyre had a knack for making me feel like I was top of the tree, even though in his list of clients I was pretty much at the tip of the roots.

Phil started promoting in the seventies with bands like AC/
DC, the Clash and Queen and the list of comedians he's looked
after reads like a *Who's Who* of comedy: Billy Connolly, Dave Allen,
Victoria Wood, Steve Coogan, Peter Kay, French & Saunders, Monty
Python, Chris Rock, Ben Elton, the list goes on.

I'd done a smaller tour already with some of the cast of *Phoenix
Nights*, as the compere. The tour was called The Jumping on the
Bandwagon Tour, an honest appraisal after two series. It was myself,
Steve Edge, Janice Connolly and Archie Kelly on the road together.
This gave me a proper taste of being onstage, and because I was the
compere I didn't really have to worry about writing a set. We all
had a blast on that tour – it was just a few mates mucking about
and getting paid for their troubles. Again Nigel McIntyre was the
promoter, and I think we ended up doing around 20 or 30 nights.
I got on really well with those three and some nights I'd be in
tears of laughter just with the chat backstage. Edgey would be first
onstage, then it'd be Janice, followed by Archie, then we'd all come
back on at the end and sing the theme tune to *Minder*.

I'd already filmed *Max and Paddy* but it hadn't been on telly
yet. I remember the first night it aired, we were doing a show in
Blackpool and we all watched the beginning of the episode backstage before the show started. Once that series started I could feel a
difference with our live audiences. I knew they wanted to see more
of me. As Nigel used to say to me:

'The McGuinness stock is rising.'

The seeds had been planted for doing my own solo tour; the
seduction had already started.

During the Bandwagon tour I got to know Janice really well. Obviously I'd worked with her on *Phoenix Nights* but I didn't really know much about her. She'd been doing a character called Barbara Nice for years on the comedy circuit (in fact she ended up on *Britain's Got Talent* as Barbara and did really well, which I totally expected because Janice/Barbara is fantastic with a live audience) and she's one of the most wonderful, beautifully stark-raving bonkers people I've ever met. There's not a bad bone in Janice's body and it was impossible to ever argue with her. I remember the first proper nice car I owned, it was an Alfa Romeo and it had cream leather seats. We'd take it in turns driving and this night it was my turn. After the shows, fans would be waiting at the stage door for autographs. Janice was in the back seat and a fan handed her a Bandwagon tour programme to sign. I heard from the back:

'Oh dear, I'm sorry, cock.'

I knew something wasn't right from the tone of her voice.

'Everything OK, love?' I asked.

Edgey was laughing his head off. I looked into the back of the car only to find Janice had taken a Sharpie permanent marker and instead of signing the tour programme had signed the back of the headrest on my cream leather seats! That was typical Janice and I honestly didn't bat an eyelid. Well, not to Janice anyhow.

Another time I was driving the car I'd bought off Phil McIntyre. We were on the motorway after a gig and from the back seat, without a hint of irony, I heard,

'Lovey, whatever you do, don't be buying a fast car if you make any money.'

We were in a Subaru WRX STi, doing 120mph at the time!

I value that time I spent with the gang on tour. We had such a good laugh and it was a pleasure to be on the road with them all.

* * *

The venues sold out fast for the Dark Side tour: 30 nights turned to 50, 50 went to 80, 80 went to 130 and I ended up doing around 180 nights. It's no wonder I was confident. Why worry about what I was going to say once I got up there? I was sold out, and stupidly that's all I thought mattered. I don't like to even think about that tour and it's certainly not something I'm particularly proud of. I wrote the entire set two days before I was due onstage, how mad is that?! The lack of thought behind that first tour is one of my biggest regrets. Yes, it made me lots of money, over a million pounds to be precise, but that didn't detract from the fact it was shite. I wish I'd had more guidance back then but no one supported me or spoke about how a stand-up show should work. I was making money for everyone – the promoters, venues and merchandise people – and that was good enough for them as well.

My main exposure to stand-up comedy came from watching old VHS tapes at Peter's house of Eddie Murphy doing his *Raw* or *Delirious* shows, Eddie looking very cool and sending his audience into fits of laughter. I never actually thought much about what he was saying, just that it was funny and it worked. I was the ladies' man from *Phoenix Nights* so my tour was basically a load of knob gags and crude shagging stories.

It was only when I did London on tour that I actually became aware of critics. I did a show at the Shepherd's Bush Empire, my first big show in the capital. There were plenty of well-known faces in the audience: Robbie Williams, Ant and Dec, Serge Pizzorno from Kasabian. I'd heard London audiences were tougher but that didn't faze me – I had Robbie Williams in the audience at the height of his powers and that's all I thought about really! That show got a right good kicking from a London critic and at the time I was fuming. Who was this prick having a go at me? Everyone in the room seemed to be having a good time; he must have been at a different show? Actually, that critic did me a favour because over time it made me think about how I went about things. I was young back then and full of bravado but as you get older and a tiny bit wiser that's how you learn.

Looking back, there was a fair bit of style over substance on that tour. I had a great big screen onstage and at the start of the show I appeared from behind eight showgirls in feathers, them not me. I'd never do that now. I mean, that's eight people you've got to pay every night! I had Phil and Nigel patting me on the back after every show, the ticket sales were off the chart, and with everyone telling me how I was smashing it every night, I thought I was king of the world. This was what I'd signed up for.

With regards to live comedy, there's two types of audience. There's the audiences who'll buy tickets to see successful mainstream comedians like Peter Kay, Lee Evans or Michael McIntyre. They might not necessarily be comedy fans as such, but they'll go because the comedy is broad, big, colourful, funny and they get it, it's a night out. Nothing wrong with that! Those are the kind of audiences I've played to for years and always enjoyed. On the other side of the coin, you've got a 'comedy' audience. These are a bit more discerning and definitely not the types to be sitting in an arena with all the bells and whistles. You'll find them in a lot of the alternative comedy clubs watching the likes of Stewart Lee, Adam Bloom, Daniel Kitson, Simon Munnery – all fantastic comedians but a million miles (and pounds) away from the big mainstream comics. I've been in front of both sets of audiences over the years and found them all to be nice but I do prefer the buzz and party atmosphere of the non-comedy audience. To use a music-based analogy, the non-comedy audience will be dancing along to Take That and Elton John, the comedy audience will be stood nodding along at a Billy Bragg gig.

Through subsequent tours, I learned to write material that appealed to the masses but was also a bit more thought out and crafted. Before my last arena tour, I spent most of the year writing, along with a couple of other comedy writers, something I never thought I'd do. Essentially the people who pay money to come and see you perform just want to have a laugh. They don't care who wrote the joke or story just as long as you deliver it right. I was also trying out new material on warm-up nights. The only warm-up I did for the Dark Side tour was the heaters in the car on the way to the gig.

When Nigel transferred the money I'd earned from that first tour I was knocked for six. From where I'd come from, and with all the struggles I'd had with money as a young man, this was momentous. It seems ridiculous to think about it now, but I was with

Barclays Bank at the time. When that money went into my account I got them to send me a statement so I could frame it. It wasn't to be arrogant or to show off to anyone, it was just for me. I used to look at it and think about my mum. She wouldn't believe it. Me from a single-parent family, using washing-up liquid in the bath and dragging old mattresses in off the streets, there it was in black and white: Mr P. McGuinness, one million pounds.

I got more savvy with touring and learned a lot from Peter about budgets and tour costs. On one of his early tours, Peter's set consisted of two paint pots with balloons tied to them. He knew that people would think he was taking the piss, making a gag out of having not spent any money on a set, but that's exactly why it was done. Out went the showgirls and in came the head mike, simple.

Even though touring had always been a financial decision for me, my last arena tour was more than that and I really enjoyed the experience. Perhaps that's because I'd finally got the balance right. I wasn't second-guessing myself or worrying about where the jokes had come from. I felt comfortable up there. Over the years, I've learned how to hone the material, and to respect it. I still know my audience. I'd like to think I could sit down and write a sharp satirical piece and put it on at a smaller alternative gig, but that's not what people want to see from me. My comedy is broad, because that's my audience, and I give them a proper show. People are parting with their hard-earned to come and see me, so it's no more than they deserve.

Another tip I picked up from Peter Kay was getting away from a gig quick – I'm talking walking offstage, pissed through in sweat, and straight into the car, sometimes still wearing your mike. After one particular show I was doing just that. I planned to be on the motorway home before all the traffic had built up with the audience pouring out. Perfect! I could still hear the audience cheering, which is always a good feeling, as I ran towards the stage door and the sound guy ripped my mike off so I could escape quickly. I shouted 'See you tomorrow!' as the door closed behind me. I was now stood in the fresh night air face to face with a lady in a long brown mac.

'Hello, how've you managed to get around here so quickly?' I said, still out of breath.

She handed me a can of beer, smiled and said, 'I've not been to the show. I thought you'd like a drink and this.'

With that she undid her mac, old-school flasher style, to reveal only skimpy underwear, Benny Hill style. As bizarre and unexpected as the situation I'd now found myself in was, I said:

'You must be freezing!'

I know women like a man with a sense of humour but this girl had taken it to the next level.

Although I look back on that first tour material-wise and shudder, the other side of me remembers how much of a good time I had. I was single, camera phones weren't really commonplace back then and there was no social media. Touring before the advent of Instagram, Twitter, Facebook and selfies was a lot less stressful. Most of the mad things that happened to me back then I'd forgotten about – it's only writing this book and properly thinking back that I've remembered them. I was fully in the middle of the most rock 'n' roll period of my life and I was definitely enjoying the ride. Fan mail was still a thing then, where people write to you and request signed pictures and generally tell you how much they like you. Honestly, I used to get hundreds and hundreds of letters a week to Phil McIntyre's office, and they would be forwarded on to me. I saved a lot of them, I think they're in my attic. This wasn't for vanity reasons either – I don't get my old fan letters out and read them to myself while necking whisky. I saved them because I knew this kind of thing wouldn't last forever and I thought it'd be some-thing to show the grandkids from the time Grandad was popular. Well, some of them, anyway – I got a lot of strange requests from women that certainly won't be shown to anyone. They'd send me pictures and ask for my old used trainers or underwear. Dear God, who'd want them?

A lot of mad stuff used to happen on the road, so I had to keep slightly level-headed. I wouldn't even have a beer before a show; I still don't now. Regardless if it's live or on the telly.

Where I grew up, glue and gas sniffing was all the rage – I'd often see people walking around with concealed cans of gas up their sleeves or little plastic bags full of glue that looked not too dissimilar to used condoms. Everyone was either doing it or knew someone who was. I could never get my head around why anyone would want to do that, so I never bothered with it. As I got into my late teens and early twenties, the rave culture kicked off. My mates and I preferred hip-hop, soul and funk. I did go to Cream in Liverpool once, and

I was blown away when I walked in – only not in a good way. I mean, where were the seats for a start? All the nightclubs I'd been to had tables and chairs around the dance floor. Cream was this huge overload of noise and light. Everyone was off their heads, dancing, but I was just wondering where the DJ was. And, as I said, there was nowhere to sit. No. This wasn't going to work for me.

I'm sure if you were into that kind of music or popping pills then that gaff would be the best place ever. I never took ecstasy, though. I didn't see the appeal in it. It definitely wasn't what I was about back then. I wasn't an angel by any stretch of the imagination and I did have a brief dabble with a few substances in my youth, but that was short-lived, namely because one night I found myself walking home barefoot, convinced my feet were full of black pepper. I've always considered myself lucky in that I could try something once or twice and not feel compelled to do it again. I don't have an addictive personality.

When I was younger drugs were a rarity, especially in Bolton. These days, though, you can walk into almost any pub and there'll be a queue of people waiting to get in a cubicle to stick God knows what up their noses.

Live shows for me are a business, and with getting older, other things take priority. These days that means a nice hotel room – with a bath, obvs – and looking after my voice. All delightfully boring, just how I like it. I will definitely tour again in some way, shape or form in the future because even though it's stressful, that buzz from a live audience, when it's going well, can't be bottled. I got standing ovations and the atmosphere was electric on that first tour, so the fact that I'm saying it wasn't any good feels a bit disrespectful to the people who came out to watch it. I definitely had a good time, but I just wish I'd done it all differently.

CHAPTER 16

FIRST ENCOUNTERS OF THE CELEBRITY HIGH LIFE

Back in 2004, Sky One came up with a show called *The Match*, a reality show where a group of celebrities formed a football team to compete against former professional footballers known as the Legends. All the celebrities lived and trained together in a *Big Brother*-style house and as the series went on, viewers could vote on who they wanted to stay in the team and who they wanted to leave. This was well before *Take Me Out* and I was still relatively unknown, so to get the chance to play in a football match at St James' Park against a team of ex-professionals was a dream. We were managed by Graham Taylor and Luther Blissett. It was a mixed bag on the celebrity front – actors, singers, sports personalities, reality stars and, of course, me.

This was the show where I first met Jonathan Wilkes. Jonny was sharing a bedroom with Ben Shephard and I was sharing with Ralf Little. We would all dip in and out of each other's rooms and I instantly hit it off with Jonny. At the time, he was known for being mates with Robbie Williams. In fact, when we did *Pantos*

On Strike together years later, I'd introduce him onstage as 'Jonny Wilkes, Robbie Williams's mate'. I know what that's like because I'd get that with Peter Kay. Even now, 20 years since I last worked with Pete on anything, people still say I get work because I'm Peter Kay's mate. So here we were, two lads with famous mates doing a reality TV show around a football match. Jonny plays up to this cheesy image but in real life he's got a fantastic sense of humour and I've got a lot of time for him – although sometimes I wish I didn't!

A few months after *The Match* finished, he called me up.

'Robbie wants to meet you,' he said.

Back then this was a big deal for me. This was Robbie 'Let Me Entertain You' Williams and he was at the height of his powers.

The meeting was arranged and next thing I knew I was in London sat in the back of a blacked-out people carrier with Jonny. We pulled up outside a hotel, the side door opened and in gets Robbie Williams.

'All right, Paddy, Rob, pleased to meet you,' he said. I was still a bit taken aback by the whole thing. He had security guards and everything. He was a proper famous person. I've met a lot of mega-famous types over the years and the one thing I've found is they're mostly normal down-to-earth people who happen to be very successful. Even though they've got pots of cash and all the trappings that come with it, they're still more or less the same people they were before they made it.

We hit it off straight away – he had the same sense of humour as Jonny so we all just had a laugh together. Rob is just a lad from Stoke-on-Trent who was thrust into an insane pop star life at an early age. I always got the vibe from him that he craved normality, and compared to his life, mine was definitely normal. He was living in a penthouse of an apartment block in Chelsea at the time, which was extremely fancy. I remember being bowled over when I discovered all the lights in his apartment were controlled by touchscreen. This was all new technology back then and something I'd certainly never seen before. In fact, 'Touchscreen' was my code name for him in my phone contacts. I remember one night I stayed over at his and we were just chilling on the couch and flicking through the Sky channels. We ended up putting Babestation on, as you do.

'Shall we ring the number?' asked Rob.

'Yes, we shall,' I said.

We put the phone on speaker and had a chat with the lady on-screen. We spoke about everything apart from the obvious. They must get some odd people phoning in to those kind of channels but I think two blokes chatting about the best Premier League managers and comedy films must've been up there with the weirdest. Bless her, she was a trouper and kept trying to bring it back to sexy time, but every time she did we just changed the subject to something like favourite biscuits of all time. So there we were, me and the king of pop, chatting away to a girl on Babestation who was totally oblivious to who she was talking to. We were on there for bloody ages, yapping away.

'Christ, Rob! It's a pound a minute, this,' I said, genuinely worried about the price of a call while I'm sat next to the UK's biggest-selling solo star. On reflection, I think he could afford the 40 quid.

Jonny turned up later and I'm not sure how it happened but we decided to play a game, never a good thing with three of the most competitive people ever. The challenge was throwing fruit off his balcony and you had to hit a buoy that was floating in the middle of Chelsea Harbour. One of us, can't remember who, threw a very ripe kiwi fruit, the perfect size and weight for this kind of challenge. It was pitch-black outside so you had to wait for the sound of it either hitting the water or the ding of it hitting the buoy. We heard neither. What we actually heard was:

'Argh! Fucking hell!'

We rushed back inside, giggling like schoolboys. Some poor sod had just been made into a smoothie. Around 20 minutes later, after we'd stopped laughing, I decided to get ready for bed. I'd stripped off and was looking for my shorts and T-shirt when I heard aggressive hammering at the penthouse door. Jonny opened the door and this security guard was stood there with bits of kiwi juice in his hair. The bloke was clearly not happy, and Jonny and Rob tried to calm him down and apologise. He was a foreign geezer and he was dipping in and out of various swear words in different languages. There was only one thing for it, I thought. *Time to snap this fella out of it.* I suddenly appeared behind Jonny and Robbie, hands on hips, not a stitch on, naked as a baby.

'Everything OK?' I said.

It worked. The bloke was that startled by me appearing with my cock and balls out, he just shook his head and walked off.

* * *

Rob invited me to his house in LA but I was apprehensive about the whole thing. I was definitely not a big flyer back then and the thought of 11 hours on a plane filled me with dread. Randomly it was John Bishop who persuaded me to go. Back then Bish was a working stand-up but not the household name he is now. I was in the Apple store in Manchester at the time, looking at these newfangled iPods, when he rang me. I can't even remember what it was for but after a bit of chat I told him my predicament.

'Robbie Williams has invited me out to his mansion in LA but I'm not sure about the flight, Bish,' I said.

'Paddy, are you fucking mad? If Robbie Williams invited me out to stay at his pad in America, you wouldn't be able to put the seat tray down for my erection.'

He then laid it out for what it was, a chance in a lifetime to witness another side of life. He talked me round and that was that. I let Jonny know I'd be coming out – he was already out there with his wife, Nic.

This was before I got the paycheque for my first big tour so there was no way I could afford the flight, but I didn't have to worry about that, Rob sorted me out. I'd never flown first-class in my life – I didn't even understand what it was till I got on that BA flight. I couldn't believe it. Beds, movies, games, drinks … and I didn't have to eat my food out of a little tinfoil container on my lap. One extra stroke of luck, especially with me being a nervous flyer, was that all the air stewardesses had been to watch me on tour the week before. They told me they'd had a great night and were going to take extra special care of me on the flight. See what I mean about that first tour? I may not have enjoyed it, but the audience loved it. The girls on that flight were amazing, they were all drop-dead gorgeous and they kept my mind off the flight by chatting to me, feeding me and throwing vodka down my neck – it was the best flight ever. Honestly, 11 hours felt like an hour to me and when we landed Jonny was waiting at arrivals.

'Alright, youth, fancy a kickabout later?' he asked.

'I do but first things first, take me for a burger,' I said.

I'd always loved the idea of going to America. Having been brought up on all those Hollywood films, I wanted to try a proper American burger and hotdog. We go to a drive-through, I get my burger and we're now on our way to Rob's house. I say house, it was a mansion on a gated estate with security, chefs, gardeners and housekeepers. There were waterfall lagoons in the back garden and a lift inside the house. Proper *MTV Cribs* stuff. Rob was already at the five-a-side football pitch, which was at another house he owned just for his staff! Gwyneth Paltrow was there, just casually watching the game – this was way beyond my pay grade but I was thoroughly enjoying the ride. Before I joined in the game, Jonny and Robbie asked if I was feeling OK from the flight, was I jetlagged or not? The furthest I'd flown was Greece so I'd never been on a flight for more than four hours and even though I'd heard of jetlag I knew nothing about it or what it felt like. I played a five-a-side match full of vodka and burgers then we went back to Robbie's house. Again the boys were asking if I was feeling OK. I was now sat on this massive luxurious sofa, still with my football kit on.

'Chaps, I'm fine! A bit of jetlag isn't gonna bother a lad from Bolton!'

Thirty seconds later I was unconscious and I didn't wake up for nigh on 48 hours. When I finally came out of the coma, I felt like a million dollars. We went out and I did all the tourist stuff: Hollywood Hills, Rodeo Drive, Venice Beach, Chateau Marmont and of course more burgers and hotdogs. It was a fantastic week. There was me, Jonny and his wife Nic, along with Pete, Rob's dad. We had a quiz every other night and one evening Shakira popped in for a coffee – that was random. Being around all that back then was so bizarre for me. We were all just normal lads in this surreal mega-successful world Rob operated in.

On the European leg of his world tour, Rob invited me out to Germany. Jonny was already there because he used to do a couple of numbers with him onstage. He was playing the Allianz Stadium, home to Bayern Munich. Before the show we had a game of footgolf under the stadium, and again with us all being so competitive, this soon descended into a three-way argument. We were busy berating Jonny for a shot he'd taken when it dawned on me that Robbie was due to go onstage in front of 70,000 German fans within the next couple of hours. That was how strange life on the road was with someone like Robbie.

Just before he was about to go on, he suggested I go out onstage and duet with him on 'Kids', the record he'd made with Kylie Minogue.

'Fuck it', I said. 'Why not?'

Just before my bit, he announced me to a packed stadium.

'Germany, please welcome Paddy McGuinness!'

A cheer went up, a deafening roar, and then nothing, as 70,000 Germans all looked confused as to who they were cheering for.

'*Wer zum Teufel ist das?*'

Google it.

* * *

Talking of being out of my depth, I became pals with former Liverpool and Bolton player Jason McAteer and his agent at the time, Dave Lockwood. (Dave incidentally became a very integral part of my life a few years later – more on that in a bit.) They were putting on a game of football to raise money for the people who had been affected by the tsunami in Southeast Asia. The game was called Tsunami Aid. All well and good but they'd got it sponsored by Ocean Finance, whose emblem was a massive big wave. I think there was only me who picked up on that one. It was fantastic to run out at Anfield in front of a full house and play with legends of the game like Robbie Fowler and Kenny Dalglish. I remember thinking how lucky I was to be doing this and I felt like I was slowly moving up the showbiz ladder just by being invited to play. I became close to Jason and Dave – they're great lads – and we did a lot together; we even flew out to watch Ricky Hatton (another great lad) boxing Floyd Mayweather in Las Vegas. Again I didn't remember much of my first day in Vegas because I was sleeping off the booze I'd ingested to get myself through the flight.

Being around footballers and ex-players is great but it became apparent very quickly that they were operating on a different level to me – in other words, they had lots of money. We were once on a night out in London and I'd forgotten to pack my top. Jason said he'd take me to a shop he knew to get me a new jumper. I was in the middle of my first big tour at the time but I hadn't received any money at that point so I was more or less skint.

'There's a shop on Bond Street where you'll get something decent. I'll give them a ring and tell them to get a few bits ready,' he said nonchalantly.

I had no idea that Bond Street was home to designer shops and jewellers. I wasn't really London savvy back then and I certainly didn't own any designer clothing.

The shop in question turned out to be Dolce & Gabbana. Trying to impress, I acted like it was nothing new for me. Inside my head I was thinking, *Can I even afford a pair of socks from here, let alone a top for going out in?* I can honestly say where I grew up I never, ever, ever saw anyone in Gucci, Prada, Dolce & Gabbana, Chanel or anything like that. Adidas, Puma, Nike and Farah were about as designer as it got for us. The shop manager and his assistant approached me and asked what I'd like. *Don't go mad, McGuinness,* I thought.

'I'm looking for a plain black jumper,' I said. I stressed a few times that it had to be plain, nothing fancy, doing anything I could to get them to show me the cheapest jumper in there without actually saying, 'Can I have the cheapest thing in here, please?'

They brought four or five different styles of black jumper out. That was a surprise in itself for me – I only knew Crew and V.

'Which would you like to try on, sir?' the manager asked.

'All of them, please.'

I thought that was the only way I could check the prices first. I took the jumpers to the changing rooms and not one had the price on. FFS! I opted for the plainest one of the lot, black with a buttoned-down collar. It didn't say Dolce & Gabbana anywhere on it apart from the label inside – *That's the one for me*, I thought. In my head I'm thinking, *I'll be lucky to have any change out of a hundred quid*, which was a massive deal for me – a hundred quid on a plain black jumper was madness but I was in London giving it the big one. By now it'd gone five and the shop was closed, they'd kept it open for me and this frigging black jumper. I gave it to the girl behind the counter while I chatted to Jason about what we were doing that evening. She folded it perfectly, wrapped it in black tissue paper, tied a black silk bow around it and popped it in a Dolce & Gabbana bag. I ended up keeping that bag for ages, as I did all the bags I got from nice shops in those days. I kept a Selfridges one, mainly because the only other yellow and black shopping bag I'd seen was from Netto. The girl behind the counter, with her perfect make-up and slicked-back ponytail, gave me a big smile, handed me the bag and said:

'Thank you, sir, that'll be ...'

The wait for the cost felt like forever.

'... three hundred and fifty pounds.'

The girl didn't even flinch, and Jason didn't so much as look up from his BlackBerry (it was the noughties). It seems I was the only person there in shock. It's a plain black jumper! I got my debit card out, thinking it's best I pay quickly before I throw up. I always had a little minus sign at the side of whatever figure was in the bank at the time but thankfully the card wasn't declined and I was now the owner of a 350-quid black jumper. It killed me at the time, but 15 years later, I've still got it. And do you know what? It still looks bloody good.

So I'd got the jumper and gone back to my hotel to get changed and have a little cry. It seemed knocking about with footballers could be quite an expensive hobby. Jason called my room to tell me he was waiting outside in a car.

'Where we going, pal?' I said.

'Chinawhite,' he told me.

I was mega-excited. Back in the day, Chinawhite was one of those places, much like The Ivy, that I'd only read about in the papers. Anyone who was anyone had been spotted partying in there, it was a magnet for celebrities, Premier League football-ers, young people in the entertainment industry, and Page 3 girls. It was a second home to Jason and his mates.

As we set off I was thinking, *Christ, I'm in a 350-quid jumper on my way to Chinawhite.* Forget the Press Club, this was one of London's most exclusive venues. The only trouble being I wasn't a Premier League footballer, celebrity or Page 3 girl. I'd already taken a hit on the jumper so I planned to buy a couple of drinks and just make them last me.

We got in there and this was my first taste of private tables and seating. I couldn't believe it when the hostess led us to this big plush sofa surrounded by champagne buckets and neon lights. Already sat there were a few of Jay's pals from the footballing world. I liked them from the off. Essentially they were all working-class lads who were now getting paid a few quid to play football. It also helped that they were all big *Max and Paddy* fans. They quoted it all night, particularly the scene we did with Noddy Holder. 'I'll do your dentist a favour and knock them bastards out,' they said while tapping each other's teeth. So I'm sat there in this roped-off area feeling like Billy Big Bananas when the hostess comes over to take our drinks order. This again well and truly opened my eyes. If you order yourself a vodka in there, they don't bring it over in a glass, you buy the entire bottle. My plan of nursing half a lager all night had gone out the window and before I could say, 'No, please stop. I've already spent all the money I haven't got on this fucking black jumper,' the drinks started flowing, and I started to get swept up in the whole evening. I forgot about paying for things and just kept ordering. It was very seductive, being surrounded by glamour girls and champagne bottles with fireworks stuck in the top. I was totally new to all this but I was loving it. What young lad wouldn't?

Before I knew it, it was the end of the night and the hostess came over with the bill. Jason had popped out to make a phone call, so I was there with this group of footballers on my own. One picked up the bill and someone shouted, 'How much?'

'Four and a half.'

Shit the bed, four hundred and fifty quid, I thought. *What's that five ways?* I only had about 40 quid in my pocket and normally that'd do me for at least two or three nights out in Bolton. Where was I going to magic another 50 quid to put my share on the table? I was thinking all this when the lad holding the bill carried on speaking.

'Grand.'

Grand!!! I thought it was 450 quid! I was honestly shell-shocked – that was the price of a car to me. Four thousand five hundred pounds on drinks?! I didn't know what to do. What was I going to say? How was I going to get out of this? Where was I going to find hundreds of pounds in the next five minutes? I was still reeling from shock from buying my now sweat-soaked black jumper. I literally didn't know what to say. I think I muttered, 'Sorry, how much?'

He said the number again, but this time, everything went into slow motion. 'Fooouur aaaaand aaaa haaalf graaaaand.'

It was the trombone shot from *Jaws*, with the walls closing in on me. There I am, in a jumper I can't afford, in Chinawhite, with a handful of professional footballers, a £4,500 bar bill, and not a Page 3 girl in sight.

Then my moment of salvation arrived. It transpired that these particular footballers had a unique way of deciding who pays the bill. They'd all take out their credit cards, then toss them in the air. Whoever's card landed signature strip up paid the bill, and the rest got off without paying. *Well, this is it,* I thought, *shit or bust.*

We all got our cards out – one Black American Express card, one Platinum Coutts, one Visa black and mine, one turquoise Barclays cash card – well, at least it'd be clear whose was whose. One of the lads took all four cards and tossed them up in the air.

Time. Stood. Still. I watched the cards flip and turn in the air. Everything went slo mo, my eyes following them up and then down, my stomach in knots. After what felt like minutes they eventually landed on the drink-stained table and bounced about. *Please, Jesus ... I'm not a deeply religious man but, come on, help a brother out.*

Eventually they landed and lay there flat. I was now sober as a judge with laser focus zoomed in on the cards. Mine was the only one lying signature strip down. I thought I was going to wee, poo and jizz all at once. I wanted to pull that black jumper over my head and dive across the dance floor, goal-scoring style. But I knew I had to hold it all in and be cool. I couldn't let them see the horrific inner torment I'd been going through for the past few minutes. I looked over to clock the lads' reaction – I thought they'd be gutted. Nothing. They just picked up their cards and paid the bill.

That night, for me, was an eye-opener of great magnitude. I realised how out of my depth I was. I was a small fish. Not in a big pond, but a massive ocean.

CHAPTER 17

THE BALL IS ROLLING

The harder I work, the luckier I get.
Samuel Goldwyn

One of the things about working in television, certainly in front of the camera, is nothing can be taken for granted. Nobody owes you a living and there's no job security. If you manage to make a career out of it, then you're either fortunate enough to have got a few hit shows under your belt or you're a grafter. I was a bit of both. After I'd finished *Max and Paddy* there wasn't any other TV work on offer for me. We finished filming and it was a case of, what next? Peter had made a lot of money from touring so he wasn't in a hurry to do anything else, and I couldn't wait around for him because I didn't have the luxury of surplus cash in the bank, let alone my own house.

I got a job through an old school pal called Paul Coleman, who years later went on to create *Car Share* with Peter. He worked in advertising at a radio station in Manchester called Key 103. A DJ by the name of Adam Cole had an afternoon show and was looking for someone to write for him. Paul mentioned my name to him and I went along to meet up for a very soft kind of interview. He wanted to read out funny stories during his show so I came up with the idea of writing a tongue-in-cheek version of Simon Bates's *Our Tune*. For those of you too young to remember *Our Tune*, it was a sad story read out live on-air during Simon Bates's Radio 1 show, followed by a song with some significance to said sad tale. I kept to the same format, the punchline always being the song that played at the end. For instance, if someone accidentally sat on a bar of chocolate, the song at the end would probably be 'Careless Whisper'. Adam liked the idea and that was that, deal done. I think I got around 50 or 60 quid a story and that got me by.

Around that time was the birth of the comedy panel show. Now there's one on every channel, but back in the day it was pretty much *8 Out of 10 Cats* that got the ball rolling for a lot of comedians and gave them some exposure. I always knew I could get a laugh and panel shows are great because there isn't much pressure – you're hired to make a few quips, job done. Also, all the focus isn't on you – there's another five people up there all doing the funnies too. The first time I was a guest on *8 Out of 10 Cats* was a shock though. I knew nothing about panel shows or how they worked and I nearly fell through the floor when a few writers came in to offer up jokes for the show. Honestly, I was so green to it all back then I just presumed comedians wrote all their own material. Even though I wasn't a full-time stand-up comedian, I liked to think that I could be funny enough on my own. Now I have writers on most of my TV shows because I understand that they are a much-valued asset to the finished article. In fact, that first time I did *Cats*, the writer who came into my room (who I quickly fired off) has ended up working with me on pretty much every show I've done for the last 15 years or so. A guy called Les Keen, who I'd say fits nicely into the comedy writer mould: miserable as fuck, cynical and pretty much hates everything. I liked him from the off.

Another thing I learned about back in those days was editing. Editing is a process where a show that takes 3 hours to record gets cut down to 30 minutes for the telly. I used to hate watching shows back knowing how much had been cut out. In fact, the last time I appeared on *8 Out of 10 Cats*, after watching it on the telly, I made my mind up to steer clear of panel shows. On the night, I got some really big laughs from the audience. You know when it's going well and it was going well. I couldn't wait for it to come on the telly because I knew I'd done a good job. In the end, not a single thing of mine made the final cut. I took that one really personally. I'd done the show in the past with no problems so I was completely vexed. These days I wouldn't be that bothered – if you're a guest on someone else's show it's always geared up towards the host and team captains and I learned that the hard way. Luckily I was confident in my own ability, and where this could knock a lot of young comedians, it only centred my focus on making it.

At the time I was getting asked to appear on a number of shows as the 'funny' guest. I was getting a couple of grand a show for my troubles and during that period I was fully integrating myself with every bar in Soho. Those years between *Max and Paddy* and *Take Me Out* were without any shadow of a doubt wild times.

When I think about those years and some of the situations I got myself in, it feels like a totally different person to who I am now.

I remember the exact day I decided things had to change with all these big nights out. I was sat on the couch with Christine in my first proper 'look at me, I'm on the telly' house, Auburn Manor. It was named after Auburn Street, a little nod to where I grew up, and I'd bought and renovated it with the money I'd made on my first stand-up tour, The Dark Side. It was late on a Sunday afternoon, we'd just settled on the couch, flicked on the telly, I'd made myself a vodka and lemonade and stupidly lit up half a joint that had been left at my house by a mate who smoked more weed than a sixties hippy. Five minutes later and boom! I was on my knees in the garden, unable to get my breath and feeling like this was going to be my last moment on earth. I mean, I can think of worse last moments, but nevertheless, I thought I was done.

Christine rang an ambulance and the next thing I know I was in hospital. Thankfully it turned out to be a massive anxiety/panic attack. I knew nothing about these, apart from seeing my mum have them when I was younger, but I never thought much about them at the time. Having never suffered from them myself, I was totally unaware of what was happening to me and that was a very scary feeling. Now I'd experienced one I knew how bad they felt and realised how my poor mum must have been feeling all those years. If you're reading this and you suffer with these attacks then please get help. Don't just live with it or feel embarrassed. They can happen to anyone at any time, rich, poor, young and old.

I absolutely hated that feeling and couldn't figure out why it happened to me. What did I have to worry about at the time? I had a few quid, a girlfriend and a nice house. I put it down to my lifestyle at the time and the fact that I was getting more and more attention.

Even though I slowed down my drinking and nights out, I kept on getting these horrendous panic attacks, and for years I just tried to manage them myself. No one apart from Christine knew I suffered with them and to the outside world I was just my usual cheery self. I didn't want anyone to have something on me, folk thinking I was a failure or weak – I wasn't thinking straight at the time because that's what being mentally unwell can do to you.

It was over ten years before I finally admitted to myself that I needed professional help. When I worked at Morrisons stacking shelves or was labouring on building sites, I would read about all these rich, successful celebrities saying they couldn't cope or they were in therapy and I'd always think, what have they got to worry about? I'm living in a two-up, two-down with my mum and I've not got a pot to piss in, I'm the one who should be stressed. Being working class, I equated money with being happy. These celebrities had got the best job in the world and pots of cash so what was their problem? Fast-forward to a tiny bit of TV fame and a sell-out tour and I'm having panic attacks and thinking about therapy!

* * *

Much like *Top Gear*, *Take Me Out* came along as a complete surprise, a very welcome curveball. Having said that, I nearly never did it. I was still with my first agent at the time, Phil McIntyre. I used to love spending time with Phil. I definitely felt like I'd landed on my feet with him. Just walking around his offices in Soho and knowing the people who'd been through those doors was enough for me but the real cherry on the cake and the reason I loved the place were the two ladies (on occasion) who looked after me during my time there, Lucy Ansbro and Adele Fowler, aka Hinge and Bracket.

One day Adele got a call from a production company asking if I'd be interested in doing a pilot for a Channel 4 dating show.

'No, sorry, he can't do it, he's busy,' she said.

I was blissfully unaware of this approach. I was happy enough doing the rounds on panel shows and earning a living from touring, I very much lived in the moment back then. A couple of weeks passed and luckily for me a chap called Andrew Newman, who was Head of Comedy and Entertainment at Channel 4, had heard about what had happened and taken it upon himself to call my agent's office and speak to Lucy Ansbro.

'We've sent this through with Paddy in mind, and I really think he should have a look at it. I think this could be a big show,' he said.

It was unusual to make that kind of call. They could have got any number of people to do that pilot – well, it'd probably have been Jimmy Carr at the time – but Andrew must've known this was ideal for me. So a meeting was set up to meet the show's producers.

I couldn't believe my eyes when they walked into the room – one of them was Suzy Lamb who'd looked after me all those years earlier when I did *The National Lottery Big Ticket*. She introduced herself and I instantly jumped up out of my seat and blurted out, 'Fucking hell! No way! I knew it was you.'

I bounded around the table, wrapped my arms around her and gave her the biggest hug. How mad that our paths had crossed again all these years later. Suzy was now an executive producer and worked for the production company Talkback Thames, who've made loads of well-known TV shows from *BGT* to *The Bill*. Everyone in the room was surprised we knew each other, especially from a National Lottery game show I was a punter on in the late nineties. From that moment, I knew I was in good hands. Suzy then explained how the show worked.

'So a single man arrives via a lift to the studio floor where a line of thirty girls look at him and turn a light on or off.'

Didn't really strike me as the next *Blind Date*. The thought of hosting my own show was appealing but this sounded a bit out there. However, like I said, I trusted Suzy so I decided to get involved. Another side of TV production that you're probably unaware of, unless you work in this game, is something called the office pilot. This is basically feeling the show out and playing the rounds, in an office. No audience, no set, no nothing, just you, the production team and a commissioner from the channel. I did quite a few of these office pilots back in the early days and I never enjoyed them. Even though they're worth doing, they always felt really eggy to me. My toes are curling even thinking about the *TMO* office run-throughs. Imagine me in a small room, a few bits of paper on the floor representing the girls' podiums, no lift and a few of the production company young-sters pretending to be the singletons. I didn't have 'Single man, reveal yourself', 'Let the sausage see the roll' or even 'No likey, no lighty' on these run-throughs, it was just about working out the rounds.

It took all my concentration to get my head around the rules of the game and how it worked. Even though it all seems straightforward now, back then we were still trying to figure it out.

After a few weeks of agonising office pilots, we finally got to the stage where we were ready for a proper studio pilot. This was more like it, now it felt real. The pilot episode was filmed with a young Channel 4 audience in mind. It was a bit more risqué, a lot more anarchic and it went really well. Suzy and all her team were really happy, and Andrew Newman and Shane Allen, the commissioners at Channel 4, gave me a bottle of champagne with a note attached reading 'Here's to the series!' That was it, job done. I couldn't believe how quickly they'd said that – normally it takes a while for these things to get the green light but it seemed Channel 4's *Take Me Out* was a go! How wrong was I… and this is another important part of learning how television works. No matter what people say to you, until you're stood on that studio floor, contract signed, with a live audience, nothing is 100 per cent guaranteed.

A week or so later, I then got a call from Lucy to say it wasn't happening. In the words of Victor Meldrew, I didn't believe it! It turns out the Director of Television at Channel 4 at the time, a guy called Kevin Lygo, had watched the pilot and overruled all his commissioners by saying he didn't want to do it. That was that, really, the boss had made his mind up and *Take Me Out* was no more.

Talk about luck! If Lygo had given it the green light I don't think *Take Me Out* would have lasted that long on Channel 4 and all those catchphrases wouldn't have seen the light of day. Although it was a blow, at the time I was more confused than disheartened.

CHAPTER 17

I couldn't understand why, especially after so much positivity from Andrew and Shane, along with that note on the champagne. Fortunately I had some tour money to keep me going and I was doing various bits and bobs on the telly.

* * *

I was also in the middle of filming a show for Channel 5 called *Rory and Paddy's Great British Adventure*. It was myself and Rory McGrath travelling around the British Isles in a VW camper van taking part in strange but quintessentially British sports like shin kicking, bog snorkelling, toe wrestling, worm charming, swamp soccer – basically all the sports the Olympics could've been. We did two series together and I was knackered at the end of each of them. Not, might I add, because of the sports they had us doing or the travelling we had to do up and down the UK. It was the drinking! Don't get me wrong, I love a drink, and I especially did back then, but I'd met my match with Rory McGrath. I love the bloke, but he'd leave Oliver Reed and Ronnie Wood in his wake, talk about rock 'n' roll.

I'd known of Rory from his work in the comedy world. I was a little nervous at meeting him because I knew he was part of that Cambridge Footlights set and I wasn't sure we'd get on or if he'd look down his nose at me. How wrong was I. We got on really well and I thoroughly enjoyed his company. (It turned out his parents were from St Helens and Accrington, so he was less of a soft southern shite than I thought. He was a hard, northern bastard like me!) Because we were now working together, I felt obliged to have a drink with him, which turned out to be pretty much all day every day while we were filming the series. I loved a night out myself but some days we'd be starting on the sauce at seven in the morning. There was only a small crew – the director, one bloke on sound and another on camera – and the director was a mate of Rory's so it was basically a jolly boys' outing with a bit of cheese rolling thrown in for good measure.

I remember one scene we filmed began in an off-licence in Cambridge, already not a good start. There was no reason for us to film anything in there, it was purely so we could grab a drink. It was around 10am and we're stood in this offy waiting for the director to shout action outside. Rory tapped me on my shoulder and said, 'Here you go.' He handed me a bottle. I looked down to see what beer he'd given me, only to find it was a bottle of absinthe!

'Fuck me, Mr McGreavy,' I said. (I had various names I'd call him on any given day.) 'Absinthe!?'

'It's good for your creative juices. Van Gogh drank it. Manet and Toulouse Lautrec.'

'But they were painters; they weren't about to do a day's lawn-mower racing! We can't do it now!'

'It's OK,' he said. 'They're still setting up the shot outside.'

We clearly had crossed wires. I'm protesting at the prospect of necking a bottle of neat absinthe at ten in the morning, Rory on the other hand thinks I'm talking about us not having enough time to drink it. I'd struggle drinking neat absinthe on any occasion, let alone in the middle of filming a factual entertainment show for Channel 5. The bottles were bigger than a normal short and a touch smaller than a regular half-size – regardless, that's a lot of absinthe.

I attempted a couple of mouthfuls but I was struggling. Rory had already drunk his when we heard the director shout action. Rory said, 'Give it here', took my bottle off me and downed that as well. Off we then went straight into a take. If I'd have done two bottles of absinthe they'd have had to call in the air ambulance but McGrath is an absolute machine. I don't think I've ever actually seen him drunk either. He's one of those steady eddies, that one mate we've all got who can just keep going when the rest of us is frigged.

One of the heaviest sessions I had with him was after filming one day. Rory, his driver and I were in the middle of nowhere and there was just one pub open. Rory's driver was more a pal, really, who didn't do much driving. I got on with him just as well as Rory, so all was good. We got a seat at the bar around five o'clock and started drinking. Closing time came and went but we carried on. Rory managed to secure us some after-time drinking with the landlord. Not really the news I wanted to hear. We'd been drinking solid since teatime and I'm quickly losing my speech and vision, along with full usage of my limbs. Everything was getting a bit spinny so I staggered to the toilets to try and splash a bit of water on my face and see if I could remember my own name. A woman walked in behind me and told me I was in the ladies'. Turns out it was the landlord's wife. Suddenly the door flung open and in stormed the landlord.

'What you doing with my wife in the toilet?!'

The state I was in, not a lot. Just as I was trying to summon the words to explain, he stormed back out, his wife chasing after him. I looked in the mirror and thought, *Well, this could only happen to me.* Out I went back into the pub to try and calm the situation down. Somehow I got myself behind the bar to reason with this bloke but he was having none of it. He squared up to me so I pushed him away, but he'd also had a bit to drink, and he stumbled backwards and subsequently ended up on his back, unconscious. I looked at Rory and his mate, who were still sitting at the bar drinking, and said, 'I'm off.'

God knows how I found my way back to the hotel. It was now silly o'clock and I was due to be up for filming at seven. I eventually made it back to my room and immediately threw up everywhere – and I mean everywhere. All over the carpet, bed, bath, toilet, cupboards … the room was covered in vomit. I then fell into unconsciousness.

I was woken by one of the crew hammering on my hotel room door to get me out of bed, and by bed I mean bathroom floor. I felt horrendous. Upon opening the door I could see the revolt on the person's face: one, I looked like an extra from *The Walking Dead* and two, a tsunami of vomit odour bellowed out of the room.

'Rory and his driver are waiting for you in the car, Paddy, you'll be travelling with them.'

Firstly, I couldn't believe they were actually in the car ready to go and secondly, had they even been to bed? I started to get dressed but the room was an absolute disgrace, it was like walking a minefield of sick bombs. I felt bad for whoever had to clean it. I had a word with one of our production crew and asked them to bill me for all the cleaning and anything I'd broken. Twitter wasn't big yet back then but there was a thing called the *News of the World*, a newspaper that came out every Sunday with a penchant for scandal.

So although I didn't have to worry about people taking selfies in the room and plastering them all over the internet, I did worry about the papers finding out. It was perfect tabloid fodder: boozing, fighting, trashed hotel room and a landlord's wife thrown in the mix! Having said that, the biggest obstacle I was facing at this moment was getting down the stairs and into the car.

Now this is what I mean about McGrath being the real deal when it comes to legendary boozers. They poured me into the back of this minibus taxi. I had sunglasses on, felt like death warmed up and was whiter than Nigel Farage's phone book.

'What time did you leave the pub, boys?' I asked.

'About half an hour ago,' said Rory.

There was a possibility, just, that he was joking!

I'm now sat in the car with my head in my hands, thinking, *This is definitely going to make the papers!*

I asked them to open the windows in the front because the bus reeked of alcohol.

'That'll be this you can smell,' said Rory, holding up a brandy they were drinking straight out of the bottle.

I knew then I was done trying to keep up with these men. My liver was waving the white flag, and my head had already retreated. McGrath was a next-level boozer, and trust me, I could do a bit back then!

As always, Rory was completely with it all day during filming. The man astounded me. Not only was he a legendary drinker but the man had some brain on him. This really fascinated me. He was also a keen bird watcher so to amuse myself during filming

I bought a massive encyclopedia of Latin bird names. I'd sit there testing him on his knowledge in between takes.

'Right, Mr McGregor, what's a *Cyanocitta cristata*?'

'Blue jay.' He was right.

'*Coturnix coturnix*?'

'Quail.' Again correct.

'*Apus apus*?'

'Swift.' Correct.

I did catch him out once, though. We were sitting in a hotel in the Highlands after dinner. He was nursing a large Laphraoig and I was necking a Blue WKD and I asked him, 'OK, what's the scientific name for a glaucous gull?' He was stumped and quite ashamed and asked me never to mention this story to anyone. So I never have. (Ha!)

His intelligence is through the roof. I actually believe he's too intelligent. I think that's why he's so rock 'n' roll – it's the only thing that stops his brain from working so much.

Back to a couple of days after the night in the pub and it turns out someone *had* rung the *News of the World* in the hope of making a few quid. The paper never even bothered with it, though – turned out myself and Rory were so far down the showbiz ladder that no one gave a toss about what we'd been up to. Oh, how I miss good old anonymity.

CHAPTER 18

TAKE ME OUT GETS THE GREEN LIGHTY!

Saturday night is the most pressurised evening of the week
for any TV show. Pass me the diving suit, I'm going in!

I was on a day off from filming with Rory and randomly I was in TK Maxx buying a lamp when my phone rang. It was Lucy.

'Remember that pilot you did for Channel 4, *Take Me Out?*'

It'd been over a year since I did it and I'd already done one series with Rory McGrath so my memory was a bit blurred and it took me a moment to remember.

'Was that the one with the lift?' I said.

'That's the one. Well, ITV want to do it and put it on prime-time Saturday night!'

'Really? Well, send Vernon Kay my best,' I said genuinely. Vernon was doing a lot for ITV at the time so I just presumed they'd give it to someone like him. All my stuff had been on Channel 4 and coming from a comedy background, along with being a bit of a naughty boy, I didn't think ITV would go near me in a million years, let alone host a Saturday night family show.

'What? No, they want you to do it!'

'Bollocks! Really?'

So there I was in TK Maxx holding on to this light, ironically, and I'd just been told I was going to be hosting a Saturday night show on ITV. Ta-ra, worm charming with Rory McGrath, hello, prime-time!

It turned out that Suzy Lamb was passionate about *Take Me Out* and hadn't been deterred by Channel 4 saying no. This happens a lot in telly: one door shuts, another one opens. She was pals with another legendary name in the television industry, a fella by the name of John K. Cooper. If you don't work in TV then you won't have heard of him but if you watched telly in the eighties, nineties and noughties you will have watched one of his shows. John had been a part of nigh on every show from my youth! *Blind Date, It'll Be Alright on the Night, Barrymore, Hale & Pace, Catchphrase, You Bet, Gladiators*, the list goes on. He was now Controller of Entertainment at ITV and Suzy kept badgering him to look at that *Take Me Out* pilot. He eventually did, and he liked it. He then showed it to Peter Fincham, Director of Television at ITV, the boss. While I was writing this book, I gave Peter Fincham a call to find out exactly why he took a risk on me. Here's what he said:

'I had two Channel 4 pilots put on my desk. One of them was *The Cube*, the other was *Take Me Out*. Firstly I couldn't believe that Channel 4 had passed on them both because I thought they were really good shows and could see the longevity in them. Justin Lee Collins was the host of *The Cube* pilot but he didn't feel right for

ITV so in steps Phillip Schofield and the rest is history with that show. *Take Me Out* on the other hand was different. I thought you did a fantastic job hosting it and although you were predominantly known for working on Channel 4 comedy shows I felt that you could easily make the move over to Saturday television, so I gave it the go ahead.'

There you go, straight from the horse's mouth. Peter could've taken that show and got any number of established prime-time hosts to front it but instead he chose me. When I was growing up, if you had a show on Saturday night TV, you were big-time. This was where the likes of Bruce Forsyth and Ant and Dec plied their trade. It's lovely how people still talk about *Max and Paddy* and *Phoenix Nights* with such affection but Peter Fincham, *Take Me Out* and Suzy Lamb's tenacity are the reasons I'm sat here in my office writing this book. If it wasn't for that show, I'm not sure what I'd be doing now. Probably in rehab after doing another series with Rory McGrath. Work, career, finances, opportunities, touring, I owe it all to being given that chance with ITV.

Once the excitement and dust had settled, it was time to actually film it. We did the first series in Manchester at Granada Studios, which suited me as Bolton was only half an hour away in the car. My life was changing very quickly. I remember being taken to The Ivy by Elaine Bedell, who was Director of Entertainment and Comedy at ITV at the time; Lorraine Heggessey, Chief Executive at Talkback Thames, the production company making *Take Me Out*; and Richard Holloway, Head of Entertainment. I'd been in the company of a lot of women over the years but sitting at that table was nerve-racking for me. I was playing it cool, no biggie – it's only a group of industry heavyweights who could make or break my career in TV, no pressure. Bang! I knock a full bowl of soup all over my lap. Someone please shoot me! The likes of Madonna eat in here and I'm now covered in lobster bisque (posh soup). Not the best first impression but such is life. Ruined trousers aside, we had a nice evening and I loved listening to stories from shows they'd been a part of over the years. I remember thinking, *Bloody hell, son, I think you're finally making it.*

First day of dress rehearsals and I'm on set at Granada Studios along with Suzy Lamb and the person who spoke to me down my ear for ten years, our show producer Mel Balac. Back then there wasn't much budget for shows like ours, all the big bucks were spent on shows like *The X Factor*, *Saturday Night Takeaway* or *Britain's Got Talent*, the monster, super-glamorous Saturday night shows. We had a cardboard *Take Me Out* sign hanging by a couple of bits of string and the Isle of Fernando's hadn't even been discovered yet. As the years went by and *TMO* got more successful, our sets got more Saturday night with flashy LEDs and lights everywhere – even the girls' podiums went digital for the last few series. Back in the early days, when one of the girls got a date there'd be 10 or 15 minutes of waiting around while our art department made up a new plastic panel to replace the girls' names on the front of their podiums.

Suzy and Mel talked me through how it was all going to work then I was told it was time to meet the girls for the first time. I know exactly how all those single men must have felt when they appeared out of the love lift – it was terrifying. There must've been

40 of them and Suzy asked me to say a few words to make them all feel at ease. Make *them* feel at ease? It was me who needed the words of encouragement – I was shitting myself. Suzy said, 'Here's Paddy, everyone!' and the entire room erupted in cheers and wolf-whistles, it really took me aback. My heart was pounding; here I was stood in a room of 40 women from all walks of life who were looking me up and down and waiting for me to come out with something funny or a few pearls of wisdom. I had neither prepared but somehow managed to blurt out a few things along the lines of I was just as new to this as they were and just as nervous. In fact, the girls seemed more up for it than me.

* * *

So I'd met the girls for the first time and I was now back on the studio floor with Suzy and Mel, running through the game play. During rehearsals I usually throw a few unscripted lines in to see if they get a laugh. If you can make a bunch of hairy-arsed TV production crew laugh, then you're on to something. Also, during rehearsals the crew fill in the part of the contestants, which was always a tricky one on *Take Me Out*. Talking to a 50-year-old bloke called Colin about his beauty regime was always a stretch of the imagination. On one occasion a crew member was in the love lift waiting for me to introduce them. Out of nowhere I just said, 'Let the sausage see the roll!' It got a big laugh on the studio floor so I carried it on throughout rehearsals.

'Let the nut see the bolt!'

'Let the cream see the horn!'

I just kept doing it. Everyone loved it and it ended up staying in the show.

Another idea I had during those rehearsals was Fernando's. I loved shows that had that element of humour that was never seen, the kind of things the viewers interpret for themselves. Terry Wogan would joke about the BBC canteen serving bad food. You'd never see it or taste it, but you'd fill in the blanks yourself. Larry Grayson would talk about his friend Everard. Again, you never saw him, so it was up to you what he looked like and that's a powerful way of getting laughs. It becomes more personal to you.

This was my thinking behind Fernando himself. The couples would always go off on a date after the show, but that felt like I'd seen it a million times before. We were a totally new style of dating show. It was a lot more entertainment based and for me it needed a little bit extra from the days of the mighty *Blind Date*. I was sat in the audience seating with Mel. Although she'd be talking to me down my ear while the show was being recorded during rehearsals, she'd often pop down to the studio floor to see how everything was going. I explained to her this idea of a bloke we'd never see called Fernando who ran a local bar to which we'd send our dates to. Mel got it straight away. We ran it by Suzy who also loved it. Club Fernando's was born.

The other thing I insisted on was making it sound not very glamorous. We didn't have the budget back in those early days to send our couples abroad and I was keen to be honest with the viewer about that, but in a humorous way. Again nothing new there, other shows like *Blankety Blank* and *Bullseye* have had those elements in the past – and people loved them.

Having said all that, the language of the show along with Fernando's and all those well-known catchphrases nearly never saw the light of day. Although Suzy and Mel had given the ideas a thumbs-up, Elaine Bedell wasn't keen. Her argument was Fernando's would cheapen the show and make it feel more low-budget.

'Elaine, we're sending couples on a date to a bar around the corner in Manchester, it is low-budget. Let's celebrate that and make something of it,' I said.

After a bit more persuasion she reluctantly went with the ideas. So now I had Fernando's and 'Let the (something) see the (something)' as part of the show. The final piece of the puzzle was 'No likey, no lighty!' Again, we were blocking things through in rehearsal when Les Keen pulled me to one side.

'Hey, Paddy, how about when the girls turn off their lights you say, "No likey, no lighty"?'

I instantly knew it'd work so we ran it by Suzy and Mel. They also liked it and that was that. Those three things became a massive part of the whole language and feel of *Take Me Out*. We were off and running and as *Take Me Out* got more popular we were given bigger studios in Maidstone and more budget to make the show. Bye-bye, Club Fernando, hello the Isle of … Fernando's!

Take Me Out ran for 10 years and we did 11 series. It never won a single award. It never even made the shortlists but even now, all these years later, everyone still quotes the show and it's firmly cemented into the British TV landscape. It was warm, silly, fun and off the success of the British version, *Take Me Out* got commissioned all around the world – we even cracked America! There was talk of me doing it in Australia but I couldn't bring myself to fly there. Funnily enough, in the end my *Top Gear* compadre Flintoff did the pilot episode of the Australian version, but I've no idea who they finally got to host it over there.

By the time it finished, *Take Me Out* was officially the biggest and most successful dating show on TV with regards to territories it'd been sold to and our hit rate of weddings and babies born. Eight weddings, countless engagements, six babies and a generation of youngsters watching the show. One of the things I've read that really warmed my cockles was written by former *Take Me Out* contestant Meera Sharma in the *Independent*:

> The *Take Me Out* format gave the show universal commonality. It was positioned as a family-friendly dating show, which you could watch before you got ready for a night out. Unlike *Love Island,* this wasn't a space limited to the Instagrammable, bikini-clad model with 100k followers – *Take Me Out* contestants were relatable women, and reflected the diverse variety of sizes, shapes, personalities, styles, ambitions and accents that real women have. The show also welcomed women from almost every corner of the UK.

That pretty much sums up the show nicely and I'm very proud to be a part of something that became a Saturday night staple and even spawned its own spin-off show, *TMO The Gossip*, a success few television shows achieve.

All this with no big marketing campaign. In fact, it was the opposite. We never got any purpose-made ads and when we started, Twitter was in its infancy and Instagram didn't even exist. It was the viewers, word of mouth and a young demographic of fans that kept us on-screen for ten very happy years.

The maddest thing about *Take Me Out* finishing was the man who turned it down for Channel 4 all those years ago, Kevin Lygo, ended up in charge at ITV and waved bon voyage to it there as well. Talk about full circle ... although to be fair to Kevin, he was very good with me during my time with him at ITV and *Take Me Out* had another few series before that happened. Kevin Lygo was also the chap who commissioned *The Keith and Paddy Picture Show*, which myself and Leigh Francis absolutely loved making.

It was Kevin who gave us the show we wanted to make in the end. We'd initially given the idea of *Movie Show* to Peter Fincham. He liked it but wanted it to be a bit more studio based. So we did a pilot episode where three celebrity guests had to answer questions about TV and film. Once they'd given their answers we'd reveal a clip of the film or TV show to see if they were correct – but the clip would be myself and Leigh doing a sketch re-enacting it. The pilot episode went well and the live studio audience enjoyed it. Then out of the blue we found out Peter Fincham was leaving ITV. Like anyone coming into a job, they want to do things their own way, so when Kevin Lygo took over we thought the pilot was doomed. In the end it actually worked out better for us. Kevin indeed didn't want the pilot episode, he much preferred the sketches. So, as opposed to the studio quiz format we delivered, Kev gave us the thumbs up to make *The Keith and Paddy Picture Show.* We couldn't have been happier.

I got on with Leigh from the minute we met. We first crossed paths in 2006 on a late-night music show on Channel 4 called *Transmission*. He's nothing like the larger-than-life persona of Keith Lemon; he's a devoted father, husband and all-round good egg – oh, and he loves a drink. During the filming of *Transmission*, I commented on how much I enjoyed his comedy, and after the show we had a drink-up. He'd brought along some of his mates from Leeds, and I was with some mates from Bolton, normally a recipe for disaster but instead we all had a great night.

It's rare for me to meet someone who I immediately connect with but Leigh was one of those people. We stayed in touch and he asked if I fancied appearing in his new show, *Keith Lemon's Very Brilliant World Tour.* I loved *Bo' Selecta!* so I immediately said yes. If nothing came of it, I knew I'd have a laugh with Leigh regardless. On the show, he wanted me to play the role of his cousin, Gary, who was a proper wrong 'un. I love playing characters like that, they're the ones you can have the most fun with. We shot it all in a day, and Leigh spread it out over the series. After that I did the odd thing with him but the thing that really cemented our relationship was *Let's Dance for Comic Relief.* The idea of the show was various celebrities recreating iconic dance routines from cinema. I got asked to do it but I wasn't sure about dancing on my own in front of millions of people so I rang Leigh to see if he fancied doing it with me.

'Fancy doing that dance from *Dirty Dancing*?' I said. 'You know, the one where they do the lift.'

'Which part am I playing?' he asked.

'Guess,' I said.

And that was that, we signed up to do the show. That's what I love about Leigh, he'll always get stuck in to help someone out and I'm the same. I know a lot of people within the industry who I like very much, but I know for a fact if I phoned them to do me a favour or help me out with an appearance on a show they wouldn't do it. Thankfully myself and Leigh haven't got that selfish streak in us, we're definitely cut from a similar cloth.

Leading up to *Let's Dance for Comic Relief*, we spent a few sweat-soaked weeks working with a choreographer to get the dance exactly right. We really took it seriously and wanted to get the routine spot on. I remember the first time I lifted Leigh above my head. He was shirtless and sweating like an influencer with no internet access. As I lowered him back down, I got a face full of wet, ginger chest hair. Spewing up aside, that was all part of the work we were putting in to get this dance right.

So we did the show and finished runners-up to Robert Webb dancing to Irene Cara's 'What a Feeling' from the movie *Flashdance.* Our *Dirty Dancing* went viral and got over two million views on YouTube – we felt there was an appetite for that kind of thing so we decided to capitalise on its popularity and write a comedy version of the movie. Our version was to be set in Morecambe, we'd more or less written it. We even had a list of people we wanted to cast. I can't remember everyone but I know we had Lily Allen down to play the part of Lisa Houseman, Baby's older sister. Cut a long story short, ITV didn't want it and we were both busy with other projects so the idea was shelved. Skip forward eight years, a studio pilot and Kevin Lygo's appointment at ITV and we were all set. That shows you how long things take in TV and how the stars have to align just at the right time before anything new gets made.

We filmed two series of *The Keith and Paddy Picture Show* and recreated films such as *Jaws, Grease, Pretty Woman, Terminator 2, Jurassic Park, Top Gun, Gremlins, Ghostbusters, Return of the Jedi* and *Rocky*, and had guests as varied as Robbie Williams, Anna Friel, Michelle Keegan, Nicole Scherzinger, Jaime Winstone, Jessica Hynes, Sian Gibson, Ant and Dec, Marc Warren, Zach Galligan, Phillip Schofield, Sarah Parish, Emily Atack, Bernie Clifton, Kara Tointon, John Thomson, Basil Brush, Tracy-Ann Oberman, Amanda Holden, Su Pollard, Bob Carolgees, Sally Phillips, Philip Glenister, Emma Willis, David Dickinson, Stephen Tompkinson, Shaun Ryder, Keith Allen, Larry Lamb, Rick Astley, Zippy and Gordon the Gopher!

After we'd finished filming the second series, we were offered a third but with a lower budget to make the shows. It was an impossible task even though we had an amazing crew along with two fantastic directors, Dan Johnston and Jamie Deeks, who both loved it as much as myself and Leigh. We just couldn't make it work with the budget ITV had offered us, so that was the end. We were all gutted – it rated really well. In fact, it was ITV's highest-rated show in that 9pm Saturday night slot for the last ten years! We all loved making it but it just wasn't to be and our little taste of Hollywood movies was stopped in its tracks by the number-crunchers in accounts. Even now, though, five years after our first episode, we still talk about films we never got to recreate and still hold out hope that we'll one day bring it back.

▶▼ My first appearance on TV, in 1996 on *God's Gift* with Claudia Winkleman. They spelt my name wrong. Where's the respect?

patrick mcguiness

▲ Me and Suzy Lamb, the first time we met on *The National Lottery Big Ticket Show* in Holland. Not sure what I was doing with my mouth.

▶ On the set of *Max and Paddy*, filming in the Crompton Place Shopping Centre in Bolton.

▲ The Dark Side tour.

▲ The Plus You! tour and the picture that became a meme.

▲ A press cutting from my first arena tour, Saturday Night Live.

▲ Me and Peter in front of Derian House, the children's hospice we raised money for on *Who Wants to Be a Millionaire?*

◀ I can count on one hand the amount of times Peter has done anything with me after Phoenix Nights and Max and Paddy . This was one of them. He agreed to come on my radio show.

▲ *We Will Rock You* press night. Before Dec, there was Pad.

▶ *Pantos on Strike* photo call.

▲ The first ever episode of *Celebrity Juice.*

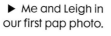

▶ Me and Leigh in our first pap photo.

▲ Bath night. Still using Fairy Liquid.

▲ Leigh, me and Sian Foulkes in *The Keith & Paddy Picture Show*. I had my first on-screen kiss with Sian in Phoenix Nights.

▶ Leigh and me on Dec's (of Ant and Dec fame) stag do.

▼ Me meeting me at Madame Tussauds, 2015. I insisted the waxwork had more hair.

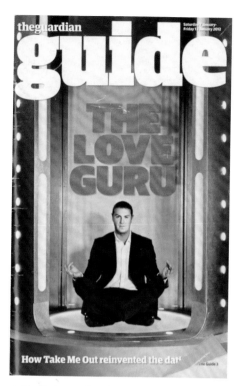

▲ My first ever front cover photo shoot, for *Take Me Out*.

▼ Very rare picture of me, Suzy Lamb and Mel Balac together in my dressing on *TMO*. Behind us are all the pictures of the girls and lads we'd go through for each show.

▲ Me, Frank Skinner and Ed Balls when I was a guest on *A Question of Sport*. Who'd have thought three years after this picture was taken, I'd be hosting it.

▲ My first Soccer Aid with Jonny Wilkes. I love this photo. It sums up our friendship nicely.

▶ Soccer Aid 2012. Me, John Bishop, Robbie Williams, Teddy Sheringham, Jamie Theakston, Graeme le Saux

▲ Soccer Aid 2014.

▲ 2016. Doing what we do best – drinking.

◀ Soccer Aid 2016. Left to right: Jack Whitehall, Danny Jones, Phil Neville, Kieron Dyer, Robbie Williams, Damian Lewis, Mark Wright, Danny Murphy, Jonny Wilkes, me, Sam Allardyce, Jamie Carragher, Ollie Murs, Jamie Theakston, Marvy Humes, Ben Shephard, David Seaman, Sol Campbell, Robbie Fowler, Louis Tomlinson, John Bishop.

▼ The eclectic mix that is Soccer Aid.

▶ The hair transplant was a success.

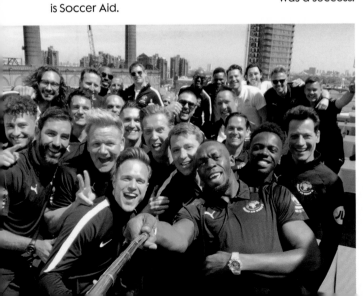

◄ Relaxing after the game. Who knew 12 months later myself and Flintoff would be the hosts of *Top Gear*?

▶ PM.

▲ Myself and Niall Horan enjoying a Guinness at the Toucan pub in Soho. I've got a lot of time for this lad.

▲ Me and Suzy Lamb, still going strong after all these years.

▶ At Suzy's leaving do come *Take Me Out* wrap party.

◄ Sarah Burrows, Suzy and me. Sarah, my make-up artist, has been making me look pretty for the telly for over ten years.

TMO 10 WRAP PARTY & SUZY LAMB'S LEAVING PARTY

8TH FEBRUARY 2018

◀ Suzy Lamb, ecstatic to see my lovely face at the global launch of *Top Gear*.

▲ The best ever hotel we stayed in on *Top Gear*. Not sure what that is hanging between Flintoff's legs, but he was clearly happy as well.

▶ In Peru with the effervescent Chris Harris. This lad always gives his best performances off camera.

▲ Two notherners enjoying the sunshine in Ethiopia

▼ Freddie, Chris and me, our first time on camera together.

▼Myself and Clare Pizey, exec producer of *Top Gear*. Here we are in Ethiopia, our first foreign trip together. Clare is now my chaperone and flying buddy on all our trips.

LETTING WHAT'S LEFT OF MY HAIR DOWN

I still can't believe what I do for a living. To be honest, I'm probably not on my own. I just don't feel a part of that whole world – I've definitely a touch of the imposter syndrome in me. When I say I don't feel like I belong, I think it's because I've managed to do the job for over 20 years but it never got beyond that – it's exactly that, a job. Outside of that, my life is still pretty much normal, apart from a nicer car and a bigger house. I'm just not a very showbiz person. I definitely don't fit into the 'celebrity' category. To be a proper celebrity you've got to put a shift in. Turning up at every party, every charity night, every movie premiere; posing for pictures, red carpets and the like. I hardly do any of that. Don't get me wrong, I've had my fair share of boozy nights out in the past, but the whole turning up to the opening of an envelope just to get in the paper has never been my thing. I couldn't care less about getting my picture taken on a red carpet. In fact, that's the worst part of those nights for me. I haven't got the skills or looks for that. I see some people on the red carpet and they look the bollocks. Me? I look like I'm sucking a boiled sweet in half the pics! I'm usually mid-conversation with someone and I certainly don't know how to pose for pics, although Flintoff's given me a few pointers on how to stand and hold my face. I'm far happier at home or having a night at a mate's house playing cards and ordering a takeaway.

I still go along to the Pride of Britain Awards, but other than that I don't really bother. In over 20 years, I've been to two movie premieres, two BAFTAs and two National Television Awards. I used to like going to the Brits because it was nothing to do with what I did for a living. I could go along with Christine and just enjoy the music and, of course, the free booze. I've had some great nights out there but that's all they were to me, a night out. Some random things can happen at these events, though.

I mean, at my first Brits, in 2011, I ended up hijacking a Thames Clipper. I was sat on the ITV table with Christine, Leigh Francis and his wife, Jill, slap bang at the front so we got a great view of whoever was performing. The free drinks were flowing and we were all having a great time dancing and singing along.

At the time Peter Fincham was Director of Television at ITV, the guy who gave me my big Saturday-night TV break with *Take Me Out*. His CV of comedy shows he'd been executive producer on was amazing: *I'm Alan Partridge*, *Smack the Pony*, *Never Mind the Buzzcocks*, *Ali G*, *Knowing Me Knowing You*, *Alas Smith and Jones*, *They Think It's All Over* and *The Day Today*. I got on really well with Peter and so did Leigh. Sometimes I'd forget what he did for a living because he was such a good laugh and so approachable. Every year he used to hold a party at his house for all the ITV talent.

The rules were very strict: no agents, no partners and no producers; it was just ITV executives and us, the people off the telly. What happened at Fincham's stayed at Fincham's and I used to love how bonkers those parties were. It was the entire gamut of ITV talent so you could be knocking back shots with Sir Trevor McDonald one minute and the next having a chat with one of the Chasers. News, entertainment, current affairs, drama, comedy, daytime – if it was on ITV, you'd be invited to Fincham's summer piss-up! I might add that's not what it was called on the invitation.

Anyway, as the night was drawing to a close at this particular Brit Awards, the talk came around to where to go next. There were loads of after-parties thrown by various record labels but they were usually invite only. Being a bit of a livewire back then, I was looked upon as someone who could get you in places. (Not sure why. I was never on any VIP lists anywhere.) So the show finished and, out of the blue, Peter walks over with his team of execs, commissioners and, randomly, Michael McIntyre.

'Paddy will know where a good party is. He'll get us in anywhere!' Peter said.

Everyone looked at me so I smiled confidently and said, 'You know it, Peter!'

On the inside I was thinking, *How the fuck am I gonna get out of this one?* I've got the entire ITV hierarchy and Michael McIntyre looking at me to deliver a great night out. The Brits was live from the O2 so most of the after-parties were being held in the bars there.

'Follow me,' I said, with literally no idea of where I was going or what I was going to do when I got there.

CHAPTER 19

I remember striding through the O2 like a light-entertainment duck being followed by all her ducklings. Christine, Leigh and Jill were also with the group and everyone was chatting and laughing, oblivious to the sheer panic I was experiencing.

'How far now, Paddy?' Peter asked.

'Good things come to those who wait, Peter!' I said.

I was scanning all the bars for some kind of corporate activity, and by corporate activity I mean middle-aged men in suits coked out of their minds. Desperation was setting in: a couple of the ITV mob had already peeled off and McIntyre was next to disappear. The group now consisted of my lot, Peter Fincham, a few other execs and Elaine Bedell, the Director of Comedy and Entertainment at ITV. These were my bosses, for God's sake, and things were quickly going tits up. Just as I thought the game was up, I bumped into someone I knew from behind the scenes in the industry. Without so much as a 'Hi, how are you doing?' I just blurted out, 'Are there any after-show parties in here?' He could see by the look on my face that I was a man in deep distress. He said he'd just left a Sony party and pointed to some steps that led up to the biggest doorman ever.

'Everything OK, Paddy?' asked Peter.

'All good, pal, it's just over there,' I said, also pointing to the steps headed by the biggest doorman ever. This was it, shit or bust, no turning back now.

Now in the unlikely event that you find yourself with your friends, family and the higher echelons of ITV trying to get into a Sony after-party, this little technique is high risk but sometimes works. I strode up the steps, head held high, phone in hand, pretending to speak to someone who was already inside.

'Yeah, I know, we're just coming up the steps now, get the drinks in,' I said, lying through my teeth. With this I looked straight at the missing link on the door and said, 'Alreet, pal.'

I then turned to the rest of my group and held my arm out to guide them in.

'He's at the bar,' I said.

The look of bewilderment on their faces. *Who's at the bar?* Before they could even ask me what I was on about, I more or less pushed them through the doors. We were in! I'd done it. Mission complete. As I mentally prepared my BAFTA speech for Best Performance, things quickly went downhill. That moment of euphoria slipped away as I looked around the room and it dawned on me. This wasn't *the* Sony after-party. It was a half-empty room of people who indeed worked at Sony, trouble being it was the Sony electrical shop. If you wanted to purchase some new headphones, a mobile phone or a flat-screen TV then this was the place to be, but if you were waiting for Beyoncé and Jay-Z to walk in it was never happening. Well, not unless they needed a new PlayStation or a digital camera. No wonder the doorman let us straight in, he was probably glad of the business. The look of disappointment on everyone's face … it wasn't even a free bar. We'd gone from front stage at the Brits to backstage at the Shits.

As I stood there wondering what to say, some bellend appeared out of nowhere and shouted a bit of abuse at Leigh, totally uncalled for. Now, Leigh is the nicest person ever, not a bad bone in that lad's body. I, on the other hand, haven't got time for idiots. Randomly, this bloke had a few pencils in his shirt pocket so I quickly grabbed hold of his collar, pulled him in close and told him exactly where I was gonna shove those pencils if he didn't piss off. It worked but Christine saw what happened and got a bit upset at me for getting involved. Obviously she was right to be upset but Leigh's a mate and that's what you do.

The mood had changed slightly so I suggested we find a nicer bar for a few more drinks. Peter and the rest of the group, apart from Elaine Bedell, had now gone home, so myself, Christine, Leigh, Jill and Elaine went off to find another bar. If you've never been to the O2, it's an absolute ball ache to get to. There's only one road in and out and the traffic is horrendous. To do a couple of miles in the car can take nigh on two hours, which none of us were particularly up for. The O2 is right on the River Thames and Elaine mentioned that there's usually a Thames Clipper or some kind of water taxi doing the rounds. This meant a two-hour journey could be done in 15 minutes – perfect!

'I'm not sure they're still running this late, though?' said Elaine.

Off we marched down to the docks and when we got there, Elaine was right, everything was closed up. This was in 2011 and *Take Me Out* was just becoming really popular; people had started to recognise me a bit more and the phrases from the show were catching on. Just as we thought it was the end of the night, I heard a voice say, 'No likey, no lighty!' It was the Thames Clipper operator from behind the locked fence. I pounced. It was time to redeem myself with the group. I started to chat to him, struck up a nice rapport and, after a bit more small talk, hit him with it.

'Any chance you can run us down the Thames, pal?' I asked.

'No chance, we're closed for the night,' he said.

'C'mon, yer bastard, let us on.'

I always find when dealing with blokes a friendly curse word works wonders. If you like someone, it's always C this or F that, it's when you don't like someone that it's usually 'mate' this or 'buddy' that. For instance, 'Mate, do you want those pencils jamming up your arse?' See what I mean?

Anyhow, after much cussing and back slapping, he opened up and let us on. I'd done it! Everyone was very pleased and none more so than me.

'I've only ever done this for someone once before,' he said.

'Who?' I asked.

'Elton John.'

'I'm in good company. Now get that paddle going, tiny dancer.'

I'd managed to commandeer the Thames Clipper just for us. In the short journey, we had a few drinks on there and a dance. He dropped us more or less right outside this hotel that was hosting the Universal Records after-party. We walked straight in, same phone trick, and this was a proper do. We bumped straight into Paloma Faith and while we were chatting I noticed Peter Jones of *Dragons' Den* fame trying to get access into the VIP section where Take That were sat. I remember thinking, *This bloke's got around 300 million quid in the bank but he doesn't know the phone trick.* Having said that, I'd gladly swap him the trick for his millions.

CHAPTER 20

DAD

*I don't think I ever fully understood my dad
or what made him tick. The one thing I do know is
he made me laugh a lot and I loved being with him.
Whenever we were together I did nothing but smile.*

All through my childhood I idolised my dad. He was funny, told me fantastic stories and I'd be bursting with excitement every weekend waiting for him to pick me up from my mum's. Skip forward many, many years and I'd now moved my dad into my mum's bungalow. I made sure all his rent was taken care of and bought him a nice car. He was very happy, especially as he'd met Margaret, a lovely lady I'm still in touch with to this day. She'd owned a well-known chippy in Bolton called Rigby's for well over 30 years and was more or less retired when my dad moved into the bungalow. Her daughters still worked at the chippy and Margaret lived above it. My dad had got friendly with her over the years and eventually they started courting (that's dating to you young 'uns). Her husband had passed away years previously so they found a much-needed companion in one another.

My dad was in his late seventies and Margaret was in her late sixties. Every time I visited them at the bungalow, guaranteed all I'd hear was laughter coming from the living room. They were mates and made each other very happy so that was good enough for me. I never worried about Margaret replacing my mum either – all I'd known in my lifetime was my mum on her own so I certainly never thought of my parents as a couple. Margaret was a godsend, especially towards the end of my dad's life. There's no way I would've been able to cope with work, looking after the kids and all my dad's appointments and medication. Margaret did all that for me and I'll never forget how much she helped or how happy she made my dad.

Having said that, there were moments when the pair of them would have me pulling what's left of my hair out. They loved getting away together but no matter where I'd offer to send them my dad would always pick Blackpool and a hotel called the Queens, right on the promenade. It's a proper old-school hotel, think Ponderosa from *Phoenix Nights*, and it wasn't cheap either – but my dad and Margaret loved it there so that's where they'd go. No matter what I said it'd always fall on deaf ears.

'Dad, what about I send you and Margaret to a lovely villa abroad?' I'd suggest.

'Queens,' he'd say.

'Dad, for that price you can go anywhere.'

CHAPTER 20

'Blackers, son.'

This back and forth would last about 20 minutes, after which time I'd give in and get the Queens booked. Also I'd have to drop them off and pick them back up a week later. It was a pain but my dad could be a funny bugger with taxis and strangers so I was not only travel agent but also designated driver. This one time I dropped them off and got on with the rest of my week. The day before I was due to pick them up, I'd popped into Manchester for a haircut. I was sat in the chair with the gown wrapped round my shoulders, mid trim, when my phone rang. It was Margaret so I answered straight away. I knew she'd only be calling if there was a problem and with my dad being in his late eighties at the time, I got that sickly feeling in my stomach.

'Hiya, Margaret, everything OK?' I asked.

Now in my experience OAPs have a certain way of asking you things. They like to give you cryptic conundrums that you have to patiently work out when all you want is an answer.

'Now what day is it?' she said.

'Erm, it's Thursday,' I said, wondering where this was going. I was also very relieved that it wasn't a call to say my dad had collapsed in the Queens!

'Yes,' she said. Then the line fell silent. It was the holy trinity of problematic phone calls. I had conundrums, Margaret's hearing and a bloke with a pair of clippers giving me the daggers because he was waiting to cut my hair.

'Hello, Margaret? Are you still there?' I asked.

'Yes, I'm here. Hello? Patrick?' she said.

'Yes, I'm still here, Margaret. I was just checking your phone hadn't lost signal. It's Thursday, love,' I said.

'Yes, it's Thursday. And what happens on Thursday?'

'Erm? Not sure? Haircut?'

'No.' Long pause. 'Me and your dad are in Blackpool.'

'Yes, I know, Margaret, I took you? Is everything OK?'

'We're waiting.'

'What for?'

'For you to take us home, remember?'

I explained to her that I was picking them up on Friday and they still had one more day of their holiday left.

'No, we're checking out today, Patrick. We're all packed and your dad's ready.'

Now the one thing that changed with my dad as he got older was that he got less chilled and towards the end he could get quite grumpy and throw his toys out of the pram at the smallest thing. I knew no matter if I was right or wrong that I'd have to get straight over to Blackpool or my name would be mud.

'OK, Margaret, tell him not to worry, I'll come straight for you.'

So I'm in Manchester, in the hairdresser's chair, loads of things to do and half a haircut.

'I've got to go, pal,' I said to the hairdresser.

'I've not finished your hair!' he said.

Even though he'd only done half of it, he still charged me full whack.

I ran to my car looking like I'd escaped from London fashion week and set off to Blackpool. The traffic was busy and it took me nigh on three hours to get there. That was three hours of weaving in and out of traffic, horn beeping, shouting and a lot of stress.

I finally pulled up outside the Queens and rang Margaret.

'I'm outside, Margaret,' I said.

Margaret made her way down to reception. She walked over to me with a smile on her face, that same smile a child gives when they've been found out for being naughty.

'Where is he, Margaret? Where's your luggage?' I asked. She stood there for a moment, still smiling, and then hit me with the bombshell.

'You were right, it is tomorrow that we leave.'

Now what you've got to remember is I'm dealing with a couple in their seventies and eighties who were both away with the fairies. I took a deep breath and said:

'I've just spoken to you a few hours ago, Margaret, and said that I'd come straight over?'

'Yes, you did, and it was only when I put the phone down and got talking to your dad and the hotel staff that we realised you were right, it is tomorrow you should be picking us up.'

At this point I was two parts perplexed, one part enraged, telling myself to stay calm.

'Margaret, did you not think of phoning me back when you realised?' I asked.

'Well, I did think about it because I said to the lady on reception that you'd be on your way over and it shouldn't be till tomorrow,' she said.

In my head there was a lot of naughty words flying about but what I actually said was:

'Oh, that's a bit of a pain, Margaret, where's my dad now?'

'He's in bed.'

'In bed?'

'Yes, when we realised it was the wrong day he decided to have a little nap before we have a walk up the promenade.'

I said I'd go up and see him before I left. I walked in their hotel room and there's my dad lying on the bed, shorts and T-shirt on, hands behind his head, legs crossed, blissfully looking out of the window. He always insisted on a sea view.

He looked at me and said, 'You shouldn't be here till tomorrow.'

I'm not a violent man but the thought of taking my dad and Margaret to the top of Blackpool Tower and throwing them off did cross my mind.

'I know, Dad, that's what I said to Margaret on the phone earlier but no one phoned me back,' I said.

He then reached for his glasses, put them on, looked at me and said, 'What have you done to your hair?'

It was at that moment I left. I told them I'd be back for them the following day.

On my way home I rang Christine to tell her what had happened. She knew how bloody dozy they were and wasn't in the least bit surprised. My stress and blood pressure had now gone down and we both had a good laugh about it. If I didn't laugh, I'd cry. Even now when I think back to that day it makes me smile. I love that generation of people – they can be frustrating at times but they're proper characters and definitely cut from a different cloth.

To be fair, though, I suppose I owed him. He'd always been calm with me – even when I crashed his car when I was 17 he didn't get annoyed. All my crew from college used to play snooker in a little club not far from mine so I asked my dad if I could borrow his car to get there. With no hesitation, he threw me the keys and told me to be careful; he was chilled like that. I was so excited – driving was a big deal for me and I couldn't wait to show off to the boys at the snooker club.

It was only five minutes from my mum's in the car so off I went in my dad's Metro. I wasn't far from the club when I spotted an old school mate by the name of Lowey. He was driving, with his girlfriend at the side of him. Lowey had passed his driving test and was fully legal. I beeped my horn: this was a big moment, that excitement when you're driving and spot a mate for the first time. Ever the bloody show-off, I decided to overtake him, not the easiest of things to do in a Metro, considering you could probably pedal faster on a pushbike. It was downhill so I slowly started to get past him. As I drew level, I looked at him and he looked at me. We both smiled and gave each other the obligatory Vs. In this moment of utter joy, I failed to notice the traffic lights we were fast approaching were on red. Bang!!! I went straight into the back of a Datsun Bluebird. The front of my dad's Metro was goosed! The bonnet was concertinaed and the radiator was haemorrhaging water. Lowey rolled past, beeped his horn, laughed and said, 'See you later, Paddy.' And that was that. I was left there alone with no idea what to do.

Naturally I was shitting myself. What was I going to say to my dad? I was still sat behind the wheel in a state of shock when the driver of the Bluebird got out. He was an old West Indian fella and luckily for me very laidback. Now the thing about those Datsun Bluebirds was they had steel front and rear bumpers and they were solid. I got out to look at the damage on the old boy's car and honestly you'd have to look very carefully to find anything. Mine on the other hand was a complete write-off.

I was stuck for words and panicking. He asked if I had any insurance. I just blurted out, 'It's my dad's.' He laughed and said, 'Don't worry, I've no insurance, too much cost.' With this a police van pulled up at the side of us and I'll never forget that moment. This copper didn't even stop, he just slowly rolled past in his van, popped his head out the window and said, 'Everything OK?' Myself and the old fella said yes in union. With that, and with his van still rolling, he said, 'OK, abide by the law.' And drove off! Abide by the law? Here was a young lad who'd just totalled a car into the back of an old bloke with no insurance!

The old geezer drove off and I was now there on my own, with my dad's car still in the middle of the road. I didn't even know about things like putting your hazards on back then. Instead I left the car there, still with the keys in, and sprinted back home to tell my dad. I'm talking full-on stiff fingers sprinting, Usain Bolt wouldn't have got close. I burst into my mum's front room and, still panting for breath, told my dad what had happened. Even though he didn't live with us my dad would often be at our house, if only for his tea and to watch telly.

'Where is it now, son?'

'It's still there, Dad.'

He asked if I was OK.

'Apart from my lungs, yes,' I said.

He chuckled and said, 'Come on, show me where it is.'

That sums up my dad's personality nicely. He was so chilled and matter-of-fact about the whole thing. In fact, the only thing he was concerned about was if I'd left the hazards on or not.

Somehow we managed to get the car back home. I felt terrible about the situation. I wasn't a spoiled kid who'd been given everything in life and didn't appreciate things. I knew that Metro was the most expensive thing my dad owned. He didn't have any money at the best of times so replacing the car or meeting the repair costs would've been impossible. Luckily, he'd been around enough cars over the years to bodge up a few of the jobs on his own. For the next 12 months we'd drive around with a bungee cord holding the bonnet down and a massive bottle of water to keep the radiator topped up.

Like I've said before, one of the most upsetting things for me was never being able to spoil my mum while she was alive because that's exactly what I would've done, although she'd probably never have accepted it. My dad on the other hand wasn't shy about me treating him and till the day he died it was always in the back of my mind about that old Metro and how he never made me feel bad about it. I loved that about him.

* * *

Dad had been married before and had a grown-up family I knew nothing about as a child. In fact, the first time I laid eyes on one of my siblings was around the time I was working at Vibroplant, so I was in my early twenties. My dad had asked me to go along with him to a nearby house. He told me about this lady who wanted to get away from her boyfriend who was a bit controlling. He said the bloke was a bit of a wrong 'un and he might turn up while we were there. My dad was a big powerful bloke and wasn't shy of a scrap but he'd done time in the past for beating up another abusive boyfriend and he didn't want it to happen again. Even though he wanted to avoid getting physical, there's always potential for things to go wrong in these kind of situations.

When we got there, this bloke was dismantling a motorbike in his front room. He was a long-haired rocker type and there was oil and bits of bike parts everywhere. He was quiet at first but as we started removing her possessions out of the house he began to get agitated.

He cast me a look and asked her, 'Is this your new boyfriend?'

I also had long hair at the time and I was in my oily Vibroplant overalls, I'd just finished work. I can see why he thought I was her new fella, well, apart from the fact that I was around 20 years younger than her and she was my sister, although at the time I didn't have a clue. I'm not sure if it's a man thing but sometimes you can meet someone you've never met before in your life and instantly know if he's a knobhead or not. He definitely was. I looked at her and could see she was nervous around him, and this wound me up. God knows what had gone on behind closed doors but I had an idea. I try not to lose my temper much because it never works out for the best but on this occasion I could feel myself getting a little heated.

The next thing I know my dad was ushering me out to the car and that was that, job done. We'd got all her stuff out and hopefully she could begin a new life.

I never saw or heard about her again after that until around ten years later when my dad told me she'd passed away with cancer. That was when he revealed it was my sister. Although I was shocked, I never showed it. I didn't want him to feel awkward so I pretended like I wasn't that taken aback. My dad was so old school I never ever saw him cry but I could feel his sadness. The last thing he needed was me asking him why he'd never told me before. He kept a lovely ornamental cat on the side of his fireplace that belonged to her and weirdly enough, even though I never knew her myself, I felt close to her every time I looked at it.

* * *

My dad's passing was different to my mum's. My mum's was sudden and unexpected but my dad had been diagnosed with pancreatic cancer and we all know how awful and drawn out that can be. For me the hardest part was seeing his deterioration, both physically and personality-wise. My dad had always been so physically strong and unafraid of death. He used to tell me that when he died, I was to just stick him in a hole in the ground without a fuss. I nearly did on that day in Blackpool.

'Son, if I ever end up in an old folks' home just shoot me.'

As a young lad my dad was my hero and to see this big power-ful man reduced to a frail shadow of himself killed me. I'm sure any of you who've been through this can relate but I was actually relieved when my dad passed away. His quality of life had gone, and his spirit had disappeared: he was just a shell.

Even when he got his diagnosis, he was quiet, and I asked all the questions. It was as if he didn't want to hear or believe what the doctor was saying. That old-school mentality of it'll be fine, I'll just walk it off. The change in him was slow but dramatic. Even in his eighties, he was always laughing and joking, loved his food and had a healthy appetite. I loved watching my dad eat when I was a kid. He'd take us out for steak and I'd sit there with my sirloin covered in ketchup, much to the disgust of the chef. My dad didn't care – I was happy and that's all that mattered.

A lot of my memories from my childhood revolve around my dad's love of food and driving. To see him lose interest in both was heartbreaking. The hardest part of it all for me was taking his car away. Margaret had told me on the quiet about her concerns. My dad had driven through a few red lights without realising and he'd become very complacent. It was such a tough decision because I knew how much driving meant to him but I couldn't live with myself if he ended up hitting a child or killing someone. I'd bought him the car, which had given me great happiness, and now here I was a couple of years later taking the keys back off him. I think he knew deep down that it was for the best but I know it hurt his pride, that it was the end of his independence.

He didn't laugh any more; in fact, he barely spoke towards the end. I'd go round to visit him and he'd just sit watching TV, scarcely saying two words to me. The only thing he'd talk about was his 90th birthday. I think it gave him something to focus on. Maybe it was a way of coping? If he spoke about it happening then in his head the cancer wasn't going to get in the way. He was also dead against going into hospital and made me promise him that wouldn't happen. He just wanted to be in my mum's old bungalow with Margaret and that's exactly what happened. He did spend one night in hospital but I was there with him to make sure I got him straight back home. At the end of someone's life they just want to be happy, they don't care about hanging around a bit longer if it's going to be in a hospital bed, they just want to be surrounded by their loved ones. All of Margaret's family looked after my dad like he was one of their own.

My dad passed away in 2013. I was sat at home with Christine. Leo and Penelope were barely 12 months old so we were up to our eyes in Bonjela and nappies. Margaret phoned and I knew from the tone of her voice something wasn't right. She asked if I could come straight over. He was laid in my old bed, that same bed I lay in when my mum passed away. He was slouched down and Margaret was struggling to lift him up. He was in a lot of pain.

'Come on, Dad, let's get you sat up,' I said.

I wrapped my arms around him and sat him up against the bed head. The strong man I knew was now frail and light in my arms. I held his hand and spoke to him for a while. We'd given him something for the pain and I asked if he'd like a cup of tea. Although he didn't, he said yes – there's something lovely about having a cup of tea made for you, it makes you feel safe and loved. I knew both my parents loved me and me them but none of us really said it out loud a lot. I make a point of telling my kids how much I love them pretty much all the time. I never really shared those words with my dad but on this particular occasion I did. I didn't want him to feel like I was saying it because he was on his last legs so instead I made a few jokes about how I couldn't keep coming over to lift him in bed so he'd have to get his arse up instead. We laughed quite a bit that night and, weirdly, for a few minutes it was like having my old dad back again. I told him I loved him that evening more than I'd ever told him in my life. He said he was comfy and I left his cup of tea at the side of the bed.

I also did something else I'd never done, I kissed him on the head. I hated that feeling of now being the person who was caring for my dad. The feeling of being looked after by your parents is the best feeling in the world. Knowing there's someone there for you who will do anything for you is an incredibly strong bond and when that gets flipped around, the reality of adulthood and life becomes very stark. I left him on the bed and spoke to Margaret in the living room. I told her to call me straight away no matter what time if she needed any more help that evening. My dad was chilled and Margaret was there with him. I got in my car and headed back home to Christine and the kids. No sooner had I pulled up on our drive when my phone rang again. Margaret was in tears and panicking.

'Please come straight back, Patrick. I've called an ambulance.'

Within no more than 20 minutes we'd gone from thinking everything was OK to my dad collapsing. By the time I got back, the ambulance was already there and they were giving him chest compressions. It was an awful feeling because I just wanted to tell them all to leave him. I knew that was it and all I wanted to do was hold him. Eventually they did stop working on him. He was unconscious but still had a very faint pulse. I went up to the hospital with him where the doctors told me that he would be gone within the next few minutes. By now some other people had turned up who I'd never met before: his children from a previous life, my half-brother and -sisters. They were all a lot older than me and even though I never knew them, it didn't feel strange them being there. After all, he was their dad too, even if he'd not seen any of them for years. I held his hand until I felt his pulse slowly fade away to nothing. I was truly heartbroken and in floods of tears; this was different from the sudden shock of my mum passing away. I was now on my own in the world, and even though I was very much independent the feeling of losing both parents was immensely upsetting. That was it, the two most important and loved people in my life were now gone.

* * *

My dad had no money and didn't own a property so I was surprised to find he'd made a will instructing what money he had in the bank to be left to my children. This was a shock as I'd been paying all his bills, along with giving him money if he ever needed it. He was a bugger for borrowing money off these doorstep lenders and I'd paid off so many of his debts over the years only for him to keep borrowing more. Every time I did it, he'd promise me that would be the last time. In the end I'd just turn a blind eye to it. Having a wad of cash on him made him feel happy, even though I'd told him till I was blue in the face he didn't need to borrow money as I was paying for everything he needed. That was his old-school mentality, I suppose – he'd borrow money without any thought of paying it back and I secretly think he used to do it to impress Margaret. He had no idea that Margaret knew what he was doing and would often phone me to let me know he'd taken out another loan. We had a good dialogue going and even though we were both pissed off with it we kept my dad oblivious to the fact we knew what he'd been up to.

My dad was also a hoarder and I'd often joke with him how I'd be the poor bugger who had to shift all his shite once he'd died – stacks of books, clothes and any old tat he could lay his hands on. He even had a massive old-fashioned safe in the bungalow. This thing looked like it came straight out of the Bank of England vault, it was huge. Myself and Franny had to put it in the bungalow and we were the poor sods who had to break our backs getting it out again after he passed away. I've still got it in my garage – I can't even give it away. I don't mind because it reminds me of him and his quirky ways. When we opened it, to my surprise I found a stack of cash. I never counted it – I just gave it straight to Margaret. I know that's what he would've wanted so that's what I did. God knows how long he'd been bunging cash in there.

I've still got some of my dad's possessions, including a stuffed toy tiger from Blackpool, and even though they're worthless to anyone else, to me they're priceless. The only things I really wanted, before everyone came out of the woodwork, were a couple of rings he'd worn all his life. I wasn't concerned by what they were worth, it was the sentiment. They were both gold, one a belt-buckle ring and the other a Claddagh ring. I finished sorting all my dad's financial affairs, which cost me around £30,000, but all I was concerned about was getting those rings. I searched everywhere for them but then Margaret told me what he'd done. My dad had pawned all his jewellery for cash. To this day, that still plays on my mind. I'm upset that he pawned the rings, that someone took advantage of him and that I'll never see them again. Then again, knowing my dad it didn't surprise me: him and my mum were chalk and cheese when it came to money. When it comes to my personal finances these days, I'm definitely more like my mum but I've also got a bit of my dad in my head telling me to spend it and just enjoy life. All I know is I wish the pair of them were still around to enjoy their grandchildren and see how far their son has come in life and what I've achieved.

CHAPTER 21

SOCCER AID AND NO KNIGHTHOOD

Apart from the joy of taking part and all those wonderful once-in-a-lifetime opportunities, the best thing ultimately about Soccer Aid is we get to do all that along with raising millions of pounds for UNICEF. I've made some lifelong pals through playing in those games and Soccer Aid feels very close to my heart. Having said that, I won't be holding my breath for a knighthood after 2016. Knighthood? 2016? What happened then? Read on, my friend!

I'd played in a few charity football matches, the biggest being Tsunami Aid at Anfield in 2005, but in 2006 Robbie and Jonny came up with Soccer Aid for UNICEF. This was the charity football match of all charity football matches, the biggest names from world football coming together to play in one-off games every two years for UNICEF (from 2018 it became an annual event). I didn't play in the first couple but after seeing the list of players who took part – Maradona, Zola, Poyet, Gazza, Matthäus, Robson, Schmeichel, Dunga to name a few – I made it my mission to play in the third. Who'd have thought I'd go on to play in seven of them and become a Soccer Aid veteran! My first Soccer Aid was 2010 and the roll call of stars I've found myself mixing with on and off the pitch has been mind-blowing: just the Rest of the World team was ridiculous in itself. Woody Harrelson, Mike Myers, Will Ferrell, Edward Norton, Gerard Butler, Michael Sheen, Jeremy Renner, Niall Horan, Gordon Ramsay, Usain Bolt, James McAvoy, Sam Worthington … I mean, it's an impressive list and on top of that the teams included nigh on every world-class legendary footballer I'd watched play the game.

I was thinking about the former pros I've played with and it's some collection of names. Deep breath, here we go: Zidane, Shearer, Figo, Roy Keane, Robbie Keane, Ronaldinho, Cafu, Berbatov, Rooney, Sheringham, Seaman, Dida, Giggs, Neville (both of them), Lehmann, Shevchenko, Keown, Terry, Ashley Cole, Andy Cole, Joe Cole, Stam, Van der Sar, Touré, Kluivert, Pires, Crespo, Ljungberg, Fowler, Owen, Evra, Le Tissier, Given, Makélélé, Vassell, Kevin Phillips, Fletcher, Carragher, Silvestre, Defoe, Heskey, Essien, Redknapp, Murphy, Del Piero, Campbell, Walker, Scholes, Butt, Seedorf, Davids, Cannavaro, oh, and Eric Cantona! Then there's the managers: Ranieri, Mourinho, Robson, Redknapp, Allardyce, Dalglish, Rush, Eriksson and of course Bradley Walsh. This is like the ultimate boyhood dreams stuff – all that's missing is Magnum's Ferrari and Jo Guest!

During the day, the teams would train separately. It was usually the Rest of the World first then the England boys – we did like a lie-in. In the evenings everyone would congregate together on the top floor of the Chelsea Harbour Hotel. With that amount of A-listers around, security was tight so anyone up there could relax knowing no one would bother them. We always got lucky with the weather and I've spent many an evening on that balcony, shorts and flip-flops on, having a drink and a laugh with the boys. I sat one evening with Mike Myers and Will Ferrell just having a beer and chatting while all the while I'm thinking, *I'm having a beer with Austin Powers and Anchor Man.* It was like if Carlsberg did holidays. I even had a selfie with Jeremy Renner. One of the lads shouted it's not every day you get a selfie with Hawkeye.

Myself and Bradders would take turns hosting quiz nights and there was always someone regaling us with a story or two. The A-list American boys like Mike, Will and Jeremy were all so lovely and down-to-earth. I remember the first year Woody Harrelson played, what a cool bloke he was. It's well documented he loves a joint – his hotel room smelt like Bob Marley's shed. One morning I woke up, went on the balcony and looked across, and there's Woody puffing away. He didn't give a monkey's who could see him either. He even spent an hour with me in my room after the match so he could have a crafty smoke; it was the least I could do after he'd just scored the winning penalty. That was one of many surreal moments that Soccer Aid has given me over the years. I'd just finished playing in front of 70,000 at Old Trafford and now I'm sat in my hotel room with Woody from *Cheers.*

Back in the early days of Soccer Aid we had a great little crew who'd always sit at the back of the team coach playing cards and chatting. It was made up of myself, Jonny, Robbie, John Bishop, Jamie Redknapp, Matt Le Tissier, Jack Whitehall, Olly Murs, Marvin Humes and whoever ventured down. I was once in a big hand with

Bish and there was only me and him left in the pot. I won't say how much I won off him but it caused me to strip off my clothes and walk down the length of the team coach in celebration. I walked past Big Sam and he didn't even bat an eyelid – all pretty standard stuff at Soccer Aid. That particular year was more like the best stag do ever. Unfortunately we lost. Understandable with all the drinking that went on.

In truth, the least enjoyable part of *Soccer Aid* was the game itself. The attack of nerves I suffered when I walked out on to the pitch in front of a full house at Old Trafford with players of such calibre was unbelievable. It also doesn't do a lot for your confidence when you miss three penalties. That's what the pressure of the game and the crowd does to you. I'm always in the five penalty takers because they get picked in training. It's simple – we all keep taking penalties until the last five consistent goal scorers are left. The trouble is, I'm so relaxed and happy during training that scoring a pen even against a legend like David Seaman seems pretty straightforward.

My worst miss was in 2018. I was the fourth penalty taker – if I scored, we'd lift the trophy. I'd played well during the game but now I honestly felt like I was going to collapse walking to the penalty spot. I placed the ball down and I was absolutely shitting myself. I'm in front of 70,000 fans, along with millions watching at home. Just before I took it, Michael Owen told me to smash it, Danny Murphy said place it and Big Sam warned me not to look up. So I had smash it, place it and don't look up all whizzing around my head. In the end, I hit the worst penalty of my life and instantly wanted the ground to swallow me up. God knows how the likes of John Terry, Gareth Southgate, Darius Vassell or any other pro who has missed a penalty in a big game cope. I was at the Euro finals against Italy, and watching those young lads Rashford, Sancho and Saka step up to the plate was amazing in itself. During the Soccer Aid penalties I could barely walk up to the spot. I'm not a professional football player and I've still not gotten over it to this day. But thankfully the Rest of the World missed their penalties as well and we ended up winning the shootout 7–6.

I've got loads of Soccer Aid stories from over the years but the publishers need this book finishing so I'm going to go with 2016 because that year was up there with the best of them for surreal moments. It was the first time a couple of the One Direction lads played – Louis Tomlinson was in the England squad and Niall Horan was playing for the Rest of the World. Two great lads who I struck up a good rapport with, especially Nialler. In fact, Nialler was the one who set my Instagram account up for me and talked me through how it works. It reminded me of being around Robbie in the early days – normal working-class lads who just happened to be global pop stars. That year England were managed by José Mourinho and Big Sam and the Rest of the World were managed by Claudio Ranieri. Both teams spent a lot of time together in the evenings in the form of quiz nights, card schools and just general fun. We'd had a blast all week and on the last night we had a proper big session planned. The following day was just the coach journey up to Manchester so we could recuperate before the game the following day.

One of the people you won't have heard of behind the scenes at Soccer Aid is a bloke called Kenneth Shepherd. Kenneth is a football agent and his family used to be heavily involved with Newcastle Football Club back in the day. I really like Kenneth, he's quiet but has a great sense of humour and is always good for a chat. On the last night he'd organised for us to go to this club/restaurant in Chelsea called Jak's, and had sorted us a private section with our own bar. This would turn out to be one of the funniest if not strangest nights of my life. From the England team there was myself and Jonny, Big Sam, Jamie Carragher, Louis Tomlinson, Mark Wright, John Bishop, Marvin Humes, Danny Jones, Jack Whitehall and our team of physios. From the Rest of the World team we had Niall Horan, Nicky Byrne, Cafu, Ronaldinho, Dida and a few others.

As the night progressed, everyone was having a great time drinking and dancing. When the DJ dropped a samba tune, the Brazilians took to the floor like they owned it. They were fantastic movers but Jamie Carragher had other ideas.

'I can dance better than that,' he informed me.

'Carra, I don't think you can match the Brazilians when it comes to the samba. We struggle with the football!' I said.

Before you could say Copacabana, the Bootle Brazilian was up having a full-on dance-off with Cafu. We made a circle around them, clapping and cheering, but as you can imagine

Liverpool's answer to Bruno Tonioli was getting danced off the floor by Brazilian legend Cafu. In a desperate last grasp (literally) of redemption, he grabbed Cafu by the knackers and attempted to pick him up. The Brazilian lads were laughing their heads off and in one last bid for dance-floor glory, Carragher attempted the windmill only to finish up upside-down against a wall. That was the point where things really got weird.

Jack Whitehall was a mate of Prince Harry's at the time and unbeknown to us had arranged to meet him in Jak's. I was already three parts pissed when someone said, 'Harry's here.' I honestly thought they were on about Redknapp. All of a sudden I heard:

'I want to go to Fernando's!'

I looked around and our group had parted to reveal this bloke standing looking at me. I gave my head a bit of a shake.

Fuck me, it's Prince Harry, I thought.

This is when it got really, really weird. He shouted, 'Fernando's!' came over to me and immediately started another dance-off. Forget samba, this was the royal edition. The lads were now all around us clapping – it was on. After Carragher, it was time for me to bring a bit of northern soul to the dance floor. To say we were dancing close would be an understatement – our chests were touching. He asked again if I could send him to Fernando's.

'I don't think you need any help in that department, pal,' I shouted back, still in a slight state of shock as to what was happening. He then proceeded to take my T-shirt off. So now I'm in the middle of the dancefloor, topless, a bottle of beer in each hand, dancing with Prince Harry. He was a great lad and I really liked him, even though the circumstances were slightly surreal to say the least.

He then disappeared and I popped my shirt back on. All the boys were in disbelief at what they had just witnessed. I was talking to Niall Horan and John Bishop about how mad that was when all of a sudden the prince pops up again. 'Can I get you a Jägerbomb?' he said.

'Of course you can, Harry.' By this point, formalities had gone out the window. The Brazilian lads were open-mouthed watching all this unfold – they couldn't believe it either. We knocked them back and made our way on to the dance floor for another round of the Soccer Aid dance-off 2016. We finished dancing and while everyone was cheering, we embraced and he gave me a smacker on the lips. That was male bonding one on one. That was that and off he went, to rapturous applause from the lads.

The One Direction boys said it was the most random night they'd ever witnessed. 'You're not on your own, lads,' I said.

What an absolute legend he was. I totally get why he wanted to step away from royal life. He seemed a genuine, down-to-earth lad to me, and being in that royal bubble must be so pressurised. Apparently he was a massive fan of *Take Me Out* and just wanted to let his hair down with the boys. We definitely did that. There was CCTV in the club but I was reassured by the powers that be that it'd never see the light of day. It's now just one of those legendary Soccer Aid nights where you had to be there to take it all in.

The following day on the coach, Jack got a text message off Harry saying to thank Paddy for such a great night and asking how my head was. I said to tell him thank you, I had a great night.

On the way up to Manchester, both team coaches pulled in at Knutsford Services. It was there that I introduced World Cup winners Ronaldinho, Cafu and Dida to their first Greggs. I bought them all a sausage roll and wished them well for the game. Just another day at Soccer Aid.

CHAPTER 22

MARRIAGE AND KIDS

Everyone needs a house to live in,
but a supportive family is what builds a home.
Anthony Liccione

Dirty dancing with royalty aside, my home life is pretty ordinary. I like to get home, put my comfies on and chill out. Myself and Christine know exactly when to give each other a bit of space as well. In fact, on paper you'd never put myself and Christine together – we are polar opposites with no common interests. We don't like the same films, TV programmes or food, we wouldn't have a night out together, and we annoy each other most of the time. I hardly know any of her mates, and aside from living in the same house we have totally separate lives. So why are we still married after a decade? Answer: we laugh and make love … a lot. Laughter and love-making is the glue that keeps us together. In fact, Christine always says to me if it wasn't for the fact that I made her laugh from the first time we met we wouldn't have lasted a month. To be fair I'd have stuck it out a bit longer as she's drop-dead gorgeous.

We first met at a big tennis event in Liverpool. Players like John McEnroe and Björn Borg were playing exhibition matches there. I've no real interest in tennis but my mate, Dave Lockwood, had invited me several times before and I'd run out of excuses as to why I couldn't attend. The day was nice enough, watched a bit of tennis, drank a few Pimm's and then food was served indoors. I was sat with Dave on his table when he said the fashion show was about to start. Fashion show at the tennis? We tucked into our food while various models walked around the room in sport and fashion outfits. I was chatting away to Dave and not paying that much attention to the proceedings until it was announced through the PA that the next part was the swimwear section. Strangely, at this point I suddenly became a bit more interested. Out walked all these models in their swimwear and straight away I spotted Christine. I'd never seen anyone as beautiful in my life but aside from that she just exuded confidence. I had to meet her. Luckily for me, Dave pretty much knows everyone in Liverpool.

'You're in luck, I know her. That's Christine.'

I don't think I've ever begged but I was practically on my knees asking Dave to introduce me.

Despite all my frolicking over the years, I was still very shy when it came to talking to women, especially those who looked like they'd just stepped off the front cover of *Vogue*. At the time I was overweight and drinking too much. *Take Me Out* wasn't even a thing and the last programme of note that I'd done on the telly was *Max and Paddy*.

The fashion show finished and I was pestering Dave to introduce me.

'Dave! Where's she gone? I thought you were bringing her over!'

'Relax, mate, I'll sort it now.' And off he went.

Five minutes later he appeared with a now fully clothed Christine. Honestly, she's still gorgeous now but back then when she walked into a room everyone would stop and stare. She looked like a Hollywood star and the sex appeal was ridiculous.

Dave introduced her and we had a bit of a stilted chat. It was awkward and I was nervous. We'd never met before and now we're sat at this dinner table, full of half-empty glasses of Pimm's and discarded napkins, me trying to think of some sparkling anecdotes. I'm not very good at the suave, romantic stuff, so I ended up going back to my default setting, which was to make her laugh. The strategy paid off because she agreed to meet me for a drink later that evening in Liverpool. Yes! I was over the moon.

A few hours later, I was nursing a drink in a bar, wondering if she was going to show up or not. Suddenly in walks Christine. She had a short gold dress on, high heels and the longest legs I'd ever seen. She turned every single head in that bar, male and female! It was like the scene from *Wayne's World* when the soft-rock ballad plays when he sees the girl of his dreams. We sat at a quiet table, which in Liverpool is a challenge of its own, and talked. I was now on form when it came to the chat and she laughed a lot. After an hour or two, she said she had to leave to meet up with her friends at a club in town but hopefully we could see each other again. I was buzzing. Like I said, back then I wasn't exactly catch of the day.

Overweight, bloated, unhealthy ... and I certainly didn't have any money to speak of. She once said to me that if I hadn't met her that night, I'd have never had the success I've had over the years.

'How do you work that one out?' I asked. 'I don't remember seeing you standing next to me while I was working my bollocks off onstage or on TV?'

'Well, if you hadn't met me, you'd have been a dickhead and cocked your career up,' she explained, and she definitely has a point. I had no responsibilities back then: my life was going out, drinking, one-night stands and touring. If I'd have worked on a show like *Take Me Out* before I settled down, I'd probably have lasted one or two series before I got myself sacked. I'd have ended up on *Celebrity Big Brother* and, shortly after, back on the building sites labouring.

At first we didn't really have a conventional relationship. For a long while we'd just meet up at hotels, have a laugh, sleep together and leave. It was all very casual and we were both happy with that. Our relationship was a real slow burner. I couldn't tell you how long it was till Christine first stayed over at my house. I know one thing, though, it saved me a few quid on Premier Inns.

Eventually, Christine started staying over more and more, until she was there more often than she wasn't. It took a while for us to settle down and commit but now we're thirteen years and three fantastic kids down the line. The way our relationship formed and grew was very natural, and I think that's been the making of it. It wasn't an intense never-apart-from-each-other relationship, it was more casual, which gave us time to grow into being a couple.

We work as a team now, as much as we can. When you have three children with autism, you have to. We don't have a lot of nights out together because we can't really leave the kids with anyone overnight. Christine's mum can manage the odd night but usually something goes wrong. I can count on one hand the amount of nights out we've had together in the last five years. The one night we look forward to supporting is the Pride of Britain Awards but even then, soon as it's over it's straight in the back of a car home for us so we can sort the kids out in the morning. Before the kids were born, we'd have lots of great parties at home and amazing holidays with our close group of friends – in hindsight we wish we'd done more but you can't predict what life will be like when you have children.

Our holidays and having friends round for parties soon fizzled out and we just got on with the business of raising three autistic children. Our twins Leo and Penelope are now eight and Felicity is five. Myself and Christine have spoken a lot about autism but there's so much more to say that I'm going to write another book just on my experiences of being a parent of autistic children. There's a hell of a lot of highs, lows and complexities that I couldn't possibly fit into one chapter so I'm not going to go too much in depth. I'll tell you how it felt becoming a parent but everything else will be for another book. I owe that to all the other families out there who are struggling or looking for answers.

Having a baby for the first time is a learning curve for any couple, but twins straight off the bat, well, that was one baptism of fire. I remember Christine doing a pregnancy test at home but the little line that's supposed to appear with a positive test was very faint.

We didn't know whether to get excited or not so the following day it was back to the shop for another test. This time the line was clear as a bell and we jumped for joy, although I was already telling Christine to take it easy. We had no idea she was pregnant with twins until our first scan. We were both very excited but nervous on our way to the hospital. In the back of my head I still couldn't believe Christine was pregnant, especially after trying on and off for a few years.

The sonographer squirted Christine's tummy with gel and set about doing the ultrasound. The moment that little image popped up on the screen was magical.

'There's the heartbeat,' she said.

I instantly burst into tears of happiness, as did Christine. It was such a lovely moment, one of pure joy. We'd done it – we'd made a baby! Then the sonographer went quiet.

'Oh, hang on,' she said. 'There's another heartbeat, you're having twins.'

Now I'm crying for the wrong reasons. Twins! How are we gonna cope? I'll never be able to retire! Joking aside, what a beautiful moment. We left the hospital floating on air. Christine had two little lifeforms inside her and we couldn't wait to meet them. I'll never forget when we got in the car. I flicked the radio on and the song 'Baby Love' was playing – what a coincidence. We sang our heads off all the way home.

The only problem with parenthood for me – well, apart from the lack of sleep, exhaustion, stress, your house being ruined and having nothing for yourself any more – is the worry. From the minute I found out Christine was pregnant I worried about my kids and they hadn't even been born yet. That's the only thing I envy about people who choose not to have children – they'll never know what real worry is like. You've got a human being to raise and all the things that come with it. I don't think I'll ever stop worrying about my kids, regardless of the autism.

A prime example of this was around about a month or two after that first scan. I was in Manchester to pick up some suits for *Take Me Out* when my phone rang. It was Christine and she was in floods of tears. She'd been at home on her own and was doing a bit of tidying up around the house. Even though I would constantly tell her to just take it easy, Christine still liked to keep active during the pregnancy. She'd suffered a massive bleed and was convinced she'd lost the babies.

Manchester to Bolton takes about 30 minutes in the car. I was home in 15! I ran every red light and speed camera! I was in bits myself and when I got home I found Christine curled up on the bathroom floor. I picked her up and carried her to bed. We rang the hospital and told them what had happened but they said we'd need to wait for the bleeding to stop and to go in the following day. That was the longest 24 hours of our lives and I held Christine all night on our bed. Neither of us slept. The day after we drove to the hospital. The journey felt like it took forever and all the way I was reassuring Christine the babies would be fine, even though I was preparing for the worst.

The sonographer got Christine ready and began the scan. God, it felt like an eternity until she said, 'There's those heartbeats, your babies are fine.'

I felt my legs buckle: the relief actually knocked me for six. We were both crying again and I was the most relieved dad ever. I'm convinced I lost a few years of my life over that but what a feeling to find out everything was OK. It turns out it was just Christine's body getting rid of various things it no longer needed after she became pregnant. From that moment on, I practically wrapped her in bubble-wrap and it was rare I even left her alone until the kids were born.

On 2 July 2013 our twins arrived and I was happy for all of two minutes. They'd just handed my son Leo to me and before I knew it they'd taken him straight off me due to some breathing difficul-ties he was having. Again, more worry – but I didn't tell Christine because she was still in the middle of giving birth to Penelope! Eventually everything settled down, we had amazing midwives and an obstetrician, Dr Bullen, who made the whole thing easy.

Our third child, Felicity, was a very happy accident. It was Christmas Eve and this should give you an idea of how roman-tic myself and Christine are. Her mum was due to stay with us over Christmas so while we were wrapping the kids' presents, Christine said:

'I think we better get a shag out of the way tonight because otherwise we won't be able to have another till my mum goes back home.'

'Good shout, love. Get yourself upstairs and I'll be with you as soon as I've finished building this Paw Patrol Tower.'

Nine months later – hello, Felicity!

Our life works now, although it's not ideal and it's certainly not conventional. We have our ups and downs but no more than most married couples. When I look at her, I still see that same gorgeous woman I first set eyes on in Liverpool but what really sets her apart is she's the best mum our kids could wish for. The kids always come first and if I'm away working or vice versa we both know one of us will always be here with them.

So my tips for a happy marriage are: laughter, intimacy and, budget permitting, separate Sky boxes and bathrooms!

CHAPTER 23

MENTAL HEALTH

It was a random chat with a friend way back in the noughties that first planted the auld Therapy seed. I can't remember how it cropped up in conversation but we started to talk about the whole therapy thing. I nearly fell through the floor when this friend told me he'd been getting help for a while – this was a person I'd put my mortgage on not being in therapy or anything like that. It made me think, *Well, if they're going through it then I've no excuses not to.* That's kind of why I'm putting it in this book – hopefully one of you reading this might feel the same way, especially the lads. Well, let me tell you this: getting help and talking about how you feel works. Not only was it a weight off my shoulders but it actually made me feel really good.

'So what do you do when you're there?' I asked my mate.

'Well, you just talk,' he said.

'Yeah, and then what happens?'

'You just work things out together.'

And that's all there is to it, really, there's no big secret, it's just talking to someone who doesn't know you and won't judge you but has the qualifications to help you understand why you're feeling this way or why panic attacks occur when you've pushed your body too far. Another thing I learned about therapists is that they're not always right for you, so don't let this put you off. Look at it like trying on a pair of new shoes. You can try a few different pairs in the shop and even though they're all the same size, some feel more comfortable than others. Eventually you settle on the pair that fits you best.

My first therapy session was arranged through my agent, Nick Worsley, a fellow Boltonian. I still felt a bit embarrassed by the whole thing and didn't want it to become public knowledge. I got the number of my mate's therapist and passed it on to Nick to make the appointment. The main reason I wanted to see the same person my mate had was down to the fact that she was a female. Again harking back to everything in my life, women were the people I trusted the most and I'd also feel more comfortable talking about my problems to a female as opposed to some bloke, because I know how all blokes' minds work. Again I was wrong.

So I was to see this lady at a hospital. Honestly, I was so paranoid about going there that Nick even booked me in after the place had closed under an alias.

I remember driving into the grounds and feeling super paranoid about being spotted. How many times have you heard about a famous person being admitted to a mental health unit for substance abuse? It was important to me to keep my treatment there away from any of that media speculation. 'Paddy McGuinness admitted to hospital.' No! So I had my cap pulled down over my eyes, never a good look when you're driving, and I was sweating like Dominic Cummings in Specsavers – oh, and at the time I was driving a black Ferrari, discretion personified. The lady was waiting for me at the door to let me in, thank frig for that! I felt instantly relieved once the door shut behind me, then that relief turned into confusion. Why am I stood in a store cupboard? In my initial panic to get in without being seen, I was looking down at the floor and walked into the totally wrong room. Not a good start, but I suppose it broke the ice. Eventually I did go to the right room and even then I was a little surprised. I wasn't sure what to expect, really. Going off what you see in the films and TV, it's normally some plush office with a leather Chesterfield you put your feet up on. The rooms I had my sessions in were always small unfurnished box rooms with a couple of office chairs and maybe, if I was lucky, a small side table to put my phone and keys on. Welcome to therapy.

So there I was, my first ever session in therapy, no frills, just the two of us and a window, which again put me on edge in case anyone could see me. On my first session, after a brief chat, she gave me some forms to fill in. These were box-ticking questions along with describing things on a scale of one to ten. After completing all the paperwork, she officially diagnosed me with clinical depression. I couldn't get my head around it! I was down from the minute I'd been given the diagnosis that my children were autistic but I was totally unaware of how much it had actually affected me. Christine knew – in fact, she was the one who really pushed me into seeing someone after I'd mentioned that I was thinking about it. She could see my behaviour and character changing at home before I could.

Being down and depressed is one thing, being clinically depressed is a whole other ball game.

'I've come to talk about panic attacks, how have I got to that?' I asked.

'This will have started a year or so ago, maybe more,' she said. 'It starts off small and grows until it's all-encompassing. Many people just don't see it coming and then find themselves in the position you're in.'

She even asked me if I'd ever thought about suicide. I'd obviously been going through day-to-day life with this huge black cloud hanging over me. I had this job, where I had to be bright, shiny and bouncy the whole time, then I'd go home and crash. This had been going on for some time and it was taking its toll, not just on me, but on Christine, the kids, and on my work too. I sometimes think about what would have happened if I hadn't got help when I did. For a kick-off, I'd probably be divorced by now, and as for my career, well, I'd probably be in the jungle eating a kangaroo's dick while Ant and Dec throw buckets of shit at me.

Remember what I said about finding those shoes that fit just right? Even though I didn't feel any kind of connection with this therapist, the shock of being told I was clinically depressed was enough to keep me going back. Eventually, once I'd started getting my head around it all, I realised she wasn't really working for me. I could sense she couldn't care less about me and I know that's not a therapist's job but at least pretend to. I'd often catch her looking at the clock and on more than one occasion, she didn't even turn up for our sessions and admitted she'd completely forgotten. I couldn't believe that a professional person could be so blasé and thought-less, especially knowing what was going on with me. I had serious mental health issues and this woman couldn't wait for the session to finish. It got to the point where I started to feel negative about seeing her. In the end, I'd get so wound up about it I felt like I needed to see another therapist to get me through the therapy I was already in. So I made the decision to see someone else. I contacted my mate again and he recommended someone else. This time it was a male therapist, who was apparently more qualified.

Unfortunately, this fella was even worse than my first thera-pist. I didn't even make it into the room with this knobhead! The session was again at the same place. Nick had sorted it for me and I was to meet him at the usual entrance, right round the corner from the main entrance. It was in the evening, around sevenish. It was winter so it was pitch-black, which suited me. I parked up and immediately felt anxious. I was starting all over again. The entrance to the room we'd used on previous visits was right at the front so you could walk straight in without any hassle ... except that the door was locked. Jesus Christ, I felt exposed. I could hear other people milling about and started to feel a bit on edge. I tried the other three doors in the same corridor, all locked. My mind was all over the place. I got back in my car and felt myself getting really annoyed. One of the things with clinical depression is you become very irritable and very angry, very quickly. When I was driving I was always ready for some kind of confrontation. It's scary how quickly I could switch from normal rational person to full-on road-rage lunatic. I'd already had the previous therapist not show up to sessions and this new one wasn't faring any better. I rang Nick from the car park.

'How's it going, my man?' he asked.

'Well, it's seven o'clock in the evening and I'm sat in the car park with no sign of this new therapist.'

Nick told me to sit tight and he'd get straight on it. He called me back and said the therapist was on his way to me. After another 20 minutes or so, I saw this bloke walking towards me, great big plumes of smoke billowing around him as he puffed away on his vape. Surely to Christ this can't be him? When he got to the car, I wound down the window and looked up at him.

'The crimson cow flies east,' he said.

I immediately felt that hot feeling I get just before I blow my top. I've never been one for fighting that much but sometimes it just happens and once the mist settles someone's usually not in good shape. So this bloke was late, in the wrong place, sucking on a vape and was now trying to make light of how we were meeting.

When I get those bad feelings, it helps to think about my wife and kids – they'll be the ones who lose out if I do something stupid like sticking a vape pipe straight down a therapist's throat. I gave him a look that said it all really. He put his vape pipe away and quickly walked over to the building. I got out and followed him in.

We got to the room and I told him it was locked, to which he tried the door and said, 'Oh, it's locked?'

He then tried the other doors that were also locked. Even though I'd already told him this, he then started swearing under his breath.

'Oh, fucking hell, they're locked as well, I'll have to go and get the fucking keys.'

I can laugh about it now but how I didn't end up doing time for strangling him on the spot is a complete mystery to me. Off he went for the keys and I got back in the car to wait. I called Nick again. I needed to speak to someone because I was now at 11 on the doing-something-stupid scale.

He came back with a caretaker, who clearly recognised me – so much for keeping it all under wraps. He then tried all the keys but none of them worked. I decided to call it a night and walked away. I honestly couldn't believe what was going on.

He followed me and said, 'I've got a perfectly good office we can use in the main facility.'

He said it in a way that was clearly putting this whole farce on to me, as if to say why do you have to be seen in this tiny building out of the way? That was enough for me, after all his unprofessionalism and lack of empathy, this tool was still being a complete tosser. The keeping-my-head-down going-under-the-radar bit went out of the window. I didn't care who was listening or who was watching, I gave it him both barrels.

There was a fair amount of swearing and it went a bit like this:

'You BLEEPing sack of BLEEP, is this how you treat all your BLEEPing patients at their first appointment, you BLEEP? You've got someone coming to you for help, and you swan over late, smoking your BLEEPing vape chatting BLEEP. You're a BLEEPing disgrace, you should be embarrassed, you BLEEP! Don't even think about billing me for this either. You can stick your session up your BLEEPing BLEEP!'

There was a lot more swearing and home truths thrown in there but you get the picture. He could see how quickly I'd turned and just stood there, head bowed like a naughty schoolboy. He knew I was right. He'd been completely offhand and flippant from the moment we met.

At that moment I was completely over therapy. It was a waste of money. The day after, Nick put in a complaint to the hospital. A gentleman there, one of the senior doctors, then contacted him. After speaking with him, Nick got back in touch with me.

'Paddy, I think you should go and see this guy. He's completely distraught at how you've been treated. He wants you to go back in and he's guaranteed that he'll see you himself as a client, which is something he doesn't normally do.'

I decided to give it one last shot, and thank God I did. Firstly, this guy had booked me into a spot that was even more tucked away. When I arrived for our first meeting, he was actually waiting for me on the car park – this was a good start.

'Patrick, let me take you straight in,' he said.

'No problem, Doc,' I said.

We got in this small, private room and I was instantly relaxed. As soon as he started talking, I liked him. All I want from a therapist is for someone to at least pretend they care, like it's not just a job, not sit there watching the clock or vaping. He was really engaged and that's all I needed. It was a completely different experience from the others I'd had, and I came out of the session knowing things were going to be all right.

I kept on seeing him for months and months. He literally changed the way I view the world. When I got the *Top Gear* job I knew my fear of flying was going to be a massive problem. This guy got me over that fear, and I can't speak highly enough of him, although professionally I can only refer to him as Doc. Those one-hour sessions every week were the best money I've ever spent, and that's including the time I went to Amsterdam in the nineties.

Eventually, I repeated that initial test to find out how I was progressing, and Doc told me I was no longer clinically depressed. It was a long road but finding that right pair of shoes made the walk a whole lot easier.

CHAPTER 24

TOP GEAR

Give it a go, life's too short not to.

*T*op Gear was a complete and utter bolt out of the blue for me. In my line of work it's easy to get pigeonholed into doing a certain kind of show and even though I'd done a car show of my own called *Stars in Their Cars* for the Discovery Channel, hardly anyone knew about it. The premise of the programme was that I'd track down cars that were once owned by a famous face and take them out for a spin down memory lane. Each celebrity had three cars they could drive: their first car, their favourite car and the car they bought when they'd started doing well for themselves. I really enjoyed doing it.

When someone leaves a high-profile TV show there's always lots of speculation in the press as to who'll be the next person to take over. If it was for hosting something like *The X Factor* or *Strictly* and my name got mentioned in the mix I wouldn't be surprised – not saying I'd get it but that's the genre I'm associated with. I'd made my name in the Saturday night light entertainment space and I was happy enough with that. In contrast, when Jeremy Clarkson embarked on a short-lived career in bare-knuckle boxing and left *Top Gear*, I would never have expected to be linked to that job because it's not what I was known for. In 2015 when the news hit, literally, about Clarkson, it was everywhere. Jezza was sacked and not long after that Hammond and May handed in their notices.

Over the following year the press went into meltdown talking about possible replacements but there was no mention of me and an ex-cricketer – why would there be? Eventually the new line-up was announced: Chris Evans would be taking over along with Matt LeBlanc, Eddie Jordan, Sabine Schmitz, Rory Reid and some prick called Chris Harris. Being a massive fan of the show, the biggest curveball for me was Matt LeBlanc. I knew he was a petrol head but on the other hand he was Joey from *Friends*. That decision was more random than me and Flintoff put together! I remember reading all the buzz about it and I was genuinely excited to see it back on the telly. Chris Evans was a mammoth name in the industry, he'd been there and got the T-shirt, so I thought the show would be in very safe hands. It wasn't long before I heard a rumour that things weren't going too well but I dismissed it as a bit of gossip.

I was in the middle of filming series eight of *Take Me Out* when the new series of *Top Gear* hit our screens. The amount of negativity towards the new line-up and particularly Chris Evans was insane. It was trending on Twitter and everyone seemed to be piling in with their opinions. I've worked in this job long enough to take all that stuff with a pinch of salt so I recorded the first episode and was really looking forward to watching it. Although it wasn't perfect, I actually didn't mind it. What I'd read online and what I watched on the screen felt like two totally different shows. It wasn't all that bad. Anyway, *Top Gear* had nothing to do with me so that was that, I got on with my life.

The viewing figures took a bit of a hit and Chris Evans parted ways after one series. Matt, Rory and Chris carried on for another three series and then Matt decided to quit. This was a pivotal time for me because Suzy Lamb and Mel Balac, the two driving factors behind *Take Me Out*'s success, had also just left. I was gutted, we'd been together on *Take Me Out* right from the get-go and the thought of doing the show without them just felt weird. The production company brought in a new producer, and although I got on well with them it never felt the same. I just had a gut feeling *Take Me Out* was coming to an end.

Just as I was fast approaching what could be a real low point, my phone rang. It was my agent Nick Worsley.

'Erm... bit of an interesting one. I've been chatting to the executive producer of *Top Gear* and they'd like to see you,' he said.

My first thought was they wanted me on as a guest. I'd been due to appear on the programme several years earlier but it never happened. It was around the time Richard Hammond had that horrendous crash that nearly killed him so all filming on the series had stopped.

'I've always wanted to do that reasonably priced car challenge,' I said.

'No, they want to talk to you about hosting it!' Nick told me.

'What? No way! How's that come about?'

Luck? Chance? This is exactly how it happened. The management company that represents me are called YMU. They look after lots of well-known faces from TV, film, sport and music. Even though Nick's my agent at YMU, he also looks after other names as well, all pretty standard stuff. At the time he was looking after Marvin and Rochelle Humes, as well as Tess Daly, and the three of them were all hosting *Children in Need*. The executive producer of that show was Clare Pizey. Cut to a week before Nick gave me the news. It's 20 June 2018 and he's having a day out at one of those Red Letter Day experiences, the ones you buy for people to go hot-air ballooning or wing walking on their birthday. Thankfully Nick's was a driving experience at Silverstone. So he's at the track watching the cars whizz past when he gets a call from Clare Pizey to discuss a few things about *Children in Need*. What I've failed to mention is Clare was also the exec producer on *Top Gear*. So they're chatting away about *Children in Need* but it's very loud due to the cars racing past in the background.

'Where are you? It's quite noisy,' said Clare.

'Silverstone racetrack,' Nick told her.

He could've been anywhere but by chance he happened to be at Silverstone the day Clare phoned him. Nick said, 'Speaking of cars, how's it going at *Top Gear*?' Chris Evans had already left and the rumours were doing the rounds about Matt LeBlanc leaving as well. You know what, I've just realised how mad that is – I'm writing about a Hollywood superstar and one of the most recognisable faces on the planet, Matt LeBlanc, and somehow we're both connected in my life story. I grew up in a two-up two-down in Bolton and I'm now talking about Joey from *Friends*! Anyway, Clare was now talking about *Top Gear* and the possibility of there being another new host. Nick decided to throw my name in the mix.

'Hear me out, Clare, but have you thought about Paddy McGuinness?' he said.

'No, I haven't. I know Paddy hosts *Take Me Out*, but I didn't know he was into cars,' she answered.

Nick then went on to explain about my love of cars and what else I'd worked on outside of *Take Me Out*, in particular the show I did for the Discovery Channel, *Stars in Their Cars*. This random, unplanned conversation that started off about Tess Daly's dresses ended up changing my life … and it was all down to chance and the fickle finger of fate. If Nick hadn't been at Silverstone that day the *Top Gear* conversation may never have even happened.

Once I'd processed Nick's news that *Top Gear* would like to see me, we both just laughed and laughed like giddy schoolkids.

Among all our excited chatter, I kept asking him, 'Are you sure this is right? They want to see me?'

'They do, my man, it's now down to you to show them exactly what you can do.'

It was all very hush-hush and I had to keep it secret that I was even being considered for it. That night I couldn't sleep, my mind had a million things spinning around it – the thought of being in the mix but with no guarantee of actually getting the job was agonising. The following day I received a phone call from Clare Pizey. We instantly clicked and chatted non-stop for a good hour or so. We had a mutual friend in Suzy Lamb and Clare, unbeknown to myself, had phoned Suzy to ask what I was like to work with prior to our call. This happens a lot in TV – word of mouth goes a long way and if you've got a reputation for being a wrong 'un that soon spreads throughout the industry. I've had producers contact me in the past asking about crew I've worked with and if I thought they were any good or not, nothing new there. When I eventually put the phone down to Clare it was so weird. I'd just been talking to someone I'd never met, seen or worked with before and it felt like I'd known her for years. This actually made me feel even more anxious. Because Clare was so lovely and supportive on the phone, the thought of not working with her on *Top Gear* was awful, especially after hearing her excitement about what she had planned for the show.

Skip forward a week to 5 July 2018 and the day of my screen test with Chris Harris. I'd been sent a script through by Clare with a review and a couple of challenges. The car I was to be reviewing and doing the challenges in was a Dacia Sandero, the UK's cheapest car – oh, the glamour. Clare had arranged for us to do it away from prying eyes at a military base near Leicester. I woke up early, it was a beautiful sunny day and I was fully prepped. I'd done my homework on the Sandero and had learned the script verbatim. That morning I decided to get a little tidy-up at a barber's, and let's be honest I've not got that much to tidy up. I told the barber I just wanted a bit of a clean-up around the edges but nothing more than that. It was early and he clearly still had his head on the pillow because he didn't take a blind bit of notice of what I'd said. The next thing I know he's put the clippers on a number one and proceeded to shear the side of my head. Now I know how a sheep feels.

'Whoa! What you doing?' I said.

The dozy prick looked at me and said that's what he thought I wanted.

'No, I said a tidy-up around the edges. Now I look like I'm off for National Service!'

The dilemma I now had was whether to stick or twist. Do I get him to tidy up the rest and just leave one side of my head with a stripe in it or do I get him to shave the rest off so it all blends in? I had to go for the latter – I couldn't turn up with just one half of my head shaved, could I? So I opted for looking like an extra from *Papillon*. I was fuming. I mean, it's not as though I was going to meet the producers of one of the biggest shows on telly! I got back from the barber's and was greeted by Christine.

'What the fuck have you done to your hair?'

'What have *I* done? Nothing. It was the silly twat with the clippers!' I said.

She sent me out for some hair dye in the hope of dying it all black so it'd at least look the same colour. It didn't work and I was now on my way to my *Top Gear* screen test with a cap on.

I'd never met Chris Harris before but the one thing I knew he loved, apart from indigo denim, was cars. At the time I owned a BMW 1M. I knew it'd make him a bit warm and fuzzy in the trouser department so I decided to rock up in that. It was a few hours' drive, which gave me plenty of time to calm down about my legalised scalping. I turned up at this military base and was greeted by a couple of soldiers carrying rifles. Due to the secrecy of it all, I couldn't even tell them why I was there but I gave them my name and one of them went to check if it was on the list to get in. It wasn't. Turns out I was at the completely wrong entrance. I rang Clare and she guided me around to another entrance at the back of the airfield. When I eventually found it, I couldn't believe my eyes. At the front of the military base it was like a scene from *Bravo Two Zero* with armed guards and military personnel everywhere. Around the back it was just some old bloke with a fag in his mouth, sat in front of a chain-link fence. He didn't even have a uniform on. Not so much *Full Metal Jacket*, more *Full Nylon Cardi.*

'Hello, I'm Paddy McGuinness.'

'In you go,' he said.

I couldn't believe it. I'd gone from SA80 rifles to some random bloke smoking a tab. The next minute I'm in and driving to the filming location. Even though I'd swanned straight in through the back gate, it still felt very cloak and dagger. This was a big deal.

When I arrived I got my first taste of the world-famous *Top Gear* hospitality – a disused shack in the arse end of nowhere. I got out of the car and Clare came over and gave me a big hug. That helped ease my nerves and instantly relax me. Straight away I said excuse the hair and told her what had happened. We had a good laugh then she took me into the shack. When I say shack I'm not exaggerating, it looked like the place the military used to reenact hostage negotiations. Harris was already in there and the three of us got chatting. There were a couple of tatty chairs and a table with some pre-packed sandwiches and drinks. I didn't mind – I was just glad I was getting on with Chris. If you're going to be working with someone who you don't particularly like then it always shows on camera and the job feels a lot more difficult.

Chris was part of the selection process because he was going to have to work with whoever got the job, and it was clear that I wasn't the only person who was up for it. At the time they'd seen a few other people but to this day I've no idea who. Flintoff hadn't been in yet and I was totally unaware he was also in the mix. Chris and I talked about cars we'd owned in the past and the fact that Chris also had a BMW 1M – we had a shared love of them. After a while Clare took me to meet the crew, who were setting everything up. This was when I first met Alex Renton, who is also an exec producer on the show and worked on it all through the Clarkson, Hammond and May years. All of a sudden it felt very real, and before I knew it someone was putting a mike on me and I was climbing into this Dacia Sandero to start my review. There were little cameras all around the car, but luckily I'd experienced this during *Stars in Thier Cars*. It can be quite off-putting because your view is somewhat restricted. I was given a two-way radio and Al asked if I was ready.

'Yep, all good, thanks,' I said.

I wasn't though. I was shitting myself. The nerves kicked in even more because I knew how much I wanted the job. I drove around this makeshift track and recited the scripted review that they'd given me. I didn't fluff any of it and I felt it went pretty well. Clare then came on the radio and told me to forget the script and do it all again in my own words. I drove around the circuit again but this time it was a lot more tongue in cheek, I just went for it.

Out went the chats about boot space and how many miles to the gallon the car would do. Instead I started to talk about the beautiful vista over the airbase and what else I could spend seven grand on, rather than this Sandero. Clare and Alex loved it.

'That was perfect,' Clare said. 'We're not looking for another car geek, we're looking for someone who can do exactly what you just did.'

Next up was a speed obstacle course challenge between Chris and myself. Harris doesn't like to show it but he hates losing. Clare had asked me to really go in on him when we were given our lap times. Soon as I read out that I'd completed the course quicker, I let Chris have it.

'You're a racing driver and I'm just a dad from Bolton? How have I won this?' I asked.

I was asking for people to bring me a copy of Chris's racing licence because I didn't believe he had one. I also picked up a traffic cone and shouted out our respective times through it and straight down his ear, which the producers loved. I'm always at my best when I'm making people laugh, and as the producers and all the crew seemed to be reacting positively to my approach, I started to relax and enjoy myself a bit more. The most nerve-racking part of the day was when they asked me to deliver those iconic lines to camera: 'Hello, and welcome to *Top Gear*.' I had to do it on a sunny afternoon, in a field, on a military base, looking like I'd just done 12 rounds with Edward Scissorhands.

Once that was all done, Nick turned up and it was back in the interrogation/green room for a quick cuppa then home. On the way back we met up at a pub to chat through how it had all gone. I felt confident that it'd gone well, Clare, Al and Chris all seemed pleased, so it was now in the hands of the TV gods. Regardless of how well I thought it went on the day with the *Top Gear* crew, it would have to go further up the ladder for approval. Executive producers, commissioners, heads of departments, channel controllers and the head of the BBC – there are so many levels. *Top Gear* is a worldwide show so a lot of research had to be done to figure out how well it would do around the world as well as the UK, hence Matt LeBlanc getting in on the job. This was my worry – I wasn't known internationally and I remembered Suzy Lamb telling me a story of how they had to subtitle *Take Me Out* when they were pitching it to the American executives. I ended up convincing myself that the BBC hierarchy were going to be of the same opinion and they'd be bringing in a big international star to launch the show again. The only thing I was clinging on to was the support and words of encouragement from Clare at how well the screen test had gone and the fact that if it was up to her the job would be mine.

A week goes by, nothing, no word off anyone. Fair enough, it's only been a week. Two weeks go by, still no sign. Then a month goes by. No matter what Clare had said to me or how the screen test went, I was now resigning myself to it not happening. I stopped ringing Nick every two minutes to see if he'd heard anything and got on with what I was doing at the time, which was getting ready to film a new game show that'd just been commissioned called *Catchpoint*. *Catchpoint* is a family teatime quiz show on BBC1 that involves answering questions while catching balls. We film it up in Glasgow and with it being a new show at the time I was totally focused on getting it right. On a side note the bloke who came up with the idea was the banker on *Deal or No Deal*. He shall remain anonymous, just in case they bring it back, but he's a lovely bloke. Myself, mystery banker and commisioning editor at the BBC Kalpna Patel-Knight all still work on the show to this day but back then it was all new.

Once a couple of months had passed I put it to the back of my mind. Most jobs you normally hear back straight away or after a few days so by now I'd convinced myself someone else had got the job. In October I went up to Glasgow to film *Catchpoint*. The first few days I was up there, I got the most horrendous flu and felt rougher than a sandpaper enema. You know the old saying, the show must go on, well, that was the position I found myself in, dosed up to the eyeballs with any medication the producers and runners could lay their hands on: Lemsip, echinacea, paracetamol, throat lozenges, the lot. I looked like shit so a make-up artist called Sarah Burrows, who's been making me look pretty on telly for over a decade, was kept very busy – I had more make-up on than the cast of *RuPaul's Drag Race*. I'd then be wheeled onstage in front of a live audience to do two shows a day. The audience had no idea I was ill but at the end of each show, I'd collapsed, exhausted, and just wanted to climb into bed. As the days went on, I started to feel really sorry for myself (man flu will do that to you). I was in a nice hotel and this was a great gig, but I just wanted to go home and curl up in bed for a week. I'd done a show the night before and was lying in my hotel bed the following morning watching *Homes Under the Hammer*. I'd been constantly blowing my nose and the bed was full of enough disused tissues to make a teenage boy blush. I'd hung the Do Not Disturb sign on the door and decided to knock up my first Lemsip of the day. My phone rang and it was Nick. If your agent phones you on a weekend or first thing in the morning, there's usually a problem.

'Bit early. What have I done now?' I said.

He laughed. 'All good, my man, I was just calling to say I'm coming up to the show tonight.'

I usually tell Nick not to bother coming along to my shows. I'm not one who needs a lot of hand-holding and the way I was feeling during that first series of *Catchpoint* I wasn't exactly up for a friendly chat after the show.

'I'm rough as fuck, pal, you've no need to come up,' I said.

'No, I want to come up and see you and I've got a meeting with Kalpna and the producers.'

Later, I was in the middle of filming the second show of the day when I noticed Nick on set behind the cameras. I gave him a wave and said I'd see him after the show.

Even though I hadn't wanted Nick to come up, seeing him gave me a bit of a pep up. He's a fellow Boltonian and he's got a similar sense of humour to me so it was actually quite nice to have a bit of a laugh. We went back to the hotel and had a drink in the bar. For some reason I ordered a bottle of red wine – I thought it'd make my flu better. To this day I'm not sure how I came to this conclusion, it just seemed a healthier drink.

We're sat chatting when he says, with a big smile on his face, 'I've got some good news.'

'You're pregnant?' I said.

'No.'

'Go on,' I said, with genuinely no idea what he was going to say.

'Clare called me earlier to tell me you've got the job on *Top Gear*!'

It was as if a doctor had walked in and injected me with some miracle cure – either that or I was right about the red wine. I was buzzing. We both hugged and I immediately ordered another bottle of flu-beating red. My heart was pounding and I was smiling ear to ear. This news had come just at the right time, especially after I'd more or less given up on the idea.

'So it's you, Chris and do you want to know who the third person is?' Nick asked.

'Go on,' I said.

'Freddie Flintoff.'

To say I was surprised was an understatement. *Top Gear* had cast two of the least likely people ever to front one of the BBC's biggest brands. A former dating show host and an ex-cricketer. It was weird filming the rest of *Catchpoint* knowing I was going to be the new host of *Top Gear*. I knew the production crew wouldn't be aware of this but I wondered if Kalpna knew. She's so lovely that I wasn't sure if she'd heard before me but wasn't letting on. I know one thing, though, for the rest of the filming days, I'd got my mojo back.

* * *

We're now in the middle of filming the fifth series, for us three, and it's doing amazingly well. The rejuvenation of the show, especially after it was at its lowest ebb, is wonderful and we're fully committed to making each series bigger and better than the last. All that success and new-found love for the show was all down, ultimately, to a risky and left-field decision to give us a shot by three people at the BBC: Charlotte Moore, Kate Phillips and BBC2 controller Patrick Holland. They're the ones who took a big risk on us so they've got to be the ones that get the plaudits. They gave us all a chance and thankfully we got the opportunity to pay that back with the show's continued success and the love it's getting again from the viewers, here and everywhere else it's shown around the world.

The BBC hadn't gone public with the news and we were all sworn to secrecy. ITV hold an event every year like the one at Channel 4 after we'd filmed *Phoenix Nights*, minus Stringfellows. Again, like with most channels, it's a chance to showcase all the new programmes due to air in the following 12 months. It's great to go along and see all the exclusive clips of new shows before they hit our screens and of course have a drink with your peers. At the time Freddie had just finished filming a series for ITV called *Cannonball*. Obviously we were both aware that we'd got the *Top Gear* job but we hadn't spoken to each other about it. Even though I'd met Fred a few times over the years, we'd never swapped numbers or anything like that. The ITV event was held at the Royal Festival Hall on the South Bank in London. I was making my way to my seat when I spotted Flintoff across the room. Our eyes locked and we gave each other a big smile and a nod of the head. We never spoke or even got near each other that night – the two new hosts of *Top Gear*, sat at an ITV do, and no one was any the wiser.

Before the news broke, the press were going nuts speculating on who the new presenters might be. This happens a lot when established shows are bringing in a new face and usually no one ever gets it right. I'd sit there with a cup of tea reading through the names, smiling. All these hot favourites with different odds at the side of their names on the chances they'd get the job. Myself and Freddie weren't on a single one of those lists – in fact you'd have got better odds on Greta Thunberg taking over the show.

Bizzarely, though, the only newspaper that actually called it was the *Daily Star*. It was literally a couple of lines at the bottom of page 12 or something: 'Paddy McGuinness tipped to take over *Top Gear*.' It was so innocuous and tucked away that no one even mentioned it again, apart from one of my mates in the building game. Popular read with the builders is the *Daily Star*. There was no way I was telling him or any of my mates: they'd be straight down the bookies. Not a mention of my name anywhere and all of a sudden there's a brickie in Ladbrokes putting his mortgage on me being the next *Top Gear* host. The odds on me taking over were that high, if you'd put a fiver on you would've probably been able to retire. Even though it was a secret, it doesn't take long for something like that to leak out to the press so a decision was made by the powers that be to do a big press launch on the banks of the River Thames to announce the new line-up.

Once again, it was all cloak and dagger. I had to travel down to London the night before, no train, back of a car job, and check into the hotel at midnight. They'd even booked me under a pseudonym so nobody in the media would get wind of it. The pseudonym the

BBC press team had chosen was 'Dougie Ryan', the name of the character I played during my short stint on *Coronation Street*. I'm on my way down to London with a fella called Jon Gittins. Jon has driven me for years and he's one of the nicest, most trustworthy blokes you could ever meet, so outside of my wife he was the only other person I'd told. Eventually, we roll up to the hotel under the cover of darkness. It's now gone midnight. Jon does a quick recce to make sure there aren't any paparazzi about. Coast clear, in I go! I'm out of the car and inside in a matter of seconds, making sure nobody sees me, baseball cap pulled down over my eyes – it was like being back in therapy! I make my way to the big, plush reception. I've checked into a hell of a lot of hotels over the years and the one thing they've all got in common, whether it's a Best Western in Blackpool or the Waldorf Astoria in Dubai, is if you're checking in past 11 o'clock at night you're gonna have problems, guaranteed.

'Hi, the name's Dougie Ryan. I'm just checking in,' I say to the bloke behind the desk.

'Good evening, Mr Ryan,' he says. 'Can I see some ID, please?'

I show him my driving licence. Now, I get this bloke is working nights and I know he doesn't have a clue who Paddy McGuinness is, never mind Dougie Ryan, but surely to God he's been told what's happening by someone?

He's looking at my driving licence, then his computer screen and back to my licence.

'Sir, this says Patrick McGuinness? I need the ID for Dougie Ryan.'

'Yes, I'm Patrick McGuinness, Dougie Ryan is a pseudonym.'

'A what?'

'A pseudonym.'

'I'm sorry, I'm not sure I understand. Do you have the ID for Dougie Ryan or is he not here yet?'

My accent is quite broad and this fella also has an accent so the two of us together are getting nowhere.

'Dougie Ryan isn't real,' I say, dropping the whole pseudonym thing. 'It's a made-up name, like a disguise. Nobody is supposed to know I'm here. Dougie Ryan is off *Coronation Street*.' (I knew that was a mistake as soon as I said it.)

'*Coronation Street?*'

'Oh, God. Look, forget *Coronation Street*. I am Patrick McGuinness! Dougie Ryan is not real, it's made up. I've been told to check in under that name by the BBC.'

Now this is where it gets even more bizarre and I promise you this is all one hundred per cent true, this whole incident happened.

'Who is the person at the BBC?' he asks.

'Kate Bush,' I say.

'Kate Bush? The singer?'

Yes, that's right. The eighties queen of baroque pop has finally run up that hill and booked me into the hotel, under the pseudonym of Dougie Ryan, on behalf of the BBC's press office, you prick! Was what I wanted to say but instead I keep it light-hearted.

'Well, if it was THE Kate Bush surely she'd have chosen the pseudonym Heathcliff?'

He's looking at me blankly. A few other members of the night staff have now appeared. None of them have a bloody clue who I am or who Dougie Ryan is. This was definitely not the place for saying, 'Do you know who I am?' By now I didn't know who I was myself. My initial excitement of checking in under a pseudonym had now all but disappeared. It's gone midnight, I'm knackered and the staff won't let me, or Dougie, check in.

So I'm stood in the hotel reception with my holdall in one hand and my phone in the other. Right, I'll try the old 'Can I see the manager' line.

'Can I see the manager, please', I said.

'I am the manager.'

'Of course you are.'

I had Kate Bush's number for emergencies but the cut-off time for calling people is eight o'clock, standard, and it's now getting on for one in the morning. Kate had said to me there wouldn't be any problems whatsoever but if there was then I should have no hesitation in calling her, no matter what time it was. I'm supposed to be tucked up in bed, all ready to launch the world's biggest motoring show, but instead I'm standing in a hotel reception wondering if this is a long-range prank by Ant and Dec.

I ring Kate but no answer, which is understandable at quarter to one in the morning. I also have another number for Phil Flemming, one of Kate's colleagues. I've never met him before and here I am ringing his phone at this ungodly hour. It's one of those painful moments. I'm stood looking at the hotel staff, who are looking back at me in silence. I've got the phone to my ear and everyone can clearly hear the phone ringing away while Phil is blissfully sleeping at the other end. I have to concede defeat, but

I'm not going without a fight. I tell the manager and staff at the hotel how unreasonable they've been and basically give them a verbal bollocking for a few minutes finishing off with…

'So you can stick your hotel and your room up your arse!'

It was at that moment I realised I had nowhere else to go and Jon was on his way back up north. An awkward situation just got even more awkward. I'd given them all a piece of my mind and stormed off… to the front of the building where I was now standing, again with all the staff looking at me, perplexed. Why is he still standing there?

I had to call Jon, who by this time was well on his way home.

'Jon, you're going to have to come back and get me, pal. They're not letting me in and please don't ask!'

Jon being Jon came straight back, no questions asked. By the time he got to me it was so late I didn't care if I had to sleep in the back of his car. We found a Premier Inn not far away and I checked in there. I'd gone from Dougie Ryan at an exclusive hotel to Paddy McGuinness at a Premier Inn within the space of a couple of hours. I eventually went to sleep around half three in the morning, not ideal when I had to be up at six.

My alarm went off and I picked up my phone, bleary-eyed, only to find a few dozen missed calls from the BBC press office. These were followed by several urgent voicemails from Kate Bush and Phil Flemming asking where the hell I was because I should have been meeting them in the reception of the hotel they'd booked. I know Kate and Phil well now and they're both fantastic at what they do, but this wasn't the best of introductions.

I gave Kate a call back and explained to her what had happened and where I was – she was mortified, not to mention furious with the hotel. They arranged to get me picked up and after a lot of make-up from Sarah, I finally stood with Chris and Fred at the side of the Thames getting our pictures taken by the world's press. That was that, the news was out. Paddy McGuinness, Chris Harris and Freddie Flintoff are the new presenters of *Top Gear!*

Over the following couple of days it really brought it home to me how big a show *Top Gear* is. I knew it was massive in the UK but I was getting messages from people all around the world. I even got a message from Stephen Moyer from *True Blood,* who said he was sitting drinking a coffee in Atlanta reading about it while he was on set and wishing me the best. It was properly bonkers but thankfully I never got too swept away with it all. In fact, the three of us are all pretty grounded in that sense.

* * *

It's the following month, November, and the dust has settled slightly. Clare and Alex have arranged for myself, Chris and Fred to meet up at a military base, standard, for a bit of filming. This wasn't to be shown on TV, it was purely to see how the three of us were on camera together. What was that much sought-after 'chemistry' going to be like? Don't forget, the three of us had never actually worked together before so this was going to be our first time doing a screen test. I wasn't too worried about it because after that day on the Thames it was clear to me that we'd be fine. If you're comfortable enough to call someone a t*sser, t**t, c**k or knobh**d, then you know it's all good and, trust me, between the three of us we've called each other every profanity under the sun. So we did the day together, insulted each other a lot and I had my first taste of playing about in supercars. Chris was in a Mercedes AMG GT, Fred was given an Audi R8 and I was handed the keys to a Porsche 911 Turbo S. It was fantastic. One of our directors, Jon Richards, a lovely bloke, took myself and Fred through different manoeuvres out on the roads for the best camera angles, and I remember thinking how surreal it all felt, that this was really happening, I'm now working on *Top Gear.*

After that day of filming I figured if we did it that way on the show, we could bring a massive dose of much-needed humour back to it. Yes, there was the usual and expected backlash on social media – the keyboard warriors couldn't help themselves. *What do McGuinness and Flintoff know about cars? Bring back Clarkson. The show is dead*, yadda, yadda, yadda, you get the picture. We all knew this was going to happen. Harris had warned us but to be honest myself and Flintoff have been around that long it wasn't really an issue for us.

Our first day of proper 'this is going to be on the telly' filming was done in the UK. I was tasked with selling the boys the idea of a hearse being the perfect family car. We had such a laugh making that film I remember thinking if the genuine fun we're having comes across on-screen then we could be on to something here. Having said that, we almost didn't get through filming down to Freddie nearly killing us all in the hearse – oh, the irony. The three of us were racing around a rally course in Wales and Fred was at the wheel. He had his foot down and we were fast approaching a sharp right-hand turn, never a good thing on a gravel road in an old hearse. It didn't help that Chris was goading Fred into driving faster – trust me, the big lad doesn't need encouraging to do that. Before you could say 'where there's blame there's a claim' we were upside down and the roof was completely crushed in. That was a genuinely terrifying moment for me. I'd been sat in the back seat so there was no way of getting out. I couldn't even hear Chris and Fred in the front because I was totally crushed in. I managed to get one hand free and somehow release my safety harness. There was a small gap I could squeeze through but I'd have to go legs first. All I could smell was petrol and it was now trickling into the back, where I was trapped. I was unaware of any injuries, the adrenaline had kicked in, and all I was focused on was getting out before the thing caught fire. I got my legs through the gap but it was too small to get my head through with my helmet on. I managed to remove the helmet with my free hand and I'm not sure if it was Chris or Fred but someone grabbed my legs and pulled me out.

It's the first time I'd been involved in a smash like that and it definitely shook me up. When I clocked the state of the car from the outside I couldn't believe any of us had survived – it was completely crushed, you couldn't even see the back seat where I'd been sitting. Not all bad, though, that evening I managed to guilt-trip Fred into giving me his hotel room. He had a bath in his and I was in need of a good soak. We were now fully baptised into the world of *Top Gear* and I had the bruises to prove it. *Things can only get better*, I thought, till Clare phoned to say we were going to Brunei.

Although *Top Gear* was a dream gig for me, there was one massive black cloud hanging over my head – my fear of flying. Even being on a short-haul flight made me extremely nervous, so how was I going to manage a 14-hour flight to Brunei? The longest flights I'd done were to America, and that was flying first-class with enough alcohol to stock the green room at *Loose Women*. Other than that I usually got on a plane for no longer than three hours tops. Anything further than that, which was very rare, and I had to revert to being blind drunk and on every sleeping tablet under the sun. The minute a plane door closed I just wanted to get off. Now, getting drunk and sedated wasn't too bad if I was going on holiday – at least I could sleep it off by the pool all day – but getting off the other side and being expected to drive a car for *Top Gear* was going to prove tricky.

With the start of filming only months away, my panic grew. I couldn't think of anything more stressful than getting on a plane for that length of time. It got that bad that I even started to get nervous about getting on trains, something I'd been doing regularly for nigh on 20 years! I got on a train home from Euston, which normally takes around an hour and 45 minutes, and soon as I heard the beeps signalling the doors were about to close, I jumped up and ran off the train. What the hell am I doing? What has just come over me? Honestly, I used to look forward to being on the train, it gave me a chance to switch off, watch a film or listen to a bit of music. I've been on trains where they've broken down on the tracks and I was stuck on there for nearly eight hours – not a problem, apart from a numb arse. Now, though, I was panicking about being on a short journey and not being able to get off when the door closed. I had a train timetable app on my phone and I worked out which trains I could get home on that stopped regularly on the way back. This turned a 1-hour-45-minute journey into a 4-hour one. I was getting off at every other station and waiting for the next train. Thinking about it now I can't believe what I was doing back then but obviously the stress and anxiety about all the foreign travel I was required to do had got the better of me and I was now in a completely head's-gone state of mind. What have I got myself into? I was screwed. I knew I had to do something about this and quick.

Once again, it was Doc I turned to. I rang him, explaining my dilemma, and he told me to go and see him. Being so close to the start of filming, the therapy was going to have to be intensive and if it didn't work I'd be forced to resign before the show had actually been filmed. I keep banging on about how helpful therapy is but I promise you it works if you find the right person for you. He told me I was suffering from cleithrophobia, which is often confused with claustrophobia, and that this, along with so many other things, had actually stemmed from my clinical depression and events from my childhood. In brief, claustrophobia is a fear of enclosed spaces, which I'm fine with, but cleithrophobia is a fear of being trapped in those places. For example, if you were claustrophobic you wouldn't venture on a plane, if you're cleithrophobic you could happily sit inside a plane all day long just as long as no one locks the door, which they have to do when you're 30,000 feet in the air. He asked if anything had happened to me that might have triggered my fear of being shut in or trapped. I thought for a while and remembered when I was about five, having a sheet on my head, pretending to be a ghost. I was at Angie's house, and her partner Ian had playfully grabbed me around the waist, trapping me under the sheet. I went absolutely nuts, screaming my head off and fighting to get out. Then there was the time when a bigger kid got me in a headlock and didn't let me go for about ten minutes. Without realising, both these experiences had stayed with me, hidden away for years. Once they're locked in your subconscious, they are very difficult to get out without some kind of help.

After Doc had explained why it was happening, we could now stop it from happening again. I had to retrain the amygdala (google it) in my brain, which is key in creating and then reversing anxiety. I had to teach myself to recognise that I was creating the danger in my head, and that I only had to look around a train or a plane at other passengers, reading their books or checking their phones, to know that same danger didn't exist for them and therefore wasn't really there. He told me you have to do something you're afraid of 20 times before the amygdala changes.

'Jesus, Doc, twenty?' I said.

Basically the only way to get over a fear of something is to do it. The therapy plays a massive part of it but ultimately you have to just do it. I reckon that'd make a great slogan for a sportswear brand.

Time was of the essence so he also prescribed me with Lorazepam, which is often given to calm people who have a fear of flying. Unfortunately, in the state of mind I was in, even that was a problem because I'd become so anxious, I thought every tablet I took was going to kill me. I couldn't even take a multivitamin from Boots without thinking it was going to fucking poison me. I'm now worried about taking a cod liver oil tablet, great! Doc told me that the tablets worked quickly but it was important to take one the minute I started to feel any kind of anxiety, even the slightest bit, or it might be too late to stop the growing panic. We agreed I would try one the next time I got on a train.

So there I was at Euston Station. I'd been driven down but agreed to go back on the train. I was sweating like Joe Wicks during half-term. The train was due in ten minutes so I popped the tablet in my mouth. Was it going to make me paranoid? Spaced out? Might it even kill me? I spat it out. I was so messed up I didn't know what was scarier, getting on the train and freaking out or swallowing a pill that might have some sort of terrible effect on me. I felt useless, hopeless and angry with myself. In the end, I got on the train, stressed off my tits, and endured the journey, hating every second of it. When I got off at the other end, I phoned Doc to tell him what had happened.

'Well, that's amazing,' he said, and I was gobsmacked.

'How?' I said. 'I spat the tablet out!'

'Paddy, you've done something that you thought you couldn't possibly do. You survived the journey, with no help, and you've proved you can do it. You've got to congratulate yourself on this achievement and start rewarding yourself.'

He was right. It might not be a big deal for someone else, but it was a bloody big deal to me. After that, I read a few relevant books and started accepting that I wasn't quite right, and that at some point I *might* flip out or have a panic attack in a situation where I felt trapped. Accepting that helped me start to relax, and after some more sessions, I felt ready to take that first long flight.

The day of the Brunei trip I felt fine. It was an evening flight so hopefully at some point I'd sleep. Doc had also prescribed me a couple of sleeping tablets just in case I had trouble switching off. It was myself, Fred, Clare and Alex on this trip. Chris had a family bereavement so wouldn't be joining us. I felt OK at the airport and then we got the call to make our way to the boarding gate. Clare knew I had an issue with flying so she was being very supportive and we were chatting away to take my mind off things. The moment I sat down in my seat, I instantly began to feel anxious, and anyone who has had or is going through those kinds of feelings knows only too well how quickly they can get out of control.

Clare, Fred and Al were putting their things in the overhead lockers, totally oblivious to what was going on inside my head. I was literally seconds away from standing up and walking off the plane. I thought about how I was going to explain this one to Christine and Nick. I thought about all those people who would give their right hand to be doing this job and then most importantly I thought about my kids. I'm the one who's providing for my family and if I quit, how will it affect them? For the first time I threw a Lorazepam down my neck. Bloody hell, Doc was right! Within minutes I felt calm. It worked fast, and although I didn't feel at all spaced out, the panic subsided. The doors of the plane shut and we were off. An hour into the journey, I took my sleeping tablet and slept for 12 hours straight. I couldn't believe it when I woke up and Clare told me we were just an hour away from landing. The thought of being on a plane for 14 hours had been unimaginable only a few weeks before, but I'd done it. The sky was blue and the sun was shining through the windows. I felt great. Before we took off I was ready to throw it all away and now I was on the other side of the world about to embark on another adventure.

Through *Top Gear* and all the flying I've done since, I've gone the other way. I'm now one of those people I used to hate – people who love flying. I look forward to a flight: phone off, films and a couple of beers for pleasure, not to knock me out. I don't even need the sleeping tablets, I go to sleep naturally on a flight, something else I never thought would have been possible. When I landed in Brunei I texted Doc: 'I'm here!' He congratulated me on how far I'd come and said it was wonderful to hear from me. It's amazing what the human mind can overcome but like a car it needs a full service and MOT to make sure it keeps ticking over nicely.

With regards to travel on *Top Gear,* Clare and Al were always very honest about it not being very glamorous. So when we arrived at our hotel in Brunei I couldn't believe what I was seeing. This place was like a palace, built on its own white-sand private beach. It was all marble and gold with the biggest swimming pools I'd ever seen. What were Clare and Al on about? This place was luxury. Typical Brits abroad, me and Fred went straight to our rooms, unpacked the shorts and within ten minutes of arriving we were laid at the side of the pool already turning a lovely shade of red. Clare joined us just as we were having a glass of Coke at the poolside bar.

'Clare, what are you on about? This *Top Gear* lark is fantastic!' I said.

'I can get used to this,' agreed Fred.

She told us that this was a complete one-off and it was the nicest place she'd stayed during her time on *Top Gear*. It was only for one night and we should be prepared for what lay ahead the following day, the jungles of Borneo.

In the morning, we had a beautiful breakfast at the hotel before being driven to a small airport. This was feeling a little bit more like the *Top Gear* Clare had been telling me about. Passport control was a bloke in the corner with a set of weighing scales. The plane wasn't that big so you had to be weighed, along with your luggage, before you got on. To give you a rough idea what state the plane was in, the passenger next to me was a rooster. This plane made Ryanair look like Concorde.

We landed on a small runway in the middle of the jungle and it was from there that my *Top Gear* baptism of fire began. Coming from the world of shiny-floored light entertainment shows, I was used to a certain level of comfort. Generally, as host, fronting a TV show, you're fairly pampered, and even if you're not, there's certainly very little hardship involved. All the crew on *Top Gear* had been there and done it but for someone like myself who loves a cup of tea and a custard cream it was definitely a culture shock. You see, a jungle isn't really conducive to filming, and by that I mean pretty much everything wants to kill you. Forget lions and tigers, in the jungle a frigging plant can put you six feet under. All that, topped with being wet through, tired and hungry, can shorten people's tempers.

For instance, in Borneo, for safety and strict insurance purposes, we all had to travel in a single convoy, and there was no deviating from the group. This meant that we were moving as one the whole time. No one could go off and do their job without the whole team. This, of course, meant that everything took four times as long as it would have under normal circumstances, which made the days a real slog. We'd generally start at first light, about 5.30am, and we'd be working until nine or ten o'clock at night. Then there'd be a drive of around two or three hours, through jungle roads, to get us to the next location for the following day. So even after we'd clocked off for the day we were still on the move. When it came to eating, any food we had was cooked by the locals and usually served on the floor, or every now and again we'd get treated to a table. I'm not a particularly fussy eater but I like what I like and when I'm staring at some kind of meat, usually covered in flies, I tend to give that a miss. Fred was fine, he'd done these kind of things before on other TV shows. I once watched him drink a cup of his own piss so a few flies on a chicken drummer weren't going to put him off.

Luckily Clare had asked me what I'd like on my rider for Borneo. If you've never heard of one, a rider is a list of things you can request, within reason, to have in your dressing room. For Borneo I went old school:

Custard Creams

Pink Wafers

Angel Delight (always strawberry)

rice pudding

Marshmallow Flumps

Pot Noodles

Everything you need for a jungle adventure and that's pretty much all I ate for the five days we were there. I even knocked up some Angel Delight for a team of Gurkhas while we floated down the crocodile-infested Sungai Belait River on the back of a homemade raft. You can take the lad out of Bolton ... When we had accommodation, and I use that word loosely, it was hardly The Ritz. On one occasion I was shown down to my room, which was essentially a wooden box with a couple of makeshift window frames cut into the side. No windows in the frames, though, just a bit of old rag hanging over them. There was no toilet or running water in there, but if you walked a bit further into the jungle they had a hosepipe hanging off a tree – that turned out to be the shower, sink and toilet in one. Even after three or four days of sleep deprivation, I couldn't sleep. The jungle in the evening is incredibly noisy, all you can hear is things moving about, and animals and insects making weird noises. I was paranoid about a snake or a bloody great big spider crawling over me so I just lay on top of this tatty old mattress, boots on, fully clothed with a beanie pulled down over my face. I barely slept a wink. I'd now gone 24 hours without sleep on a diet of Pink Wafers and Flumps. In the morning I staggered up to the area where the crew were all having breakfast. Once again, all the food was already laid out and covered in flies but I did spot a few boiled eggs that were still in the shell – lovely, nature's clingfilm. At last, something I could eat.

I'd just sat down with a black coffee and a boiled egg when Clare came over and said we needed to leave.

'Clare, I've not slept for twenty-four hours and I've just spent the night in a coffin with windows! I'm having a boiled egg and a coffee!'

Sleep deprivation is the worst. I'm not a bawling and shouting kind of person but I felt myself getting really annoyed by the whole thing. I looked at Clare and Al, picked up my stuff and left the situation before it escalated into anything more.

We set off to our next location and I was quietly seething. I could feel it building more and more as the morning went on. Clare has been in the game a long time and knew I was inwardly having a moment.

'Paddy, can we please have a talk?' she said.

What Clare didn't know was that in my head I'd had enough. I wasn't well travelled and I'd never gone that long with so little food and sleep. I'd effectively quit and if it wasn't for Clare spotting something wasn't right I honestly think that could have been a possibility. It feels like I've known Clare forever, she's so lovely and I always listen to what she has to say. That's the reason I got in the car with her to clear the air. We both expressed our concerns and had a really serious but good chat, which was totally undercut by the sight of Flintoff flying past clinging on to the back of a rogue water buffalo for dear life. We both laughed about the absurdity of it all, had a big hug and got on with the rest of the day. If I've learned anything from getting older, it's flying off the handle straight away is not the right way to do things. In the words of Bob Hoskins, from the BT adverts in the nineties, it's good to talk.

So before *Top Gear* even hit our TV screens I'd already nearly been killed by Flintoff in a hearse and almost quit the show twice. As Yazz once said, the only way is up.

Yazz was right. We finally left the jungles of Borneo and made our way back to a little town where I spotted something that almost brought me to tears... a KFC. After five days of Flumps and boiled eggs this was like an oasis in the desert. Myself, Fred, Clare and a girl called Gemma, who was in charge of the kitty, all marched down there and filled our faces – they even did mash!

When I look back at that first trip abroad with *Top Gear* I do nothing but smile. Yes, it was arduous, and yes, the image of Flintoff having a shit in a bush will never be erased from my mind, no matter how much therapy I get, but all those moments brought us together and some of the things I experienced I would never have seen in my lifetime. During that first series of *Top Gear* I'd visited the Afar Triangle in Ethiopia, driven a sports car through the jungles of Borneo, had a near-death experience in a hearse, been electrocuted in Telford and seen Chris Harris assaulted by a watermelon. It was now time to face the ultimate test: the *Top Gear* live studio audience.

The three of us together were still an unknown quantity for the viewers. We were all comfortable with each other and I knew from what we'd filmed that there was some really good stuff in there. Chris had warned me how difficult the audience can be; he said we'd be lucky if we got one laugh, never mind a round of applause. He'd been a part of all the shows with Chris Evans and Matt LeBlanc, the viewing figures were down and public support was at the lowest it'd been for a long time. All Chris's concerns were genuine, he'd lived them for the last three series, but if I know one thing, it's how to work a studio audience. Chris will be the first to tell you that's not his thing – the man's a genius when it comes to cars but stick him in front of a live audience and he clams up. During rehearsals and the day of the studio shows, he comes out with some funny stuff, but he forgets to do it when the cameras are pointing at him!

The original thought was to start the episode in our dressing room (portacabin) with Fred reading an *Autotrader* and me reading one of Jeremy Clarkson's books. This got binned at the very last minute so we began in the studio. When we were first introduced to the audience, in this big aircraft hangar at Dunsfold, the applause and cheering really took me aback. I'd had Harris telling me how bad it was going to be, only to be greeted by the warmest, friendliest audience ever. This was a great start. I then did a bit of chat with the audience, which didn't happen with Chris and Matt. I told them about what we'd been filming, did a few jokes, got them laughing and we were off. The first time I uttered those immortal words 'Welcome to *Top Gear*' in front of that live audience in the very spot Clarkson, Hammond and May had done it for all those years felt exciting and nerve-racking, but mainly I was proud of us all.

If you're fortunate enough to get a ticket for the studio shows one of the things you get to see, before it goes on telly, are the films we've done. This was going to be the real acid test. How were the audience going to react? The first film we showed them was our trip to Ethiopia. All the lights went off in the hangar and the audience all looked up at the big screens. Myself, Chris and Fred sloped off into the shadows to watch everyone's reactions. They absolutely loved it and the round of applause they gave it was fantastic. We looked at each other and smiled. We were buzzing.

'I told you,' I said to Chris.

The rest of the run went exactly the same – all the films we'd made went down a storm with our live audiences and that was a really good barometer of how the viewing public might react.

When the night of the first episode arrived, I felt sick with nervous excitement. Knowing how hard we'd all worked on the show and how well it'd gone down with our studio audience, I'm not sure I was ready for any kind of negativity online. It turns out I didn't have to worry. We all know what Twitter can be like but the feedback we got was unreal – I found myself scrolling through it actively looking for something negative. It was a tsunami of positivity and the critics had given us glowing reviews as well. As the weeks went on, the viewing figures grew and the *Guardian* declared *Top Gear* to be the best it'd ever been. One of the funniest tweets I read at the time was: 'I thought it was going to be shit! I wanted it to be shit, but you've proved me wrong. I'm loving it!'

Something I'm particularly proud of is the new audience we've brought to the show. There's a hell of a lot of viewers out there who aren't necessarily fans of cars but they love how entertaining the programme is. We're still working hard on the show and thankfully the viewing figures keep going up every series – long may it continue because we love it!

 **CHAPTER 25**

IT'S THE FINAL CHAPTER! (EUROPE)

Speak softly and carry a big stick; you will go far.

Theodore Roosevelt

We all have a common goal in life, being happy. In the past, I've looked at someone and thought, *I'd like to be like them.* With the advent of Instagram, everyone looks like they're living their best life. Most of the time, though, when you scratch the surface, the people you think are blissfully happy or amazingly successful have just as much strife and drama in their lives as the rest of us. Just look at the Kardashians. Yes, they've made a lot of money but at what cost? I try and keep a healthy balance in my life and, yes, I'm busy with work most of the time but when I stop filming, I stop being that bloke off the telly. I think that's what keeps me sane. Some people immerse themselves in the job I do 24/7 and more power to them if it works for them, but I choose to step out of it all until the next job. I think that's why I still have an appetite for it. If I was at every single red-carpet event or showbiz gathering I'd quickly become sick of it all. It's important for me to enjoy my down time, which is the least glamorous life ever.

It takes a while to figure out what truly makes you happy – for me it's being at home and seeing friends. We all have our own views and opinions on happiness, whether it be health, wealth or having a lie-in for once. For me it's only now, when there's more sand in the bottom of the egg timer, that I think I've found what makes me happy but the quest still continues. I'm a believer in *now*, always have been. What's the point in waiting? We have one chance at life, and if there's something you want out there, and it's within your grasp, then do it. Don't wait. Enjoy it.

While I was coming to the end of writing this book I got offered the job of hosting *A Question of Sport,* an iconic show for the BBC, much like *Top Gear.* Now I'm the host of two of the BBC's biggest and longest-running shows. I loved them as a kid and now I'm bloody well hosting them.

Yes, it's a big deal when someone new steps into a show, but that's all part of the excitement for me. If things don't work out it's not the end of the world, regardless of what the underbelly of Twitter say. I'm giving it a go, I'll try my best, I'll work hard and then the rest is up to the viewers and the TV gods. Simple really. You can't let other people's opinions become yours. Be true to yourself. Enjoy the highs and learn from the lows – trust me, I've had my fair share of both. If there's one fibre of you that thinks you can do something, go for it! Having said all that, if I get a call tomorrow asking me to play Hamlet for the Royal Shakespeare Company then chances are I'll say no. In the words of Dirty Harry, 'A man's got to know his limitations.'

I like to see my mates whenever I get chance and I'm always the one to suggest us getting together. It can be hard work persuading them but when it finally happens it's always a laugh. I've got a group of mates who love a good drink up and insist on paying their way, I've got another group who only come out if everything is free and I've got another who sit somewhere in between. For me none of this matters. If I have to jump through hoops to get them out, or make sure all the food and drink is free, then so be it. At the end of the day, it makes me happy and I've never been with a group of friends where I've not laughed, a lot!

I once hired this mega-villa in Portugal for a mate's 50th. It was the group who always insist on chipping in towards the bill, the Hateful Eight. Even though they want to pay their way, I never let them know the full cost of the things I sort for us. That way they don't feel like freeloaders and I know they appreciate whatever we do. This place cost a fortune to rent for a week but I thought, *Sod it, I've known these lads all my life and you're a long time dead.* It was owned by a pharmaceuticals multi-millionaire and had its own walkway to the beach, a separate four-bedroom villa within its grounds, swimming pools, basketball court and a mini golf course. We even had our own chef. I'd also booked a private yacht for a day. I was buzzing for the lads – they're all grafters who work hard so to give them this treat was well worth it. No point in doing well for yourself if you can't share it about now and again.

After the initial excitement of entering this mega-villa and dumping our bags in the rooms, I was still in my bedroom when I heard a familiar voice. It was Jeremy Clarkson. I wandered down to the palatial living room to find my mates all sat there, drinking beer, watching *The Grand Tour*.

'What the fuck are you lot doing?' I said.

'We like this,' one of them said. 'It's that *Grand Tour* thing.'

'I know what it is,' I said. 'What I don't know is why we're in Portugal's answer to Buckingham Palace and you tools are sitting here watching it. We've got a private yacht waiting for us and you men are all sat watching my show's biggest rival!'

That's exactly why I'm still the same person I was before I worked on telly – with my mates it's impossible not to be.

I've been working in the entertainment industry for over 20 years now and I've had my share of ups and downs but ultimately the secret to my longevity and success is not being very successful. Sounds mad, that, doesn't it? In the UK we love to build people up but also relish pulling them down. If you can keep your head down, work hard and treat people with respect you'll be accepted and forgiven for the odd mistake. If you're mega-successful and winning awards, the slightest thing and you're done: the house of cards will soon tumble down. For the rest of us, though, the rules are simple: don't get too big for your boots. I thoroughly enjoy not being top of the tree, there's less drama when you're further down and you still get to enjoy the sunshine.

So there you have it. I've no TV awards, I don't trend on Twitter and my name is never linked to any jobs that become available on the telly. Yet I've never stopped working in 21 years of being in the public eye, the job offers keep coming in and, most importantly, people still smile when they see me on the street.

That'll do for me!

ACKNOWLEDGEMENTS

Thank you, Christine, and my three beautiful children, Leo, Penelope and Felicity. I'd be lost without your unwavering support and cuddles. I love you all more than you'll ever know.

For my family, although we don't see each other much, the bond is still strong and you're never far from my thoughts. Thanks to our Kathryn for the numerous bollockings throughout the years. Never change. Thank you, Lorraine, for the hours of laughter and fantastic nights together. Thanks to my uncle Tony for teaching me how to be a man. For my cousins, Domonic, Katie, Lucy and Aaron, I've watched you all grow up into fine people. Thanks to my brother, Tony, for never questioning getting your kit off in the name of comedy and live entertainment. Thanks to Brenda Winnard for always making me feel loved and wanted. You're the last of a generation. For Margaret Rigby, thank you to you and all your family for making my dad's final years happy ones. Thanks to Peter for giving me a platform to build on from *Phoenix Nights* and *Max and Paddy*, and for the endless, countless nights of laughter when it's just the two of us together. To all my mates from Bolton who knew me when I had nothing! That's you Taz (Knock Knee), Anton (Palance), Danny (Dick Fingers), Andy C (Giuseppe), Shaun (Ruprecht), Cleggy (Buscemi), Rick (Angry Man), Bernard (VVIP), Rob (Bobby B Bad), Si (Zola Budd), Stotty, Niggi, Del and Bully. None of it would be worth it without you lot. Let's keep those good times going, boys. To my agents past and present – Phil, Lucy, Adele, Nick, Paul, Daz and Emma – thanks for pushing me on, having my back and hopefully reducing your percentages.

And finally to my best mate/brother of over 34 years, Franny. Having someone that you know, without a shadow of doubt, will be there for you through thick and thin is invaluable. I love you, pal, and thanks for always being there for me.